ROCK HUDSON

Books by Sara Davidson

LOOSE CHANGE

REAL PROPERTY

FRIENDS OF THE OPPOSITE SEX

ROCK HUDSON

His Story

Rock Hudson

and

Sara Davidson

William Morrow and Company, Inc.
New York

Grateful acknowledgment is made for permission to quote from the following material:

Rock Hudson interviewed by Ronald L. Davis, Southern Methodist University Oral History Project Number 276, August 24, 1983.

"Rock Hudson in an Interview with Gordon Gow," *Films and Filming*, Brevet Publishing Ltd. (U.K.), June 1976.

"Rock Hudson from A to Z," by Robert Osborne, columnist-critic, *The Hollywood Reporter*.

Rock Hudson interviewed in *Coronet*, June 1976.

Rock Hudson interviewed in *McCall's*, February 1967.

Rock Hudson interviewed in *Chicago American Magazine*, February 19, 1967.

Library of Congress Catalog Card Number: 86-61181

ISBN: 0-688-06472-8

Printed in the United States of America

First Edition

1 2 3 4 5 6 7 8 9 10

BOOK DESIGN BY HOWARD PETLACK

I've always been a private person. I've never wanted to write a book, I've never let my house be photographed and I've never let the public know what I really think.

Now that's changed—there's a lot I want to say and not too much time left. I want the truth to be told, because it sure as hell hasn't been told before. So I've asked those who know me best—my real friends—to work with Sara Davidson in telling my story.

Rock Hudson

September 5, 1985

ACKNOWLEDGMENTS

This book was greatly facilitated by the collaboration of Mark Miller, George Nader and Tom Clark; they revealed information to me that they had never discussed with anyone, and I am grateful for their trust.

I would like to thank my research assistants, Sandy Ferguson of "Legwork," who did a marvelous job of locating obscure facts quickly, and Michael Levin, who was wonderful in elucidating legal and medical issues.

For their confidence, I thank my agent, Lynn Nesbit, my publisher, Sherry Arden, my editor, Lisa Drew, and Paul Sherman.

For typing transcripts, I thank Pat King and Gina Daramparis. For caring for my children while I worked, I thank Blanca Rosa Garcia.

For his love and faith, I want to thank Glen Strauss; this book could not have been undertaken without his vision.

—SARA DAVIDSON

On August 24, 1983, Rock Hudson gave an interview to Professor Ronald L. Davis of Southern Methodist University, which became part of the S.M.U. Oral History Collection on the Performing Arts. It was the first time in Rock's life that he gave such a candid interview, ranging over all aspects of his career, and it is the most lengthy, surviving record of his thoughts about his work. The interview is one of hundreds in the S.M.U. collection, which is becoming a major preserve of oral history on the performing arts. We are grateful to S.M.U. for permission to publish excerpts from that interview.

ROCK HUDSON

INTRODUCTION

On the fourth of September in 1985, I drove for the first time to Rock Hudson's house, called "the Castle," at 9402 Beverly Crest Drive. The house was high on a ridge, looking out over the city of Beverly Hills. When the air quality was good, which it was not, you could see clear west to the Pacific and east across Los Angeles to the San Gabriel Mountains. But on this day, water and mountain disappeared behind clouds of yellow-brown haze.

There were twelve cars parked in front of the house. A blond young man was waxing an antique blue station wagon. This was Marc Christian, who had moved into the Castle with Rock Hudson in 1983. He looked like a surfer, with flaxen hair and bare, tanned chest. Recently, Christian had been asked to leave the house, but he had refused. He had moved into the theater behind the garage, where he was sleeping on a convertible sofa.

I rang the front doorbell. The carved wooden door was opened by Mark Miller, Rock's personal secretary. Miller, a large man who once was an opera singer, welcomed me and gave me a tour of the house and grounds. The Castle had two living rooms, two front doors, a theater with a real stage and footlights, a steam room, gym, pool, four fireplaces and six ice makers. But there were only two bedrooms. One was Rock's; the other was being occupied by Tom Clark, who had lived with Rock for ten years before Christian. Tom and Rock had been reunited at UCLA Medical Center after the news had been released that Rock had AIDS (acquired immune deficiency syndrome). When Rock came home in August, so did Tom.

Tom met us at the foot of the grand staircase. He was nearly as tall as Rock, with white hair and vibrant blue eyes. He was determined Rock would get well. "I believe in miracles," he said. "We're gonna beat this." He wore a button that said I LOVE ROCK, with a heart in place of "love."

Mark Miller took me to the kitchen, where, he said, "everything happens." He introduced me to the butler, James Wright, who spoke with elegant British diction and carried a little Shih Tzu with a red bow in her hair. Next to James was the gardener, Clarence Morimoto, a saintly-looking Japanese man of eighty who was fixing himself an ice-cream sundae. Behind them, at the kitchen table, was Rock Hudson.

Rock was dressed in light-blue pajamas. He was smoking a cigarette, opening mail. He picked up a telegram, waved it at me and said, with a glint of merriment, "Baby has arrived." He opened the telegram—it was from a fan in New York, urging Rock to try a cure of herbs and grasses. Rock tossed it in a pile. Then he reached out his arm—pale white, firm, ramrod straight—and shook my hand with a stiff motion. "Let's go in the living room. We can talk."

Despite the heat of September, Rock put on warm socks and asked for the furnace to be turned on. He looked stooped and uncomfortable in the oversized upholstered chair. His face was so thin you could see the bone structure, and there were dark folds of sagging skin under his eyes. He crossed and uncrossed his legs, looked at me and waited.

I had already met with Rock's attorney, his business manager and publisher in New York as well as with Mark Miller. We had understood that Rock might not be able to give me the time generally required to write a book about one's life. Rock had told Miller, "You know the whole story. You'll have to do it for me."

I asked Rock why he had decided to undertake the book. "So much bullshit has been written about me. It's time to tell my story. It's time to set things straight." He said he'd always wished he could write. I asked why. "Because I can't." He paused. "I mean, goddammit, write it well if you're gonna write it."

Under normal circumstances, I would have spent days with Rock before we started interviews. But time was precious, so I took out my list and began with what I thought were harmless, basic questions. He answered in short phrases, with many stops.

"When did you first want to be an actor?"

"I always wanted to be an actor. In Winnetka, Illinois, where I grew up, that was unheard of. You worked for the fire department. You didn't dare want to be an actor." He said that when he first came to Hollywood, he was so green that when he saw people riding the bus to Twentieth Century-Fox wearing tuxedos, "I thought, those are stars!" He chuckled. "They were extras. That's what I knew."

He was quiet. Suddenly he shouted: "Come on, open up!" I

thought he was addressing himself, referring to our interview. But he said, "My sinuses. Drives me crazy."

"Do you need a pill?" Tom Clark said.

"No. Not yet."

"Good. I don't want you to have one."

Rock talked about his first agent, Henry Willson, who had given him the name Rock Hudson. "It's still hard to answer to," he said. "I think of myself as Roy."

The phone rang. Rock's eyes moved to the instrument, and it seemed he had to forcibly restrain himself from reaching for it. I learned later that Rock loves to answer the phone, go to the door, open mail, even though staff members are there to screen calls. Rock kept his eye on the phone until the ringing stopped.

"Strange man. Henry," he said. "Big ego. He felt he knew everyone and everything. He did some good for me at the beginning, but he got lazy. He didn't plan ahead. He sat back in the office and waited for the phone to ring. I told him, finally, 'You better get off your ass, 'cus it's time to start hustling.' He said, 'Why? You're working all the time.'"

Rock snuffed out his cigarette, and immediately lit another.

"I told him, that isn't the answer, and it wasn't. Because I ended up doing what I think is a lot of crap."

I asked what he thought were his best films.

"*Giant. Seconds. Pillow Talk. Lover Come Back.* I *love* the comedies. I got to learn from Doris . . . talk about knowing your craft! If I have to do a comedy with, say, Shelley Winters, that's hard labor. She's not funny, and she thinks she is. She's got a voice that goes right through you. Wha wha wha. To try to do a comedy with someone who has no conception of what comedy is—that's a killer. But Doris knows."

We talked for another half hour and Rock began to grow tired. "This is very difficult," he said. "I'm sitting here, racking my brain, saying nothing."

I told him I lived nearby and could come back whenever he felt up to it—night or day. He thanked me. "It's nice to have that freedom." He rose and, with Tom beside him, walked slowly, stiffly, up the grand staircase to his bedroom.

When I left the house, James, the butler, was hurrying across the patio wearing nothing but a towel. I drove out the front gates feeling panicky, disoriented. It was one of the most bizarre scenes I'd ever witnessed: the old lover and the new lover brushing elbows in the hall, the old lover reclaiming his place while the new one refused to give ground. Friends gathering in the living room, laughing and telling stories while the movie star lay dying of a terrifying disease—the plague of our time. The eighty-year-old gardener eating ice cream in the kitchen. The butler in his towel. What was I getting into?

For the next four weeks, I went to the house almost daily, and talked with Rock when he had the strength. Slowly, I began to be caught up in the drama that was taking place. The house was indeed like a castle, with Byzantine plots, intrigue, people whispering and choosing sides and listening behind pillars and scheming to gain access to the throne. One friend said, "The currents in that house are dangerous. You never know who's telling you what for what reason."

Rock died on October 2, 1985, and immediately was cremated. I went to the memorial service at the Castle, where several hundred people drank margaritas and ate chili and listened to mariachis. The next day, I sailed with his closest friends on the yacht, *Tasia II*, into the Catalina Channel. The motors were cut and in the hush, Tom Clark threw the ashes of Rock Hudson into the ocean. We tossed flowers, which continued to float in a brilliant ring while the ashes formed a gray cloud on the water, then sank and disappeared.

After the burial, I continued the task of piecing together the complete story of Rock Hudson's life. I had no idea, at the outset, how complex and fascinating the task would be. What struck me was how deeply Rock Hudson had been loved, not merely by his fans but by a relatively large number of friends. What I saw, at his death, was not *pro forma* grief, but real, raw pain and loss.

To his friends, Rock had possessed something unique: the ability to make them laugh as no one else could. He was childlike and silly and broke people up. He laughed until tears ran down his cheeks, and took special delight in laughing and making people laugh when they weren't supposed to. His deep, rippling laugh and tall body shaking with mirth were infectious. Actress after actress told me she'd never had more fun on a stage, more helpless fits of hysteria than with Rock. Most of us can laugh and play like this with one or two people, but Rock could do it with everyone, young and old, women and men. The gift, the twinkle, resided in him.

On screen, he projected the image of a simple soul, not ambivalent or tortured. He was warm and good and pure. He seemed completely what he was at the moment: completely in love, completely brave, completely repentant. Yet in life, Rock was anything but simple. He was a master of illusion, devious and secretive, capable of being extremely kind and utterly heartless. Like the Trickster, he appeared to different people in different guises. George Nader, the actor and writer who was Rock's friend for thirty-five years, said, "There is no Rock Hudson. There are many Rock Hudsons. He projects what will appeal to the person he's with, and he will get that person's heart at any cost. The larger the audience, the more bland and one-note the performance will be."

Rock Hudson rarely talked to anyone, even his lovers, about his fears or feelings, his inner life. He did not have long conversations about relationships or the state of one's soul. He never complained or admitted to having troubles. "If there was torment of the spirit," Nader says, "no one saw it."

Rock went for the joke, the game, music, gardening, water-skiing, and laughter—always laughter. Warmth and love were communicated without words. He was the first person to help a friend in trouble, the first to pack boxes and move furniture, to show up with buckets and a shovel to dig someone's house out of a mud slide. He would leave the studio early to take a friend to the dentist. Yet he would not let that friend know what he wanted, what he was planning, where he was going that night. His face, which seemed so blank and untroubled, made people think, at first, he was a naïve country boy. But the happy, simple face was a tool he cultivated.

Trying to understand Rock Hudson was like trying to penetrate a sphinx. The more I looked, the more mysterious and disturbing the details of his life became. Every day there was a surprise, a new contradiction to resolve, and before long, there was nowhere I could put a foot on firm ground. It was like treading on a spider's web.

I found that nothing could be taken at face value. Even if Rock had told the same fact to ten people, it might not have been true. He loved secrets and seemed to enjoy throwing people on a false scent. Often, Rock told different friends conflicting stories, and I would be reduced to making a scorecard: How many said yes, how many said no? Then I would weight the sources and try to ponder Rock's motives.

As I looked up the men Rock had been romantically involved with, I had the feeling I was meeting the same person at different ages. The farther back they went in Rock's life, the older they were in 1985. It was almost comical: I would knock on the door and when it opened, there, once again, was a figure who was blond, tall and well built, manly, who could easily be taken for straight. Usually, he had a mustache. But none of these men had had a relationship with the same Rock Hudson.

The more elusive the story became, the more determined, the more obsessed I was to find out: What was the truth? The work that has resulted is not a conventional "as told to" biography, where the celebrity speaks, edited and assisted by the writer. Because of Rock's health, he asked his friends to help tell his story, and I have put together the narrative from many views.

I began with Mark Miller and George Nader, who were Rock's "family"—a tight unit who had been devoted and loyal to one another since 1951. Both Mark and George had kept journals, and Mark had been Rock's secretary, overseeing all that happened in the Castle, since 1972. We worked together for three months, conducting interviews all day, four times a week. At the beginning, Mark and George were cautious, censoring what they said, but at the end, they held little back. We became collaborators, trying to crack a puzzle they had been grappling with for three decades.

I next turned to Tom Clark, who had lived with Rock on closer terms and for more years than anyone. Tom was invaluable in sharing his recollections and guiding me to others who were important in Rock's life. Mark, George and Tom provided the basic outline. To fill it out and gain additional perspectives, I interviewed sixty-two people, who spoke at length and on the record. Where there were conflicts and disputed facts, I have indicated this in the text.

At the beginning of each chapter and interspersed through the book, there are passages where Rock speaks for himself. For these sections, I have drawn on the interviews I did with Rock and on interviews conducted elsewhere. The sources of his quotes are listed in the chapter notes at the end of the book.

Before he died, Rock signed a letter asking his friends to cooperate with me, to tell the truth, the "whole story." For many, this was a strange and difficult request. Rock had trained his friends to observe "total silence," especially with writers. Anyone admitted to the inner circle was told: Never speak about what happens in the Castle to the press. Those who broke this rule were dropped.

Why, now, was Rock releasing his friends? Many agonized about being interviewed. Had Rock been in his right mind? Did he know what he was doing? Should they reveal things that Rock had never publicly admitted during his lifetime?

Some decided not to participate, but the majority I contacted agreed to talk. It was Rock's wish, and Rock was a Master. He had stayed up on the high wire for four decades. He had remained a fixed star in a galaxy where new stars rose and fell each season, and he was going to stay fixed and visible for some time after his passing.

An hour before the memorial service for Rock Hudson was to begin, Mark Miller sat alone in the largest living room of the Castle. On the croquet lawn in back, a white tent had been erected, a string quartet was playing and guests were taking their seats. Marc Christian was in the wings, threatening to file a multimillion dollar law suit against Hudson's estate, and Rock's picture stared out from every tabloid in the supermarket.

I sat down beside Mark Miller. "Gorgeous day." The sky was brilliant blue and it was ninety degrees.

"Rock ordered it," Mark said. He gestured toward the heavens. "Rock's up there having lunch with Marilyn Monroe. He looks down and says, 'We left a mess, didn't we?'"

We laughed. Mark continued: "Marilyn agrees. 'We're both on the cover of *People* this week,' she says.

"Then Rock says: 'Yeah, and I got top billing.'"

CHAPTER 1

Paris. I don't want to hear about Paris. It's cold there. I'm sick and tired of going to doctors. They don't know anything, they can't do anything. I'm not going to go to fucking Paris!

In July of 1985, Rock Hudson's health was sinking at an alarming rate. James Wright, the butler, found his bedsheets soaked with sweat every morning. Rock had dropped from 225 pounds to 170. He could barely keep food down. His body was covered with rashes that itched and drove him mad. He started to forget appointments, and wandered around the house and grounds in his jockey shorts.

Besides his doctors, only four people in the world knew Rock had AIDS: Mark Miller, his secretary; George Nader, who lived with Miller; James Wright; and Dean Dittman, an actor friend whom Rock had confided in shortly after learning he had the disease. For a year, these four had watched helplessly as Rock faded before their eyes, yet insisted on working and keeping up the illusion that nothing was wrong.

Periodically, they urged him to go back to Paris, where he had gone in 1984 for injections of the experimental drug HPA 23. It was believed the drug could inhibit the AIDS virus, but it worked like insulin—one had to take it continually. Without the injections, the virus would grow back. When Rock had left Paris, the treatment appeared to have been successful. His blood was cultured and no AIDS virus was found. Rock promised his doctor, Dominique Dormont, to return in a few months, but almost a year had elapsed and Rock would not go back. When friends suggested it, he said, "I don't want to hear about fucking Paris!"

Instead, he appeared in nine episodes of *Dynasty*, and when Doris Day asked him to be the first guest on her show, *Doris Day's Best Friends*, on the Christian Broadcast Network, Rock accepted. The night before he was to leave for Carmel, California, to tape the show, Mark Miller said to Rock, "I don't think you should go."

"Why not, I'm fine."

"You're not fine."

"What do you mean?"

"You don't look well. You shouldn't be seen in public. There's going to be a press conference—photographers will be there from all over to catch the reunion between you and Doris."

Rock waved his hand—a gesture he used when he wanted to dismiss or silence someone. "Doris is counting on me. I won't let her down."

Later, Mark called Dale Olson, Rock's press agent, who was to accompany him to Carmel. Mark asked Dale to dissuade Rock from going. Dale said he would try. The next afternoon, Dale drove to the Castle with a limousine to pick up Rock. He found Rock dressed and packed, but lying sound asleep on a wooden bench beside the door. Dale woke him and said, "Rock, this is ridiculous. I don't know what's wrong but you seem sick. I'm canceling . . ."

Rock sat up. "Come on. We're going!" Like an old man, he walked with obvious pain to the limousine and, grunting, got inside.

He slept in the car all the way to the airport, and slept on the plane to Carmel. Dale kept saying, "It's not too late, we can cancel . . ."

"No way. I promised Doris, I'm going to do it and that's that!"

Rock was late for the reunion at Pebble Beach. He had gone to sleep on arriving at the Quail Lodge, and Dale had hoped he would sleep right through the press conference. But Rock woke up, looked about helplessly for his shaving things, found them, shaved and went over just in time for the last five minutes.

When he walked into the room, Doris Day says, "It was devastating. I didn't show what I was feeling, but it broke my heart. I wanted to get him out of there and look at him and say, why are you doing this?"

Later, when segments of the press conference were shown on television, Rock's hair looked stringy and greasy and his clothes did not match. But he held his arm around Doris and looked at her with such tenderness. "I was watching another film of yours," he said in a soft voice, "and then I saw a film of you with me. You know where the difference was? In you."

"Really!" Doris said.

Rock ran his finger over her cheek. They looked so at home, so peaceful together, like a man with his cherished partner in their sunset years. As he stroked her face and looked into her eyes, he seemed to be saying, "We had a good life, didn't we?"

The following morning, Doris tried to convince Rock not to tape the show. She made breakfast for him—scrambled eggs and croissants and cottage-fried potatoes and coffee—and they sat in the sun on the terrace of her home. She noticed Rock only picked at his food. "I'm worried about you," she said. "I don't want you to do this show if you're not up to it. What's the point?"

"I'm *gonna* do the show," Rock said.

"Will you stop that! You don't have to . . ."

"I want to."

Doris looked at him squarely. "You're not leveling with me."

"I've had the flu. I lost a lot of weight and I can't gain it back."

"Are you anorexic? Are you thinking you're fat and wanting to be skinny?" Later, Doris would say, "AIDS did not even occur to me."

Rock told her it was just the flu. She asked what he was doing about it, what did his friends say? "I think you need another doctor. I think you should get another opinion. I think you should *do* something."

"You really think I should?" Rock said.

"Yes."

"Okay, I will."

Rock and Doris drove out to Stone Pine Ranch where they taped *Doris Day's Best Friends*. Doris says, "We didn't push at all. We let him go at his own pace, and we laughed so much, just like the old times. I think he had more laughs—we were practically on the ground with hysterics."

The show called for Rock to arrive on a rickety old bus, to walk around the grounds with Doris and her dog, and to sit and reminisce. At every chance, Rock went to his trailer to lie down. At the end of shooting, on the second day, he was invited to stay for dinner with the production staff and Doris. "Oh, no," he said, "I've gotta catch a plane. I have to go to a birthday party."

Doris says, "I knew he was not going to a birthday party. He made that up. I knew as sure as I'm sitting here he wanted to go home and get in bed." Of course, she was right. The television show would be Rock Hudson's last performance, and it seemed fitting, satisfying, that it had been with Doris Day.

Rock arrived back at the Castle more emaciated and weak than when he had left. He seemed to be hanging by a thread. Mark Miller was firm: He said he had bought tickets for Rock and Dean Dittman to fly to Paris in two days. He had arranged with Dr. Dormont for Rock to receive treatment. He showed Rock a letter from a friend, Bob Darcy, who also had AIDS and had been in Paris for thirteen months getting HPA treatment. Bob Darcy wrote that he had gained weight, he was swimming two miles a day and he felt strong.

Rock heaved a sigh. "Okay, I'll go . . . but not with Dean. I want to go with Ron Channell." Mark had picked Dean Dittman because Dean knew Rock's condition and would know what to do in an emergency. He had not considered sending Rock with Marc Christian because Rock and Christian had been estranged for some time. They were leading separate lives, though Christian continued to sleep in the Castle in a separate bedroom. When Rock said he was willing to go with Ron Channell, Mark said he would cancel Dean and switch. Anything to get Rock back to Paris.

Ron Channell (pronounced like the name of the designer, Chanel), was a personal trainer Rock had hired in 1983 to come to the house and exercise with him. Ron was a tall, muscular, strapping young man with thick black hair, who possessed a childlike sense of humor that clicked with Rock's. They became buddies. Ron started coming to the Castle for an hour in the morning, several times a week; then it was five times a week; then he was staying for lunch and most of the afternoon. He and Rock horsed around and laughed and did jigsaw puzzles. They exercised together and Ron would encourage him, "Come on, guy!"

Ron made it clear to everyone in the house that he was straight and wasn't interested in anything but Rock's friendship. But the staff saw Rock grow steadily more infatuated. "He would practically sit by the window and wait for Ron," Mark Miller says. "The first thing he asked when he woke up was 'Did Ron call? When's he coming by?' Everything Ron did was wonderful."

In 1984, Rock had asked Ron to go with him to Europe for seven weeks, to attend the Deauville Film Festival and take a holiday. Rock would keep him on salary as a physical therapist. Unbeknownst to Ron, Rock was going to Paris to receive infusions of HPA 23 from Dr. Dormont. The treatment required Rock to be in Paris every other week, and to have infusions for three hours in the morning. Rock told Ron he had to go to script conferences in the morning; he would leave the hotel with his briefcase and secretly take a cab to Percy Hospital.

In between their weeks in Paris, Rock and Ron traveled to London, Rome, Barcelona and St. Tropez, where they went sailing in the Mediterranean. It was Ron's first trip to Europe, and Rock loved being his guide, taking him everywhere first class. Rock and Ron both said they had never had a more fantastic trip.

A year later, when Rock asked Ron to drop everything and return to Europe with him, Ron jumped. He was packed and ready to leave the following day.

This time, Mark Miller and James Wright told people Rock was going to Geneva to a special clinic, to be treated for anorexia. The flight was set for Saturday night at ten. On Friday, Mark drove to Palm Desert, where he and George had a home and spent their weekends. Mark could not sleep that night. He woke George at four in the morning. "Something tells me we should go back and make sure Rock gets off all right." Mark was frightened, and George tried to calm him. "I'm afraid we'll never see him again," Mark said.

On Saturday, James called from the Castle. "Mr. Hudson is terribly weak, he can hardly walk. He hasn't eaten at all. I don't think he can make it on a plane." Mark and George got in their car and started driving back to Los Angeles.

At the Castle, James kept looking in on Rock, who did not leave his bed. "Mr. Hudson," he said, "we have to pack." James always called him "Mr. Hudson." James was a lovable character, an enchanting mixture of wildness and propriety. He wore casual clothes and sometimes, nothing but a towel, but he never sat at the table with Rock, he sat on a stool behind the cooking island, and he always called Rock by his last name. "Mr. Hudson loved it—it kept us at a distance, you see, which is correct. Familiarity breeds contempt."

Rock looked at James in confusion. "Pack? For what?"

"You're leaving for Paris."

"No, I'm not. Not today."

"Yes. Tonight."

"I need a suitcase. I've gotta go out and buy a suitcase."

James was perplexed. "He had all kinds of suitcases upstairs."

The doorbell rang—it was Ross Hunter and Jacque Mapes. Ross Hunter had produced many of Hudson's most important films, including *Magnificent Obsession* and *Pillow Talk*. Hunter and Mapes had been constant guests at the Castle over the years. They said they had a lunch date with Rock, and James went up to announce them. Rock had forgotten the date, but he dressed and came downstairs.

"I hear you're going on a trip tonight," Ross said.

"I'm going to Paris."

"*No*," James said. "You're going to Geneva."

Rock told Ross and Jacque he had to buy a suitcase. They offered to drive him to a luggage store but Rock said, "No, *I* will drive. I've got a new Mercedes." They argued, but Rock was adamant. He had just bought a black Mercedes 500 SEL sedan because, he told Miller, he wanted to go on "double dates" with Ron Channell.

Rock, Ross Hunter and Jacque Mapes got into the Mercedes, and as Rock was pulling out of the driveway, he banged the new car into the gate. He swore, then laughed, then continued out to the street. "He was in no condition to drive," James says.

When Rock returned, without having eaten lunch but with a new suitcase, he went straight back to bed. James went up to the bedroom at four. "Mr. Hudson, we have to pack. You lie there. I'll collect your things."

James packed two suitcases and asked, "Can I get you anything?"

"No," Rock said, and went back to sleep.

Mark and George arrived at the Castle around 7 P.M. Marc Christian answered the door. "We're here to see Rock." Christian made a sweeping gesture toward the stairs, as if to say, go on up. They found Rock nude, walking aimlessly around his bedroom. Mark and George were shocked at his skeletal appearance. "He looked like a famine victim, his skin all wrinkled and hanging in flaps." When they learned he hadn't eaten all day, they started a chant for a chocolate milk shake. "James makes the best chocolate shakes in the world! Milk shake! Let's have a milk shake!"

Mark and George jollied Rock into the shower. James brought up

23

the shakes, and Rock came out of the shower and collapsed in a chair. George helped him put on his shirt and pants, then pulled on his socks and shoes for him, all the while giving him sips of the milk shake. "Praise whatever powers," George says, "he finished the whole milk shake."

Ron Channell arrived, the limousine appeared and they left for the airport at 8:30. Mark sat in front with the driver, who was new and didn't know how to find the airport. Rock and Ron sat in the back-seat, and George was in the jump seat facing them. Rock, with a sweet smile, hooked his arm through Ron's. "I was moved," George says. "Rock looked happy. In thirty years, I had never seen him put his arm through a man's when other people were present. I wouldn't have believed Rock was capable of showing that kind of affection and warmth. I almost broke down. It was as if he was telling me, 'George, this is the one. This is it.'"

A representative from the Mark Allan Travel Agency, which provides special service to celebrities, met them at the International Airlines Terminal. "Don't go any farther," he said. "Air France has been tipped off that Rock's not well and in no condition to fly. They may not let him board." Mark got Rock and everyone to sit down in the lounge and engage in spirited conversation while the travel agent took the tickets and passports to the check-in counter. George stood in front of Rock, blocking him from view. The staff at the ticket counter stared in their direction. The agent told Air France that Rock was fine.

Ron Channell asked Mark to step aside with him. "I'm nervous— what are we doing?" Ron said. "What am I getting into?" Mark realized, at that moment, he should be going on the plane in place of Ron, but he had no passport. "I'm sorry to put you through this," Mark said. "If I had a passport, I would get on that plane right like I am, with no change of clothes or anything. Please, the doctors have ordered him to go to Paris. Try and get through it. I'll make it up to you. There'll be a limousine to meet you at the airport and take you to the Ritz."

The agent returned with boarding passes. Air France had cleared Rock for departure. The agent and Ron each took one of Rock's arms and walked on either side of him, supporting him, through the gate and onto the plane. The agent told Mark and George, "It's better if

you don't go any farther—so nothing will look out of the ordinary."
Mark and George headed out of the terminal.

As they walked away from Rock, they were in agony. All year, they
had been trying to get Rock on this plane, but now, they wondered,
was it too late? Would he make it? He couldn't dress himself. Would
he even live through the flight? Mark had the impulse to turn around
and bring him back, but he thought, "At the other end of the rain-
bow may be help. Here, there's no help at all."

Mark and George waited around the airport until the plane had
taken off and they could be sure Rock had not been turned back.
Then, sick at heart, they started the three-hour drive back to Palm
Desert.

They did not make it to the desert that night. They had to stop
north of Los Angeles and continue Sunday morning. When they
reached Palm Desert, there was a frantic message on the machine
from Ron Channell in Paris. Rock had refused to eat or drink on the
eleven-hour flight, had refused even water. At the airport in Paris,
there had been no limousine. So Ron had been stuck with three
suitcases and a movie star who couldn't walk. Ron had maneuvered
Rock through customs and into the VIP lounge, found a cab and
gotten bags and movie star into the vehicle. When they had checked
into their rooms at the Ritz, Rock had collapsed on the bed and was
breathing irregularly. "What do I do!" Ron said on the machine.

Mark called Rock's doctor in Los Angeles, Gary Sugarman, and
called Ron back. "Get Rock immediately into the American Hospital, by limousine, taxi, I don't care how you do it." He also told him
to call Dr. Dominique Dormont. Mark said he would renew his own
passport and catch the next flight to Paris.

When doctors at the American Hospital examined Rock and saw
the scars from his heart-bypass surgery, they assumed it was heart
trouble and put him in the cardiology section. Ron Channell did not
know and could not tell them about AIDS. Rock was severely dehydrated, so they started intravenous feeding. Meanwhile, Ron called
Dr. Dormont at home and left four messages on his answering machine. The first said, call Mr. Hudson at the Ritz. The second said,
come as soon as possible. The third said, come quickly. The fourth
said, Mr. Hudson is in the American Hospital.

Dr. Dormont had been out of the city on Sunday. When he returned home at 1 A.M., he tried to call the hospital but didn't know under what name Rock had been admitted. "I asked for Roy Scherer, because I had treated him under that name. There was no Scherer in the hospital."

Dr. Dormont, thirty-six, was a lieutenant commander in the navy, who had been doing research on AIDS for three years. He conducted his work at the Percy Hospital, a military research hospital in Clamart, on the outskirts of Paris. He was in his car, driving home Monday evening when he heard on the news: Rock Hudson was dying of liver cancer, and had been brought to the American Hospital. Later, he would learn that a scan had been taken at the hospital, which had showed abnormalities in the liver. The news had leaked out that it was cancer.

Dr. Dormont received a call that night from Dr. Sugarman in Los Angeles. He asked Dr. Dormont to take Rock out of the American Hospital and put him in Percy. Dr. Dormont said, "In France, it's not like that. The best thing is for someone close to Rock to come to Paris and together we will go to the American Hospital and talk to the physicians."

Mark Miller arrived in Paris on Tuesday, July 23. He and Ron Channell went to the American Hospital where they met the cardiologist, Florent de Vernejoul, who had taken charge of Rock's case. Mark did not speak French and the cardiologist spoke passable English. Because of difficulties in translation, there was a miscommunication. The cardiologist meant to tell Mark that he suspected liver cancer, but that Hudson was too weak for exploratory surgery. What Mark understood was: Rock had liver cancer and it was "inoperable."

Mark walked into Rock's room and found him half unconscious. Mark grabbed Rock's foot through the blanket. "I'm here," he said. "We'll take care of everything." Mark broke down and wept. Later, he said, "When I entered the room, I knew he was going to die. Before Paris, I had thought he could turn it around, but when I saw him in that room, I knew."

Rock murmured he was glad Mark was there. Mark said, "I just got in, I'm going to the hotel and I'll see you later."

That night, there were reporters and photographers swarming all

over the Ritz Hotel. Ron Channell was in a state of distraction. He
had finally reached Dr. Dormont the night before, and Dr. Dormont
had told him Rock had AIDS. "Why didn't Rock tell me! My God,
why wouldn't he tell me!" he said, and broke into tears.

"He would tell no one," Mark said. "He wanted to live a normal
life."

Ron Channell was sick for Rock and frightened for himself. He
and Rock had horsed around and shared food. Rock had kissed members of Ron Channell's family when he met them. What if the disease could be transmitted through saliva? Ron was worried the press
would identify him incorrectly as Rock's lover, and that his own career would be ruined because of the taint of association with someone
who has AIDS. Mark arranged for Ron to take the Concorde to New
York the next morning. "How can I leave? I don't want to be photographed!" Ron said.

"Ron, this is not my first day in pictures," Mark said. "I'll get you
out with no one knowing." Mark said he would order a limousine for
"Mr. Channell" to wait at the front door of the hotel at 9 A.M. At 7
A.M., he would take Ron down a back hall and out a service door,
where he would have a taxi waiting. Ron would miss the press entirely. The plan worked.

Before Ron left, Mark said to him, "While we're here—I'm sure
Rock will approve—let's go buy you a Rolex watch. He was planning
to give you one for Christmas." They sneaked out of the hotel, found
a Rolex store, and Ron wore the watch home on the Concorde.

On Wednesday, July 24, when Mark went to the hospital, he
found Rock much improved, due to the intravenous feeding. There
was color in his cheeks and the deep creases seemed to have been
smoothed. Mark started to tell him how wonderful he looked, but
Rock waved his hand and said, eagerly, "Where's Ron?"

"I put him on the Concorde to New York. He left two hours ago."

A veil seemed to drop over Rock's face, wiping away all traces of
expression. His next words were toneless. "Two hours ago. Why?"

"He went to pieces," Mark said, "into total panic, when he found
out you had . . ."

Rock finished the sentence. "The plague." He stared past Mark. "I
knew this would happen. That he'd desert me when he found out."

"He was shaking with fright," Mark said. "He cried most of the night. I booked his flight and then got him out of the hotel by the usual routine . . ."

There was desolation in Rock's voice, though his face and eyes still showed no expression.

"Nothing. Not even a good-bye."

"He wasn't thinking," Mark said. "He couldn't. He's afraid the press will peg him as your last lover. Which they will, if they get to him."

Rock turned on his side, away from Mark, and faced the wall. Mark walked to the picture window and stood, studying the apartment complex across the street. He wondered if there were cameras or telephoto lenses pointed at him from behind the shaded windows. He asked the private nurse, a young Irishwoman named Ann, to be sure to keep the curtains drawn far enough to screen Rock from view. She hurried over and drew the curtains.

On his way out, Mark stopped to talk with Dr. de Vernejoul. To Mark's surprise, the doctor still was unaware that Rock had AIDS. Mark had expected that one of Rock's doctors in California would inform him, but none had, so Mark told the cardiologist himself. The doctor was upset. The American Hospital did not accept AIDS patients. The staff would be furious that they had not been warned before examining Rock so they could have taken special precautions. Rock would have to leave the American Hospital, but where could he go? He was too weak to travel.

Mark took a limousine to the Percy Hospital to meet with Dr. Dormont. The press chased him clear across Paris. From this point on, Mark could not go anywhere without being tailed and photographed. When his car drove into the military installation, the gates closed behind him, leaving the press outside.

Mark was surprised at Dr. Dormont's appearance: He looked in his twenties, although he was thirty-six, had short blond hair and was dressed in blue shirt, khaki pants, argyle socks and loafers. Dr. Dormont told him he had asked his commanding officer for permission to transport Hudson from the American Hospital to Percy, but the commander had refused. Dr. Dormont was treating Americans on an out-patient basis, but he could not admit Americans, particularly "show business people," to the hospital. Dr. Dormont had asked for permission to visit Hudson at the American Hospital, but this also was refused. "If you have contacts at the White House, perhaps they could intercede with President Mitterrand."

Mark returned to the Ritz, called Dale Olson in California and asked him to notify the White House.

"I'll work on it," Dale said. "How are you doing there?"

"I've got fifty messages under my door," Mark said.

"Do you need someone to get between you and the press?"

"Yes," Mark said, and Dale said he would find someone.

An hour later, there was a rap at the door. Mark answered it in his blue nightshirt. The visitor was Yanou Collart, a French publicist whom Olson had called. Yanou is forty-two, with streaked blond hair, a youthful figure and an air of femininity and savvy. She represents celebrities and the great chefs of France, and likes to entertain them at dinner parties in her home near the Champs Élysées. She had met Rock and had become friendly with him during his European trip of 1984. Mark told her, "This is the first time in my life the press has been chasing me for statements. Can you take over?"

"Yes, of course."

Mark then told her the problem: Rock had AIDS. He had to leave the American Hospital and could not be accepted at Percy. Yanou was shocked. "I knew he was homosexual but I was not expecting AIDS. In Paris at that time, we knew very little about the disease. We heard it was a new sickness in America that homosexuals were dying from."

Yanou began calling her contacts at the Ministry of Defense, to see if the commander's decision could be overruled. Some of the people she needed to reach were out of Paris, and by midnight, she had failed to get an answer.

Thursday morning, July 25, Mark and Yanou went together to see Rock. Mark told her, "Don't cry," so, Yanou says, "I tried to make it fun."

They found Rock sitting up in a chair while the nurses made his bed. "Hey, it's great to see you," he said to Yanou. "Isn't this a hoot? Here I am, back in Paris, my favorite city, and I'm in a hospital."

Yanou said, "That is not important. Anyone can be in a hospital, and in a few days you'll be feeling better."

Rock said, "Listen, stay around because I won't be in here long, and when I'm out, I want you to cook for me. Make that wonderful chocolate mousse."

Yanou says Rock had "fallen in love" with the chocolate mousse she'd served him at a party the year before. "I do the best chocolate mousse in the world," she says. "It's a mousse of bitter chocolate, made from my mother's recipe." She promised to fix it for Rock as soon as he was released.

Later that morning, Yanou and Mark learned that the commanding officer of Percy Hospital had reversed his decision and told Dr. Dormont that Rock could be admitted. It is unclear who intervened on Rock's behalf. Some say it was Nancy Reagan, who called Mitterrand; others report that the French minister of defense made the decision. The day before, however, President Reagan had called Rock in the hospital. Rock reported it to Miller: "I got a call from the President."

"Oh, what did he say?"

"He said, 'Hi. Nancy sends her love.' I said, 'Good. I send my love to Nancy.' Then Ronnie said, 'We're both not in the best condition. [Reagan had cancer of the colon.] I hope we'll both be better in a while.'"

Rock added, "It was like a script. We both read our lines perfectly. But . . . Why did he call?"

Dr. Dormont came to the hospital to see Rock later that morning. Rock's face lit up when he recognized the doctor. Dr. Dormont examined Rock, drew blood and was shocked at how debilitated and dehydrated he was. He was far too weak to benefit from injections of HPA 23.

At 11 A.M., there was a meeting at the American Hospital to determine what would be done with Rock. Mark, Yanou and Dr. Dormont attended, along with the cardiologist and staff members of the hospital. Everyone had a different concern. Certain members of the hospital staff wanted Rock removed as soon as possible. They could not cover up the fact that he had AIDS and told Mark that if he did not make an announcement disclosing the disease, they would. Some of the staff hoped that Rock could be moved before the announcement was made, so the hospital would not be associated with AIDS patients.

Dr. Dormont, on the other hand, wanted Rock to stay put until he was stronger. Mark Miller wanted Rock to get the best treatment and to have his life prolonged. "We were dealing—trying to get Rock what we could." Yanou sent word to the press that there would be a statement at 2 P.M., and began to draft the release. The statement was only one paragraph, but the group argued about it for two hours until it was satisfactory to all parties.

Mark went back up to Rock's room. "Rock," he said, "I'm sorry, but, unfortunately, we have to announce that you have AIDS."

Rock stared at Mark, then waved his hand in dismissal. "Who cares. Go ahead. We've hidden it for over a year. What's the point."

Mark brought Yanou in. "I have to read you the statement I will be reading to the press, with your approval," she said. She sat down at the foot of his bed and began to read the draft, in French-accented English. As she spoke, her eyes filled with tears. "Mr. Rock Hudson has acquired immune deficiency syndrome." Except for her voice, the room was still, so still that every sound was magnified. A sheet rustled. The hand on the wall clock ticked. "Mr. Rock Hudson has acquired immune deficiency syndrome, which was diagnosed over a year ago in the United States."

Rock lay motionless. He was witnessing the death of the image he had created. For thirty-six years, he had planned, plotted and protected his image as the romantic hero, the leading man. For thirty-six years, he had lived with the fear of being exposed. There had been years of furtively exchanging phone numbers and sneaking out at three in the morning. Years of taking beautiful women to premieres, then going home to the man he lived with. Years of being careful not to go out in public with "too many boys." Three years of marriage to a woman he thought he could love, which proved impossible. And, finally, after the social changes of the sixties and seventies, and after Rock's position as a star had become secure, there had been a relaxation. The press knew and protected him. The entertainment world knew and didn't seem to care. Now, everyone would know. Rock Hudson would be unmasked.

Perhaps there was some relief in the unburdening. There would be no further tension or anxiety. He could let go. Everything was over: life, career, the world. What did it matter? Rock could not know or even guess, at that moment, that with the death of the illusion, something new would be created.

Yanou finished reading. Rock stared at her, then said, "Okay. Go out and give it to the dogs."

Mark Miller watched from the window of a private conference room as Yanou walked out to face the press on the hospital steps. She read her statement. They listened in stunned silence. When she finished, they ran, knocking each other down, to get to the hospital phones. A British woman cried, "He's got AIDS. He's finished."

Mark Miller knew the news was explosive, but he had not expected it to be the lead item on the evening news around the world. Within hours, there were hundreds of telegrams and messages for Rock at the hospital. Over the next two weeks, Rock would receive thirty thousand letters from fans in every country. What was more astounding than the numbers was the content of the letters. With few exceptions, people wrote: Your private life is your own affair. We love you and are praying for you.

That night, Mark was awakened by a call from Marc Christian in Los Angeles, who had heard the news on television and was enraged. According to Miller, the conversation went as follows. Christian said, "How dare you not tell me!"

Miller said, "It was up to Rock to tell you. Rock had the disease, not me. Rock ordered me not to tell anyone."

"But why the hell didn't you tell me anyway? You should have told me. I've been exposed. It's not fair to me!"

"I couldn't tell you," Mark said. "My loyalties are to Rock Hudson and you know that. I'm not a friend of yours for thirty-five years. I tried to give you clues. I asked you to get a complete physical last year, remember? The doctor who examined you knew you'd been exposed to AIDS and said you had no sign of it. I doubt you have it now." Miller told him they would bring him to Paris immediately so Dr. Dormont could culture his blood.

On Friday, July 26, when Mark arrived at Rock's room, Rock looked at him with a glint in his eye. "Got some brush fires out there?"

"It's a fire storm," Mark said.

"Thought it might be." Rock made a spiraling motion with his finger.

"I can't leave my hotel room without being photographed," Mark said. "I've become a little media star."

Rock laughed. "Remember how Andy Warhol said everyone should be famous for fifteen minutes? Well, you've been on sixteen. Get off!"

The twinkle had returned to Rock's eye, Mark thought, because Rock had always loved it when controversy was swirling around him. "He was happiest when he was putting out brush fires." Though he protested that he hated publicity, he knew the power of keeping his name in print.

Mark told him Elizabeth Taylor had called and said that Rock, by coming forward and admitting he had AIDS, was going to "save millions of lives."

"Why?" Rock said.

Mark showed him some of the telegrams: from Frank Sinatra, Gregory Peck, Marlene Dietrich, James Garner, Carol Burnett, Ali MacGraw, Jack Lemmon, Richard Dreyfuss, Ava Gardner, Mickey Rooney, Milton Berle. There was one from Madonna: "To Rock Hudson, my heartthrob since childhood. Saying lots of prayers for you. All my love, Madonna."

Rock was puzzled. "I don't know Madonna. I barely know Gregory Peck."

Then there were the cables from motorcycle policemen and switchboard operators and teachers, sending love and wishes of encouragement. Rock could not make sense of it; he had expected the opposite.

Late on Friday, the doctors decided Rock was strong enough to undergo a biopsy of the liver. They would have the results Monday. Dr. Dormont told Rock he had two choices: He could return to the States, to UCLA Medical Center, and at a later date come back to Paris for treatment; or he could go to Percy Hospital and stay two to three weeks until he was in a condition where it might be possible to give him HPA 23. "Think about it," Dr. Dormont said. "You can give me your answer Sunday."

Over the weekend, Yanou flew to St. Tropez, where she had a prior commitment to do publicity on a film. Mark went to the hospital Sunday morning and was met by the public-relations director,

Bruce Redor, Dr. de Vernejoul and another specialist. They sat him down in the conference room and told him Rock was in very serious condition. No matter what they found in the biopsy, Rock's white-cell count was so low he would not survive. They said he would probably die within three days. They asked Mark to tell Rock.

Mark agreed, but said he wanted them to come with him. Rock was sitting up in bed—he'd been expecting Mark's visit. Mark grabbed his foot through the covers and held onto it. "I have bad news for you," he said. "You've got three days to live."

"Oh, fuck." Rock turned to the window. He made the spiraling motion with his finger, the gesture he always used to suggest, with irony, "Whoopee." Then he looked at the men standing opposite him with dour faces.

"What'll I do for an encore?"

They laughed—it broke the tension and they were grateful.

"You can go to Percy Hospital," Mark said. "That's been cleared. Or you can go to California . . ."

"I want to die in my own bed," Rock said.

"You're on."

Mark asked if he wanted to see Phyllis Gates, his former wife. Rock made a rocking gesture with his palm, meaning he wasn't sure.

"I'm leaving you with a mess," Rock said. "And believe me, it's going to be a real mess. I'm sorry."

Mark did not focus on that statement or what it meant. He had one mission: to find a way to get Rock home.

Sunday night, Mark called Yanou back from St. Tropez, and all that night and Monday, they worked on chartering a plane. A commercial flight was impossible because Rock needed to travel with medical personnel and intensive-care equipment. They found a 707, but it could not fly to Los Angeles without stopping. Europe Assistance offered to rent them a 747 for $250,000, including the intensive-care unit, doctors and a nurse. Later, when Dr. Dormont heard the figure, he stood up from his chair. "What? That's my research budget for four years!" Then he reflected: It was Rock's money, he had earned it and this was his last wish.

The money had to be wired from New York before the plane would take off. The wire was sent, and departure was set for 11 P.M. Monday.

Yanou rented an ambulance to take Rock from the hospital to the heliport near the Eiffel Tower. To throw off the press, she gave out a statement saying Rock was stable and would stay at the hospital one more week. It rained Monday evening, and when the ambulance drove out with Rock, there were no reporters around. Dr. Dormont and Dr. de Vernejoul followed in a separate car. When Rock was transferred to the helicopter, they said good-bye to Yanou. "I don't think we can be of further assistance."

Rock was sleeping—he'd been given a sedative. The helicopter landed at Charles de Gaulle Airport in an area beyond customs, where photographers were not allowed. Rock was carried on a stretcher into the 747, and the stretcher was placed across a row of seats.

Rock woke up and saw Yanou standing by him.

"Where am I?"

"Rock, you are in a plane taking you back to Los Angeles," she said.

"Am I flying?"

"Not yet. You will be flying in about forty minutes."

"Who's with me?" He looked about. "Where's Mark?"

"Mark is not here. He has to stay in Paris to pay bills and take care of paperwork. He'll return the day after tomorrow."

Rock looked disoriented.

"Be happy," Yanou said. "Everyone is waiting for you on the other side. Dale Olson is there . . . your doctor . . ."

"But, how did I get on a plane?"

"Listen, I will explain it." Yanou told him how she'd rented the ambulance, rented the helicopter, issued a false statement to the press and landed with the helicopter beyond customs. "So we avoid all the press!"

Rock started to laugh—the deep, rippling laugh that so enchanted his friends. "I love that," he said. "Fuck the press."

The nurse walked by and Rock asked Yanou, "Who is she?"

"That's the nurse who's going with you."

"She's very pretty."

"Rock, please don't start, because I am very jealous," Yanou said.

"But . . . you're flying with me, aren't you?"

"No, I cannot."

"You're not coming with me either?"

She said she was sorry, and explained that she had work commitments.

Rock started to cry.

He was alone, a dying man on a deserted jumbo jet, with two doctors and a nurse who did not speak his language. Yanou took his hand, but after a moment he stopped crying.

He swallowed, regained control. He smiled. "You know, it would have been great if you could have flown with me. You could have made the chocolate mousse at my house."

She kissed him on the cheek.

Rock looked at her with wonder. "You're really not afraid . . . to touch me?" He gestured toward her hand in his.

"No," she said.

The flight attendant came up. "The plane is ready. We can leave."

Rock said to Yanou, "I'll call you when I get home."

It was one in the morning, Tuesday, July 30, when the plane landed in Los Angeles. No personal friends were there to meet Rock, just the press, who were kept at a distance. He was taken by helicopter to UCLA, where he stayed for a month before returning to the Castle, where he would die, as he had wanted, in his own bed.

CHAPTER 2

Nobody is discovered. Ever. Publicity departments loved to say that Lana Turner was discovered sitting at a soda fountain counter, drinking a chocolate soda. . . . It isn't true. I mean, there are too many interesting-looking people on earth for that to ever happen.

But the movies themselves have created this myth—this monster. It's been fictionalized a thousand times. Warner Baxter said to Ginger Rogers or somebody, "Come with me and I'll make you a star. You don't belong in the chorus, you belong in the lead," or "The star has broken her ankle, so you are going on in her place tonight, and that will make you a star." Trash.

I wasn't discovered. I knew I wanted to be an actor when I was a little boy. But living in a small town in the Middle West, I didn't say so, because that's just sissy stuff.

I once asked my stepfather if I could have drama lessons. The old man said, "Why?" When I said I wanted to be an actor . . . Crack! (makes striking gesture with arm) and that was that.

But I think I saw just about every film. When The Hurricane came out, with Jon Hall and Dorothy Lamour, in 1937, I was twelve years old. Jon Hall did a swan dive from a crow's nest into the lagoon and swam to Dorothy Lamour. I'd always been a diver, so that clinched it. I had to be an actor, and go to Tahiti and be like Jon Hall. But I never said anything. I just kept my mouth shut.

In 1931, when Rock was six, he lived with his maternal grandparents, James and Mary Ellen Wood, in a bungalow at 719 Center Street in Winnetka, Illinois. It was the Depression, and there were six adults and five children living in a one-bedroom house with one bathroom. Grandma and Grandpa Wood slept in the glazed-in sun porch. One of their sons, John, his wife and four children slept in the room upstairs, a converted attic. Rock, who was then Roy Scherer, Jr., his mother, Katherine, and father, Roy Harold Scherer, slept in the one bedroom.

37

Young Roy was Grandma's favorite, and Grandma Wood was the reigning spirit of the house. "When Grandma said, 'Jump,' you said, 'How high?'" one of her grandchildren remembers. "But whatever Roy did was fine with her. He got away with murder." Roy once ate a pound of raw bacon and took a bite from every apple in the ice box, mischief he refused to admit he'd committed and for which his cousins were punished. It was a family joke that in *Giant,* when Rock Hudson got beaten up at the end of the film, he was "finally getting the licking he'd deserved at Grandma Wood's."

Roy and his cousins—three girls and a boy—had great fun in the house on Center Street. They did not experience it as hard times, nor were they aware that they were a working-class family in a suburb inhabited by the wealthy. They ate a big dinner together in the dining room every night at five-thirty. They said grace, and Grandma Wood proceeded to eat her dessert first. Grandpa, who worked for Winnetka Coal and Lumber, dished out the plates: It was meat and potatoes and gravy and vegetables, except on Friday, when Grandma made her baked spaghetti, a family treat. She told her children she had a special dispensation from the bishop to use bacon in the sauce. After dinner, the adults sat down for a game of 500, and the kids played in the porch or listened to *The Witch's Cave* on the radio.

When he became a movie star, Rock Hudson told people he'd been an altar boy and had gotten in trouble for giggling in church. But that was not so. "No way Rock was an altar boy," says his cousin Dorothy Raychek. "Grandma Wood was a strict Catholic, but Roy's mother, Auntie Kay, defied her." Kay sent Roy to public school while his cousins went to Sacred Heart; Kay and Roy were the only ones in the family who did not go to church on Sunday. Family lore is that while Kay was working, Grandma Wood secretly took Roy off to be baptized at Sacred Heart Church in Hubbard Woods.

Kay Wood was a large woman, handsome, and she could be overbearing. "Grandma Wood the Second," her nieces called her. She made her own rules and bowed her head to no one. In Winnetka, at that time, divorce was a stigma, practically unheard of, but Kay was to be divorced three times. Roy Scherer was her first husband. He was an auto mechanic, but in the Depression years, he could not earn enough to support his family.

In 1932, when Roy was seven, his cousin Dorothy was home from school sick one day. "Uncle Roy came out of their bedroom carrying a suitcase, and gave me a nickel not to tell anyone he was going," she recalls. "I cherished that nickel! I didn't say a thing. I watched him walk down the street and that's the last I saw of him."

Roy was devastated when his father left the family and went to California. It was the most bitter rejection of his life, but it was never discussed in the house. No one actually told the children Uncle Roy was not coming back. "We were brought up not to ask questions," Dorothy says. "What happened in the adult world did not concern the children."

Not long after Scherer had left, Kay started dating Wally Fitzgerald, who came to the house in a marine dress uniform. Fitzgerald had a job shoveling coal in the "Water Works," Winnetka's water and electric plant. He married Kay and adopted Roy, who became Roy Fitzgerald.

At New Trier High School, there seemed to be nothing promising or exceptional about Roy Fitzgerald. He didn't earn good grades, he didn't go out for sports or activities, even though New Trier was renowned for its drama and music programs. He was not in the most popular crowd and was not even considered especially attractive. He was tall, skinny and gangly—he had shot up to six feet four and not filled out—and he was embarrassed about his size. His pants were never long enough,and he had to cinch in the waist with belts.

He was shy, partly because his home life was chaotic. Wally Fitzgerald used to beat Roy, saying he wanted to "make a man out of him." Sometimes, when Wally was arguing with Kay, he would go into Rock's room and start hitting him. "We used to see Roy covered with bruises," says his cousin Helen Folkers. "One day, Auntie Kay showed up with two black eyes." Kay divorced Wally, married him a second time, then divorced him again when Roy was fifteen.

Roy and his mother were extremely close. "She was mother, father and big sister to me," he said, "and I was son and brother to her, regardless of who she was married to." Kay played piano and Roy learned to play by ear, for they never had money for lessons. Kay took jobs to support them; briefly, she worked as a live-in housekeeper for a wealthy family, and she and Roy shared a bed in the servants' quarters. For several years, they lived in an apartment above Walgreen's Drug Store. As soon as Roy was old enough, he took part-time jobs, which is one of the reasons he didn't participate in after-school activities.

His cousins remember him as happy and likable. "He always had a smile in his eyes, and the most infectious laugh. He would start to giggle and everyone would giggle and couldn't stop." He played boogie-woogie on the piano, and he could jitterbug better than any of them.

His best friends were Jimmy Matteoni and Pat McGuire. Roy was to remain close to Jimmy all his life. "We laughed all the time," Jimmy says. They had private jokes, buzzwords they could utter at any moment and break each other up. One was from a Danny Kaye movie, *Up in Arms*. Danny Kaye did a lot of nonsense patter, and one line tickled Roy: "Hey, hey, cockda bina cerza." Roy would say "Bina cerza" whenever he wanted to undercut something serious. It was sure to send Jimmy into hysterics.

They had a game of "last tag" that was to run for forty years. "I'd say good-bye and start home," Jim recalls, "then I'd tag him and run like hell. He'd chase me all the way to my house, laughing, then I'd chase him back to his house and we'd go back and forth three times." After he became a star, Rock would arrange to meet Jim whenever he passed through Chicago. "One time, just as he was about to step on a plane, I tagged him and ran. He turned right around and chased me out of the airport—two grown men in suits!—with everyone yelling, 'Mr. Hudson!' But he caught me—he'd never give up."

Roy and Jimmy used to go down to the South Side of Chicago to buy blues and boogie records. "We'd listen and try to play them on the piano. Roy had an excellent ear and could pick up anything." They rode the bus one hundred miles to see *The Gold Rush* and *The Great Dictator* with Charlie Chaplin. When they liked a movie, they would see it dozens of times. One of their favorites was *Fantasia*, which introduced them to classical music. They would sit at the piano in Jim's living room and pick out a Bach concerto, with Roy playing one hand and Jim the other. Jim would go on to become a music teacher and start his own school. Roy did not tell Jim he wanted to be an actor, even though Jim was his most trusted friend.

On the weekends, they would go on double dates, sometimes triple dates, to a movie or a dance with a big band. They took out many girls, but there were two Roy liked—Nancy Gillogly and Sue Ford. At the end of the evening, they would park and neck. Jim says he had "absolutely no inkling that Roy was homosexual. Quite the contrary—he chased girls with great care and perseverance. When Pat joined the navy, we went to Saint Louis for the weekend and picked up girls at a dance. Roy talked his girl into going up to his room at the Jefferson Hotel. Pat and I didn't have success, so we went up and pestered him and he was mad."

Rock Hudson, many years later, told friends he had had some awareness he was attracted to men from the time he was nine years old. There had been an incident with an older man on a farm where he was visiting, and it had been pleasurable. In fact, Roy had encouraged it. "But I was convinced I was the only guy who felt as I did." He became more conscious of his sexuality while he was in the navy, where he had encounters with several men, but they were secretive and fraught with risk.

February 22, 1944

Dear Jim,

Well, goddamit, if you don't write to me I guess I'll have to write to you. Meat!

Right now we're waiting for the tailor, then we get our service stripes. Yesterday we had our strength tests. They had us do jumps, situps, chinups and some other shit-ass things. The only thing I did very well was the situps. I did 108 of them. Boy is my stomach sore.

I don't know if Ma told you (if she didn't, don't say anything) she's leaving for California March 15—3 days before our first visiting day, March 18! You be sure and come up here that day. Bring some others up too.

Of course we aren't going to have any parties in my apartment on my leaves and liberty or anything. Oh no! What a poor time . . .

I believe we're being pushed through here because we've been here only 63 days and we're getting our service stripes. We also know how to use a rifle and bayonet too! So I'll be home before you know it.

More later,
Write sooner,
Roy

Roy Fitzgerald enlisted in the navy in 1943 and was shipped on the S.S. *Lew Wallace,* a Kaiser Liberty ship, to Samar, a sandy island in the Philippines. He was assigned to AROU 2—Aviation Repair and Overhaul Unit—and worked on the airstrip, unloading naval planes from carriers. Rock Hudson would later say in many interviews that as a mechanic, he had made a mistake that caused two planes to be demolished and as a result, he was demoted to the laundry. But later he admitted, "I made that up."

Roy was transferred to the laundry in August 1945, when the war ended and there were no more planes to unload. He had a buddy, Eddie Kraft, and in their free time, they would take a jeep, go for a drive on the beach and make ice cream from a powdered mix. He was called "Fitz" by the men who shared his barracks—a quonset hut. One, Darrold Miller, who lives in Spokane, Washington, says, "We heard rumors about Fitz for thirty years, but we dismissed them because we never saw any evidence of that in our barracks. He was a great guy—one of our bunch. When the news came out last July, I told my friends: It must have been that dang Hollywood down there. It ruins people, with this homosexual business or the damn drugs."

Roy was shipped home in 1946, and as the carrier approached the Golden Gate Bridge, the seamen crowded on deck to try to spot the orange towers in the fog.

"There it is!" someone shouted. "We're home, we're home!" The lights on the bridge came on, winking in the fog. Fireboats sprayed water, and there was a banner on Angel Island saying, "Thanks, boys, for a job well done!" An escort ship brought out cases of Coca-Cola, and the green, frosted, hourglass bottles were passed out to every hand.

Rock remembered how, when he had sailed out of the Golden Gate to start his tour, Doris Day's voice had come over the ship's loudspeakers singing "Sentimental Journey." The seamen had fallen silent. They were eighteen-year-olds, going off to war, and Doris was singing about the journey home. "She had the whole ship in tears, including me," Roy said.

He could not have believed, had anyone told him, that thirteen years later, he would be on screen with Doris Day in one of the most successful comedies of the era. That he and Doris would be a team— the embodiment of all that could be beautiful and true between a man and woman. Doris Day—the voice on the speakers—was as far away from Seaman Roy Fitzgerald as the moon.

*   *   *

Roy decided to go to California instead of New York to break into acting because his father, Roy Scherer, was living in Long Beach, a small town south of Los Angeles. Roy hoped to renew his closeness with his father, but Scherer had remarried and adopted a daughter, and having Roy in the house created tension. Roy tried working for his father, selling vacuum cleaners door to door, but after a month he had failed to sell a machine.

He moved out of his father's place and into a rooming house, and found a job driving a truck for Budget Pack. He bought a suit and whenever he had a free moment, stood outside the gates of studios, waiting to be discovered. He was lonely. "People weren't friendly like they were in the Midwest," he said. "It was very difficult for me to make friends."

But Long Beach had a homosexual community, and in 1947, Roy stumbled upon it. There was a gay bar where men would sit around on stools and listen to a black woman sing bawdy songs. On the weekends, gay men would gather on the sand and take the sun in front of the Villa Riviera, an apartment building on Ocean Boulevard.

For the first time, Roy was introduced to a large group of men who were open about their sexuality. One of the men Roy met was Ken Hodge, who had worked in radio for many years, producing Lux Radio Theatre. Ken was thirty-six and Roy was twenty-one. Ken seemed the essence of sophistication: His blond hair was beautifully styled, he was well dressed, and he lived in a penthouse with a sweeping view and beautiful antique furniture, in the Chateau Marmont, a building owned by his Aunt Bernadette. Ken was the first person Roy had met who had any connection to show business. Ken had left the business and moved to Long Beach to manage his aunt's properties, but he was casting about for a way to return.

Ken and Roy became lovers. It was Ken who arranged for Roy to have his first publicity pictures taken. Ken offered to become Roy's agent; he would groom him, guide him, and together they would launch a new star.

Before he died, Rock Hudson told me the following story of how he got his name from his first agent, Henry Willson:

Henry thought he knew what was best for me. I remember he said, "We have to change your name."

"Why?" I asked. "I don't want one of those silly names."

"You have to," he said, "so it looks good on the marquee. Roy Fitzgerald is too long."

"What about Geraldine Fitzgerald? Is that too long?"

But Henry insisted. He hit me with Hudson. Then he had some real macho, cockamamie first names. Like Dirk. Lance. Finally he said, "What about Rock?" That clicked. "Yeah, that sounds pretty good," I said. *It was not too far from Roy, and no one else had it. So that was it.*

Rock told this story, in different words, so many times and so consistently that it is part of the canon about Rock Hudson. But shortly after Hudson died, I received a letter from Herbert Millspaugh, a retired clerk in San Francisco, who said he had been present the day Roy Fitzgerald was named Rock Hudson. He included names, dates and supporting photographs.

In the summer of 1947, Millspaugh said, he was living in Long Beach, working for the Texas Oil Company, hanging out by the Villa Riviera and going to parties at the penthouse of Ken Hodge. Ken introduced him to an extremely handsome young man he'd just met, Roy Fitzgerald, who wanted to be an actor. One Sunday, a group of Ken's friends walked back from the beach to Ken's apartment, fixed gin and tonics and started trying to think up a name for the actor. Most stars changed their names when they began—it was part of the process of being reborn, of bringing a romantic character to life.

"Ken wanted a name that suggested strength," Millspaugh said. "Someone came up with Rock. Then we looked through the Long Beach phone book to find a second name that sounded right. We came up with Hudson. Everything you've read in the press during the last forty years about the origin of the name is malarkey. It originated in Long Beach on that long ago Sunday afternoon."

According to Millspaugh, Roy Fitzgerald and Ken Hodge left Long Beach and moved to Hollywood, where they shared a bungalow in the hills. Ken began working his contacts; he used his savings to throw parties to introduce Roy to people in the business. At one party, Henry Willson showed up, took Roy aside and told him to call him at his office—he was head of talent for the David O. Selznick Studio. Without telling Ken, Roy called Willson, went to see him "and when he left," Millspaugh said, "he had signed a contract, something Ken had not thought to do with his protégé. Henry Willson became Roy's agent, and Ken moved back to Long Beach and proceeded to go to pieces."

Rock Hudson told different stories about how he met Henry Willson. He told one reporter that he had been a mail carrier and discovered Henry Willson was on his route, so he delivered him a picture of himself. More frequently, he said he sent his photos to hundreds of agents, directors and producers, and only one called him—Willson. Rock went for an interview and was signed.

Ken Hodge, Henry Willson and Rock Hudson are no longer living, so there is no one to verify the story. When Millspaugh's letter arrived, though, I read it to Mark Miller and George Nader. They exchanged glances. "It sounds like Rock," Mark said. He went to the files and dug out the first check Rock had received for acting. For sentimental reasons, he had never cashed it. The check was dated March 19, 1948, for ten dollars, payable to Roy Fitzgerald from Vanguard Films, Inc., Culver City. The check was issued shortly before Rock signed with Willson.

On the back it was endorsed:

ROY FITZGERALD
PAY TO THE ORDER OF ROCK HUDSON
KENNETH G. HODGE

Henry Willson was a notorious homosexual. He had an entourage of young men who accompanied him to nightclubs and came to his house in Stone Canyon for swimming parties. Willson was not attractive: He was short, with a soft chin and flaccid body, a prominent nose and receding frizzy hair. He always wore a dark blue suit with a vest.

"He exuded evil," George Nader says. He was rumored to have Mafia connections, and to possess a voracious sexual appetite. He would drop names of his famous clients to seduce hopeful young actors. As they talked about business, he would reach under the table and place a hand on the young man's thigh.

But Willson was a shrewd observer of talent and brilliant at launching careers. He could take a new actor to a studio and convince them to sign him and give him good parts. He was known for discovering and renaming stars. He changed Art Gelien to Tab Hunter, Merle Johnson to Troy Donahue, Francis Timothy McCown to Rory Calhoun and Elmore Rual Torn to Rip Torn. He also named Rhonda Fleming, Guy Madison, John Saxon and James Darren. The names all have a similar ring to "Rock Hudson," which would argue for Henry's having created that name.

When Henry met Rock, the Selznick Studio was disbanding and Henry wanted to start his own talent agency. He signed Rock, who told him straight out that he had no training. Henry enrolled him in evening acting classes and began to set up interviews and screen tests.

The major studios gave screen tests to decide if they wanted to put a new actor under contract. Rock was tested five times and received no offers. He was callow, overeager, like the amateur who smiles even when the gun is pointed at him. One of the screen tests is still shown by Twentieth Century-Fox to young actors as an example of how bad one can be and still, through hard work, become a star.

Undaunted, Henry took Rock to meet Raoul Walsh, a director at Warner Brothers. Raoul wore a patch over one eye, and friends have speculated that Raoul saw Rock as the camera did—with one eye. Because of the way Rock looked, Raoul gave him a bit part in *Fighter Squadron* and told him the film would serve as a screen test. Rock called Jimmy Matteoni in Winnetka, delirious with joy. "I've got a part! I'm gonna make a hundred twenty dollars a week. I'm rich. Rich!" He called Budget Pack and quit.

In *Fighter Squadron*, Rock played an air corps officer who had three lines. There was a scene in the squadron's rec room where he had to say, "Pretty soon you're going to have to get a bigger blackboard." But it kept coming out "bligger backboard." The harder he tried, the more tongue-twisted he became, until, after twenty takes, they changed the line to "Pretty soon you'll have to write smaller numbers." But Rock looked breathtaking on the screen. "He had a face which the camera loved," a friend said. "He looked ten times better on screen or in a still photo than he did in person. It was his face. You can learn to come alive on screen, but for the camera to say, this is a truly beautiful or handsome person—it has to be in the face."

*   *   *

After *Fighter Squadron*, Raoul Walsh signed Rock to a one-year contract, which would pay for his living expenses while he studied acting.

During that year, then, I started going to class and going to diction lessons, learning how to lower my voice . . . learning anything I could. Because something within this midwestern hick stupidity of mine told me that if you are going to do something, do it. And do it the best you can.

Now, I'm often asked by young actors, "How do you approach a scene?" You just do it! That was Raoul Walsh's attitude—you just do it. When he said that, it made it so simple in my head.

Don't try to act, he said. Remember, up on that screen you're magnified forty times. Be natural, underplay, and it will look great.

Raoul Walsh did not use Rock in any more films, but he asked him to paint his house and wash windows. In 1949, he sold Rock's contract to Universal-International Pictures for $9,000. There had been an offer from Warner Brothers, but Raoul and Henry Willson thought that Rock would learn more at Universal in their stock-player training program.

Universal was known, then, as a B studio, where low-budget pictures were churned out fast. But it had the best publicity machine in town and the best training program. Rock went to acting classes taught by Sophie Rosenstein, a brilliant coach who possessed the ability to draw out each person's natural gifts. On Saturday mornings, Sophie would show old Garbo movies without the sound. She said that if you watched movies without sound, you could tell if a person was acting or if he was faking it.

Rock took fencing lessons, lifted weights in the gym, learned to ride horses on the back lot. "I even studied ballet," he said. He worked with a voice coach, Lester Luther, who had a technique for lowering the speaking voice. He asked Rock to stand at the piano, preferably when he had a cold or throat infection, and yell as loud as he could. This would supposedly break down the vocal cords, and when they healed, the voice would be lower. The technique ruined

Rock's voice for singing, but it gave him the unusually low, sensual voice that was to become his trademark.

The wardrobe department made a dummy of his body and outfitted him with a tuxedo and suits. No more pants that were too short. The new clothes were part of a complete make-over by the Studio. Roy Fitzgerald had walked in off the street, gone to makeup, to wardrobe, to hair, to coaching, to publicity and come out as the rising new actor Rock Hudson. He learned the way to enter a restaurant like a star, how to step out of a limousine, how to smile while keeping his eyes open, how to walk down a staircase without looking down. "If you're hungry, you don't walk to the commissary," Rock was told, "you call a car."

While he studied, Rock was placed in bit parts. He had gone from driving a truck to acting on a sound stage, and he scrambled to learn as he went. He listened to everyone—script girls gave him advice on how to read lines, and electricians told him where to stand to get a better light.

His contract ran for seven years. The Studio decided what films he would make and paid him $75 a week whether he appeared in no pictures or a dozen. He worked forty weeks and was on hiatus for twelve, but he could not work anywhere else. If he wanted to make a film for another studio, Universal might give him three months off, but they would add six months to the end of his contract. He received a raise at regular intervals, and the Studio had the option to drop him after a year.

Some actors felt these contracts were "slavery," but Rock thought it was a wonderful system. "The Studio took care of everything. They could get you a house, a car, airline tickets, special shoes. All you had to do was concentrate on your performance. There was no better method of training."

The point of all the training and grooming was to build stars—properties—that would be money-makers for the Studio. Publicity was essential, and Universal maintained a large staff of publicists who worked to keep the players' names in the press. Rock was required to go to premieres and nightclubs with young actresses under contract, so that both might get their pictures in the paper. Another publicity tool was the layout for a fan magazine. Rock would be asked to fake a "date" with an actress and take a photographer along, who would shoot them as they played tennis by the beach, or danced at Ciro's, staring into each other's eyes.

The movie magazines always wrote flattering stories. In their thin, cheesy pages, everyone was beautiful, everyone was in love, everyone wore jewels and evening clothes or sat around a swimming pool in a bathing suit and no one was in pain.

One of the actresses Rock was coupled with in the magazines was Vera Ellen, a dancer under contract to M.G.M. Vera Ellen was more well known and older than Rock, so she was able to pull him up. In 1950, they conceived the idea of putting on skimpy bathing suits, painting their bodies gold and going to the Hollywood Press Photographers Ball as Mr. and Mrs. Oscar. It was daring, and all the photographers rushed and jostled to take their picture. Louella Parsons, who was doing a live radio show from the ball, invited Vera to the microphone. She brought Rock along, which is how he got his first interview with Louella on national radio.

Going out with Vera had been a crafty professional move, but Rock came to care for her, and at one point, toyed with the idea of marriage. He put Jimmy Matteoni on notice, for they had promised to be best man at each other's wedding. But Rock and Vera drifted, her career began to fizzle and Rock's continued on an upward trajectory.

Universal was a close-knit studio when Rock came there, and the same people worked together on picture after picture. Rock liked to go to dinner with his makeup man, his wardrobe man and a script girl, Betty Abbott, who was the niece of Bud Abbott. "You knew everyone by first name," Rock said, "from the carpenters to the Studio head. You never locked your door. It was a family."

Everyone rooted for the contract players, but each year, many fell away. Those who became successful included: Tony Curtis, Jeff Chandler, Piper Laurie, Rod McKuen, Julia Adams, David Janssen. But none was to achieve the level of fame and survive as long as Rock.

At the Studio, people could sense fairly quickly that Rock was going to pull away from the pack. Roger Jones, who worked in publicity, says, "I just knew Rock would make it. He had something special—it was almost a spiritual quality—something about the eyes."

George Nader says Rock possessed a gift for moving an audience, even as a beginner. "Every major star has a tremendous motor inside that can generate animal magnetism. They rev that motor up and the emotion comes out the eyes, through the senses—we don't know how—but it can reach off a screen and touch people sitting in a darkened theater."

Nader says you can learn techniques to act, "but for the audience to *feel* something, there has to be that motor inside to begin with. It's a gift, and Rock had it."

CHAPTER 3

M*ark Miller? What else can I say about the man? He runs my life. He's my man Friday. He makes me laugh. He's my best friend drunk or sober. I couldn't exist without Mark Miller.*

George Nader? I can trust him to tell me the truth. If you ever need to know something, ask George. George is always right.

You know how many people have tried to break us up? Every new person that's come along—the first thing he does is try to get rid of Mark and George. It's never worked.

In 1951, a young agent, Dick Clayton, was invited to dinner by Mark Miller and George Nader. Clayton called on his way over. "I want to bring a guy you might like. He's just been put under contract at Universal and he's lonely, he doesn't know anyone in town."

"Bring him along," Mark said.

Mark was twenty-five and George was thirty, and they were living in one of a string of connecting cottages that trailed up a hillside in Studio City. When the newcomer appeared, they were startled at how tall and attractive he was, yet how bashful, awkward. He wore jeans that were too short, a Pendleton shirt that needed to be cleaned and loafers with no socks. His name was Roc Hudson—the Studio had decreed that he drop the *k* from his first name.

Rock, Mark and George liked each other instantly. They were all starting out, eager to make it in the business, and all had grown up in small towns during the Depression. Rock still felt bewildered and out of his element. He told them how Henry Willson had taken him to dinner to celebrate the signing of their contract. They had driven to the Biltmore in Santa Barbara, a formal old hotel that reeked of money and the splendor of early California aristocracy. Rock had never eaten at such a place. The dining tables were set with antique china and crystal, silver candelabra and hand-embroidered linen. When Rock finished eating, he stacked his dishes as Grandma Wood had taught him—the butter plate, salad plate and dinner plate on top of each other—and set them in a corner of the table. Henry told Rock, "I see, right off, we got problems. The first thing is, we do not stack dishes. You're a movie star, not a busboy!"

Mark and George laughed with Rock until their sides hurt. The following night, Rock came back to Mark and George's. He hated to be alone, and started calling from the Studio. "Hi! What're you doin'? Can I come over for dinner?" Or he'd say, "I'm taking you out to dinner tonight. You have to pay, I don't have any money." Before long, Rock was seeing Mark and George three or four nights a week.

Mark and George had been together since 1947, when they met while performing in *Oh, Susannah!* at the Pasadena Playhouse. Mark was a singer, playing Clem, and George was a student at the Playhouse, dancing and singing in the chorus. During the six-week run, their friendship was cemented and they have not been apart since. "Both of us were brought up to believe you fall in love and stay in love for life," George says. "The relationship had to have meaning and be for the long run."

From the start, they pooled their resources. They realized that if they were to stay together, they could not pursue two careers. Mark wanted to study opera seriously, which would take him to New York, while George would have to stay in California to succeed as a film actor. So Mark gave up his singing and took jobs to support George. "You couldn't work full time and become a movie star," Mark said. "George had to be available for interviews at two P.M. on Thursday."

Mark worked as a carhop at Jack's Drive-In, sold ladies' shoes at Chandler's and bought a Foster's Freeze in Alhambra, which he ran for a year. By 1952, George was earning enough as an actor so that Mark could stop working. He became George's business manager, handled mail, invested the money George was earning in real estate, restored houses and eventually got his real-estate license.

They have always been known to friends as "MarkandGeorge," yet they possess distinct personalities. Mark is like a big, huggable bear. He has brown hair, a brown mustache, warm brown eyes, and when he's home, will pad around wearing sweat pants and mukluks. He loves laughter and shenanigans, is a great storyteller and is loyal to the point of fierceness. "That's the Iowa farm boy," he says. "I remember being snowed in for six weeks in 1936, during one of the great snows that hit the Northern Plains. There were fifteen-foot drifts, we had to make tunnels to go to the barn and we couldn't go two miles to town to get coal or food. You know how we survived? By the wagons forming a circle. Three families that lived close together pooled everything—canned food, potatoes, coal—and shared it three ways. Otherwise, we'd have frozen to death. That's when you learn you don't desert in time of need, because you weren't deserted then."

George Nader, in his prime, had a perfectly proportioned body, dark hair and blue eyes, but it is his character that continues to dazzle: kind, truthful, dear, wise. His word is gold. Where Mark can be excitable, George is like a river, calm on the surface with powerful currents deep below. He does not stew over what is petty or trivial, but has a knack for seeing beyond. He uses tact and gentleness to persuade people and resolve problems. Yet he has no love of crowds or society. In his later years, he has chosen to live in the desert, to avoid parties and gatherings. He has begun writing novels—his first published was *Chrome*—and seems more suited to the reclusive life than to that of an actor.

Mark and George had different relationships with Rock. Neither was involved with him sexually. Mark's friendship with Rock was playful: "I never talked with him on a deep personal level," Mark says. "He'd immediately freeze—he was embarrassed by it. Instead, we loved to giggle, and I could make him laugh anytime. No matter how bad a mood he was in, I could break him up and have him rolling on the floor."

If Rock wanted to talk about serious matters, he went to George. Yet even with George, he would open to a point, then withdraw. George expected and demanded the most of Rock; he always urged Rock to aim higher as an actor, to try Shakespeare, to seek greatness. George says, "When everyone else was fawning, I'd say, Rock, the Emperor has no clothes. The fucker is naked." Whenever Rock made a film he was proud of, he asked, "Has George seen it?"

One of the reasons the three became so close was that in 1951, when they met, they could not go out freely and be seen with other men. This was the "Dark Ages," when there was no such word as "gay." Homosexuals were "fairies" who were ridiculed and shunned. Rock, Mark and George were deep in the closet, although they did not use those words. They rarely spoke about being homosexual, or if they did, they used code phrases, like "Is he musical?"

If they went to a restaurant, they could go as three but not as four, because four men would look like two couples. Often, a group would be gathered at Mark and George's and someone would say, "Let's go to DuPar's." George would look around and shake his head. "Too many boys. Let's order in."

George says, "It was more fun to stay home anyway. If you didn't go out, you didn't get in trouble. We had a piano, Mark was a marvelous cook and Rock loved to play games." They played Boccaccio, Dictionary, Hearts, Essence, Twenty Questions. Rock hated to lose and would never give up. "Don't tell me," he'd yell. "I'll kill myself if I don't get this." He'd go home and call back at three in the morning. Without saying hello, he'd blurt, "Is it Thomas Alva Edison?"

"No," George would say, and Rock would hang up, only to call back later.

Mark tried to teach Rock and George to play bridge. Mark told Rock, "If you play bridge, you'll get out more and move in different social circles, because people are always looking for a fourth." Rock said, "Okay, come to my place. We'll learn bridge and I'll cook steaks." They needed a fourth, so Mark brought a friend of one of the carhops at Jack's, a young man named Floyd.

Rock was living in a small furnished house on Long Ridge in Sherman Oaks. Like a true midwesterner, he loved to barbecue, but he invariably burned the steaks. "He thought he was the best steak man in the world," Mark says. "He bought the most expensive cuts, and would say, with a flourish, 'I will do the steaks.' But he'd cremate them because he wanted to have another Scotch and soda. I'd say, 'Rock, don't forget mine, I like it rare. . . .' but he'd say, 'Oh, no, it hasn't gone long enough!' When they started to flame, he'd squirt them with water. In thirty-five years, I never had an edible steak that he cooked."

Along with the charred steak, Rock made salad and corn on the cob. There was a lot of drinking before and during the meal, and afterward the four men sat down around the coffee table and Mark started to explain Culbertson's method. "The ace is high, you follow suit . . ." Everything he said sounded hilarious to his pupils. He described how to bid, and there were peals of laughter. He talked about how to finesse. "You can even finesse a nine . . ."

"Do what?" Rock said.

"Finesse a nine."

The three fell on the floor and roared.

Mark had had it. "Come on, George. We're going home." The barbecue was still smoking, the kitchen was a mess. Floyd said, "I'll stay and help clean up."

The next day, when Mark came home from working at the drive-in, he found a dozen roses from Floyd, with a card that said, "Thank you." Floyd had stayed the night at Rock's. A week later, Floyd was drafted and shipped to Korea, where he was killed.

Mark had no luck teaching Rock bridge, and it took him a year, he says, to make Rock do something about his "abominable clothes. He wore those Pendleton wool shirts, which he sweated in and rarely had cleaned because he couldn't afford it. He had a definite body odor that needed correction. Henry Willson told him, 'For God's sake, wear deodorant,' but Rock wouldn't, because he thought it was sissy." There were no deodorants for men on the market at that time; the deodorants had names like Tussy and Mum. Eventually, Mark bought a jar for Rock, which he tried, but he broke out in a rash and got angry.

On Sundays, Rock, Mark and George often drove to Point Dume, a secluded beach in Malibu where they could body surf and sunbathe nude. They'd have dinner at the Trancas Restaurant, then drive back to town and stop at Wallich's Music City. Rock loved Wallich's because they had soundproof booths where you could listen to new records to see if you wanted to buy them. Rock spent all his spare money on records; his favorite was Patti Page singing "Mockin' Bird Hill," which he played again and again until one night Mark shouted, "If I hear Patti Page sing 'Mockin' Bird Hill' one more time, I'm going to fling it out the window!"

The three took a trip to Lake Arrowhead in Rock's red convertible with the top down. Rock always did the driving; he had to be the first at a stop light and the first to pull away, and he couldn't stand having cars in front of him. "Get outa my way!" he'd shout. They played Twenty Questions all the way to the mountains, except when Patti Page came on the radio and they had to be silent for "Mockin' Bird Hill." They stopped at a rustic diner to eat, and checked into mock log cabins near the lake. The next morning, they rented a boat and Rock taught George to water-ski.

What they loved about Lake Arrowhead was that it was far enough removed from the movie colony that for a weekend, they didn't have to worry about being seen with too many boys. They didn't have to look handsome. They could giggle with abandon, play miniature golf and have nutty fun. On Monday, they would be back on the sound stage.

Rock and George knew that if they were going to be stars, they had to present a masculine image without a chink, without a suggestion of softness. To this day, no actor who plays romantic leads has been open about being homosexual, even though many stars are. If exposed, an actor could not continue playing sexy parts, making love to women. The audience, it is feared, would lose their ability to believe him.

Rock was terrified of being caught in a sexual situation with a man. He always had two phone lines when he lived with someone, and made sure his roommate never answered his phone. He was careful not to be photographed with a man. On the set, if he met someone, they would exchange phone numbers with the stealth and caution of spies passing nuclear secrets. Rock would wait until one in the morning to make the call. If it was all right, he would drive to the person's house, park two blocks away, look around furtively and then run to the door. "It was as if the Russians were watching," Dean Dittman says. "And in fact, they were."

American culture in the fifties had rigid definitions of masculine and feminine. Women wore girdles and bras that made their breasts stand out in artificial points. Men had short hair and held their cigarettes—everyone smoked—between the thumb and first finger. Veterans were returning from Korea, and the military look—a flattop haircut and dog tags around the neck—was sexy. Fag hatred and fag jokes were rampant.

The accepted wisdom was that men were either normal or queer. There was no such thing as bisexuality. The consensus in both the straight and gay communities was: If you were bisexual, you hadn't come all the way out of the closet.

In reality, there was a wide range of homosexual types, from those who were effeminate and lisped to those who looked virile and straight. Rock, according to one friend, Stockton Briggle, was "the straightest homosexual I ever met. He had no feminine traits or mannerisms, even when in private among friends." Tony Randall, who starred with Rock in three comedies, says, "He was a marvelous-looking man—so big and muscular and healthy. His skin was healthy. His teeth were healthy. He was Tarzan."

Rock had enormous sexual energy. Mark Miller used to tell him, "Just because it wiggles, you don't have to fuck it."

"Oh, I do," Rock would say.

He was attracted to women, he enjoyed flirting with women and occasionally had affairs, but all things being equal, he preferred to be with men. He liked blonds, with blue eyes, in their twenties, who were tall, well built and manly. He never responded to men who were obviously gay. He preferred it if they had also slept with women, if they "had a story." The fact that a man liked women made him more masculine in Rock's eyes. If he met someone straight who showed any wedge of curiosity, any sliver of receptivity, Rock would move mountains to win him.

When the Kinsey report on male sexuality was published in 1948, Rock purchased the 804-page volume, read it carefully and discussed it with Mark and George. The book, *Sexual Behavior in the Human Male*, was reassuring to them because it overturned many of the prevailing ideas.

What Kinsey found, after studying twelve thousand people, was that "males do not represent two discrete populations, heterosexual and homosexual." Rather, there is a continuum of sexual tendencies among men, from those who are exclusively heterosexual to those who are exclusively homosexual. Few men warrant being placed at either extreme, and most fall somewhere in between. At least 37 percent of the male population has had some homosexual experience between adolescence and old age, Kinsey said. "This is more than one male in three that one may meet as he passes along a city street." Kinsey said that homosexual relations were not rare or abnormal, nor did they constitute evidence in themselves of neuroses or psychoses. He urged psychiatrists to refrain from trying to redirect homosexual behavior but instead to encourage self-acceptance.

"For the first time," Mark Miller says, "homosexuality was validated by a respected scientist, an impartial observer." Yet the Kinsey report did not change attitudes in the general public, and gay men were still viewed with horror and treasted as outcasts.

57

Rock found, with Mark and George, a haven of security and tolerance. George says, "We felt rejected as homosexuals by everyone
else, but in our group, we were accepted. There was a bonding between the three of us, and we've remained absolutely tied together no
matter what. We've had fights, we didn't speak for two different years
in two different decades. We've been excluded by Rock and we've
turned him down, and none of that has made any difference. Because here we are, at the end of our lives, grieving at the loss of the
best friend we ever had."

In 1951, Rock and George talked incessantly about how to get
ahead in films. How do you get a lead? What pictures are coming
up? Who's casting them? What are the other studios doing, and why
do they always pick New York actors for the good parts?

While Rock was under contract, George was independent and was
about to get his first lead role in *Monsoon*. The critical difference
between Rock and George was that for George, his relationship with
Mark came first. Rock always said, "I'd like to have a Mark in my
life," but for Rock, career was everything. "He'd throw aside whatever was necessary to become a star," George says. "It was the only
important thing."

Rock had played small parts in eleven films, but many were what
he called "T. and S." movies—tits and sand—with lots of bouncing
breasts and bodies hitting the sand. Rock had fought and prevailed
with the Studio to let him put the *k* back in his name. He had started
working on scenes with Jimmy Dobson, an actor from New York who
later became Rock's dialogue coach, and with Marilyn Maxwell, who
was to be a lifelong friend. What drew the three together was their
desire to improve. Dobson says, "Rock was a good actor but he didn't
know he was good. He had no confidence at all in his ability. He
didn't even know he was good-looking. I was able to act as a mirror,
to show him what he did well and what he didn't do quite as well."

Dobson says Rock was a "thinking actor, and in film, thoughts
show on the screen. If he was in love and had no lines to say, you
could tell it from the look on his face. His sense of timing was incredible, which came out in the comedies. And he worked hard—
I've never known an actor to work as hard."

In January of 1951, Rock was chosen to play Speed O'Keefe in

Iron Man, the largest role he had yet been given. Seen today, in the context of Stallone's Rocky films, *Iron Man* looks hopelessly primitive. Jeff Chandler and Rock were cast as two boxers named Coke and Speed. Jeff Chandler had the starring role, as a coal miner who was reluctant to fight, but once he started, became determined to win and was booed by the crowds because he was a "dirty fighter." Rock was his friend and polar opposite—wholesome, clean, cheered by the fans. Rock's acting was still green and flat-footed, but he felt suited for the role. "I liked playing Speed because he was a completely happy person. He loved fighting and just about everything in his life."

Rock was nervous about his performance, so he sent Mark Miller to see a sneak preview. Mark came back to Rock's house and said, "You're gonna be a star."

"I am?"

"It's Chandler's picture, but the audience loved you. You're gonna be a star."

Later that year, Rock was given a supporting part in *Bend of the River*, a western with James Stewart, Arthur Kennedy and Julia Adams. Rock got fourth billing and had few major scenes, but the film would be a turning point in his career. He played a gambler from Missouri, heading west to the Oregon Territory with a wagon train of people trying to start a new life.

To promote the movie, the Studio sent Rock on his first publicity junket, a tour of the Northwest with co-stars Julia Adams and Lori Nelson. The tour was grueling—they were scheduled to give interviews and make public appearances from dawn until late in the evening, with hardly a break to eat. Gail Gifford, a publicist who accompanied them, says, "On a tour like this, people get exhausted and their real natures tend to show. You either come home hating the person or wanting to be dear friends. Rock was a joy. He saw humor in everything. He could break up at the slightest provocation and we literally laughed our way through Oregon and Washington."

The movie had been shot in Oregon, and the world premiere was held in Portland. James Stewart flew up for the event, which began with a parade through the city. The stars rode in convertibles decorated with flowers and their names in large letters on the side of the car. Rock waved to the crowds, and began to hear chanting, faint at first. "We want Rock." He thought it was a mistake, but as he continued up the parade route, the chanting grew louder. "We want Rock!" He had never been cheered before—he had hardly been recognized. Was it a trick? Had the Studio paid a bunch of kids to yell his name?

The parade ended outside the theater, where there was a wooden platform set up with lights and a microphone. Jimmy Stewart walked on, said a few words and was applauded. Rock walked on and before he could speak, the young people screamed and pushed so hard the platform started to collapse. Rock had to be escorted away by a wedge of policemen. To everyone's surprise, the fans had yelled more for Rock Hudson than they had for James Stewart.

It went to my head—I was floating! Me over Jimmy Stewart? I went back to the hotel that night and got drunk. I couldn't sleep, I wanted more! I got up at the crack of dawn, ate breakfast and went out in front of the hotel so the people on their way to work could see me. But no one recognized me. I took a walk, and my picture was in the window of practically every store—beauty parlor, supermarket, cleaners—and still, no one recognized me. I finally stood right beside my picture. No one paid any attention. Nothing. Nobody knew who I was. They just kept walking.

It was sad, but I learned a great lesson. Mob scenes—cheering fans—don't mean a damn thing. It's temporary, and if you try to grab on to it, you get nothing but air in your hands.

After *Bend of the River*, the Studio realized Rock could attract a large following. "The Push" was on. He was given lead roles in B pictures—*Scarlet Angel* with Yvonne de Carlo; *The Lawless Breed*, directed by Raoul Walsh, in which he played John Wesley Hardin from youth to old age; *Sea Devils; The Golden Blade* and *Taza, Son of Cochise*. While making *Taza* in Arizona, he sent Betty Abbott a telegram, "I'm eating red clay. At night, I stand in shower and red dirt pours off." His favorite line of his career came from that film: "Taza will build Una's wikiup." Rock broke up every time he had to say "wikiup," and it became a buzzword on the set. Later, he said he never felt comfortable playing an Indian, his features were too blatantly European. "I looked like Joe College with a long wig and dark makeup. It was ridiculous."

Rock was assigned to a special publicist at Universal, Roger Jones, whose assignment was to get Rock as much coverage as possible. He set up interviews anywhere he could, and accompanied Rock to photo sessions and beauty contests and openings of shopping centers. Jones was witty and intelligent, and he and Rock developed a special closeness.

"He was my son my son," Jones says. "He became my charge, and he came to me for everything: How do you dress? How do you judge a beauty contest? What do you say to a director who's steering you wrong? Rock was a real farm boy, and a lot of people wanted to stamp that out of him, but I told him, that farm-boy innocence is a wonderful quality. Don't give it up."

Roger and his wife, Pinky, loved music and taught Rock to sight-read. Often Roger and Rock would sit at the piano in Roger's home and play four-handed until early morning. "Rock had a phobia about being home alone at night," Roger says. "Many times he'd say, 'Can I sleep in the den?'"

Roger was a student of yoga, and one night he was sitting in his living room, facing the wall, meditating, trying to visualize a red rose. He heard the back door open and Rock's footsteps in the kitchen. Rock always let himself in without knocking. He heard Rock ask Pinky, "Where's Rog?"

"In the living room. Developing his mental powers."

Rock sneaked up behind Roger's chair and said, in his deep voice, "Hi!"

"Shhhh."

"What are you doing?"

"I'm concentrating on a rose."

"I don't see a rose."

"Go away and leave me alone!"

Rock went back to the kitchen and started cooking hamburgers with Pinky. "I love hamburgers, and before long, the aroma was all through the house. I couldn't concentrate on anything but hamburgers," Roger says. He went back to the kitchen and saw Rock and Pinky sitting side by side in chairs facing the wall, eating hamburgers.

"What's going on?" Roger said.

"Shhhh," Rock said. "We're concentrating."

"On what?"

"A hamburger. Can't you see it?"

They started to laugh, and "that was the end of my East Indian period," Roger says.

Rock was not yet being written about in national publications, but he was featured every month in at least two fan magazines, usually with his shirt off. "I became the beefcake king," he said. He was photographed—stripped to the waist—washing his car, carrying a ladder, painting a house, watering his garden. The captions read "Looking at him from any angle, the conclusion is: what a man!" The theme of all the articles was: how to meet and marry Rock. One headline said "So you'd like to be Mrs. Hudson? Here's how to handle Hollywood's 'Big Rock.'"

Rock would laugh, thirty years later, when he was going through scrapbooks with Dean Dittman and came across these pieces. In a spread called BACHELORS' BEDLAM he was shown in the house he shared with Bob Preble, an actor under contract at Twentieth Century-Fox. In one shot, they were seen in Rock's red convertible with Rock driving. "Best friends: Rock Hudson and Bob Preble." In another, Rock was in bed with his shirt off, while Bob stood over him, holding a clock. The caption said, "Rip Van Hudson invariably sleeps through the alarm, which awakens Bob in the next room."

But the house only had one bedroom. The bachelors slept in two single beds pushed together and covered with a king-size spread. Bob Preble, who met Rock through their mutual agent, Henry Willson, now sells electric motors. He says he and Rock decided to live together for company and to lower their expenses. Preble had never shared a house with a man before Rock, and he moved out after three years to marry actress Yvonne Rivero.

Rock told Mark and George that Preble was straight and they were just roommates. But other friends had the impression they were intimate. Preble says he and Rock did "a little experimenting, on a couple occasions after we'd had a few drinks, but nothing you would call a definite relation. I guess he hoped the barriers would come down.

The situation did come close to spilling over to something that would have been foreign to my whole being, my whole behavior. But before that happened, I left and married Yvonne."

Preble had studied drama at the University of Maine and Carnegie Tech, and found that Rock "needed a lot of refinement. He didn't know Mozart existed, and he'd never tasted wine, except the cheap stuff for cooking." When they met, in 1950, Preble was staying in Malibu with four guys and wasn't getting anywhere with his career. Rock was living by himself and lonely, so the two went house hunting.

Preble knew Rock was gay, "and I was a little nervous, but I said to myself, just roll with the punches." He tried, several times, to fix Rock up with women who were known to be "easy," to see if "maybe I could turn him around a little. Secretly, I really did want him to be straight so we could take out girls like any two guys. But it never worked. None of the girls could get to first base with him."

The three years they lived together were, in Preble's memory, "a blast—one great glorious good time." They lived in four different houses, and the last, on Avenida del Sol, was spectacular: all wood and glass, which, in its day, looked futuristic. To reach it, they had to climb steep wooden steps up a hillside, and from their windows, they could see across the entire Valley to the farthest mountain range.

They gave parties; they drove to Las Vegas in Rock's convertible with the top down and the radio blaring; they went to Grauman's Chinese Theatre with bottles of Kahlúa and straws and got slowly bombed while watching Tyrone Power. "There was always music in the house. Rock bought a player piano and hundreds of rolls, and he could set it up to play for hours."

Preble dropped out of the entertainment business after his marriage to Yvonne, but he continued to weave in and out of Rock's life. "He was like a talisman," Mark Miller says. "Whenever Rock got in trouble or had bad news, Bob Preble would show up." He appeared right after Rock had a car accident, and when Rock needed surgery to remove a lymph node.

Preble says, "My work takes me all around town and sometimes it's like a light bulb going off. I'll think, I need to see Rock."

The last time Preble dropped in, unannounced, was an afternoon in June of 1984. Rock and Mark Miller were sitting alone in Mark's office. Rock had just found out, and was telling Mark, that he had been diagnosed as having AIDS. Within minutes, Bob Preble was knocking at the door. Rock looked at Mark in dismay.

"How does he know?"

Chapter 4

Magnificent Obsession *was the first solid dramatic role where I had no physicality to rely on. Now I give the Studio credit. . . . They put me in all of those westerns and Indian pictures to get some training. Where if my scenes weren't all that good dramatically, it didn't matter that much. I knew that, and so I'd try different things to see if it would work. And I would say "Oh, no, no. Don't do that again" or "Yeah, take that further." And that was wonderful experience. So by the time* Magnificent Obsession *came around, I was ready.*

While Rock was getting to know Mark Miller and George Nader, he was not romantically involved with anyone and wanted to be. With that in mind, in 1952, Mark and George, who had moved to a house by the beach in Venice, invited Rock to dinner with a young man they'd met, Jack Navaar. Jack had just returned from army service in Korea and was floating. He had met Henry Willson, who had offered to represent him and had tried to change his name to Rand Saxon.

Jack was twenty-two. He had been hearing "You should be in pictures" most of his life. He was tall, lean and fit, with blond wavy hair, blue eyes and a beautifully sculpted, heart-shaped face. He also possessed a sharp mind and caustic wit. "When I heard Rock Hudson, *the* Rock Hudson, was coming," he recalls, "I was nervous and kind of excited and a little embarrassed." Rock arrived, but sat in a corner and didn't say much. Jack went into the kitchen where Mark was cooking dinner. "I don't think he likes me," Jack said. "He's not even talking to me. I should go home." He had broken a date with a woman to come to dinner. Mark told him to give it a chance.

Rock was quiet through dinner, but afterward he surprised everyone by saying, "Let's go up to my place and listen to records." Rock had just bought a hi-fi system he was excited about, so they trooped up to his house on Avenida del Sol. "It was thrilling for me because it was way up in the hills and had a view like nothing I'd seen," Jack says. Bob Preble was away, and Mark started turning off lights, setting the mood, "playing matchmaker"; then he and George slipped away.

Rock and Jack sat up late, talking, joking, playing records. Rock asked him, "Is it easy for you, do you usually get what you want in life?"

"I don't know," Jack said. "I'm not sure what I want exactly."

"For me, that's the hardest thing. To get something when I really want it."

"What do you mean?"

"Well, I'd like to have you stay over tonight. I'd like to get to know you better, and I'm really screwing it up . . ."

"No, as a matter of fact, you're not," Jack said.

The next morning, Rock cooked breakfast. He liked to make what he called "Greyhound Bus Station Eggs"—he would crack eggs right into the skillet and scramble them fast so the white and yellow didn't mix—along with lots of toast and bacon and fresh orange juice and coffee. He and Jack spent the day together and in the evening, Rock called Mark and George. "Hiya! What're you doin' tonight?" He surprised them by bringing Jack back down to the beach, and they had another dinner together. From then on, Rock saw Jack four or five nights of the week.

Jack was flattered and exhilarated that Rock was pursuing him, but he was not entirely comfortable in a homosexual relationship. When I met Jack, in 1985, he was married to a younger woman, they were raising three small children and considering having a fourth. Jack had become a clothing manufacturer. They lived in a gracious home in a rural part of Southern California, with a white fence and five pumpkins on the porch in preparation for Halloween. They rode horses and kept four in a corral behind the house.

Jack said that when he had been in high school, he had fallen into a homosexual relationship, "and in those days, if you had sex with a man, that put you in a category from which you could not deviate. You were a fruitcake, and destined to be that all your life. But I had had relations with women and part of me still wanted to."

When he met Rock, his parents were getting a divorce, "my family was falling apart and Rock made me feel secure and loved." In May of 1953, when Preble moved out of Avenida del Sol, Rock and Jack started living together. But they found a new place, a two-story house on Grandview, because, Jack told Rock, "I don't want to live in the same house where you lived with Bob."

Jack took a job at Hughes Aircraft, but Rock wanted him to quit so he could be home and free when Rock was free. Rock liked to come back from a week's shooting and say "Let's drive to the Grand Canyon." They'd throw a few things in the car and take off, sleeping in motels or camping out and then daring each other to swim in a cold stream. "We lived a reclusive life and were very involved with each other," Jack says. They went to movies constantly—Lana Turner was Rock's favorite star. They had a running game called "Last Word." Julia Adams would call, say "last word" and hang up, then not answer her phone. So Rock and Jack sent her a telegram that said "last word." Another game they played was "Gotcha," in which they tried to scare each other. Jack says, "One person would hide in the closet, the other would come to reach for a shirt and you'd jump out and yell 'Gotcha!' You'd be amazed how many times you would fall for it and scream. You'd let down your guard, walk outside to empty the trash and you'd get caught. Maybe that's why we both had heart attacks later in life."

They had a private code, "1-2-3," which meant "I love you." When people were around, Rock would rap three times on a counter, or nudge Jack three times under the table, or say, "One two three." "He was a very romantic man," Jack says, "and I responded to it."

On Sundays, they would get dressed up and alternate going to visit Rock's mother, who was living in Arcadia with her third husband, Joe Olsen, and Jack's mother, who lived in Santa Monica. Rock's mother called Jack "Cookie," and always made roast lamb with mint jelly because she thought Jack liked it. Finally, Jack asked Kay if she might make something else. "Of course, Cookie," Kay said. "I can't stand lamb. I was making it for you."

For Jack's twenty-third birthday, Rock threw a party and gave him a stack of presents—boxes piled upon boxes—from an expensive Beverly Hills store, Gifts for Men. "There was a yellow cashmere sweater and a black cashmere sweater and belts and socks and shirts. He was just like a kid, he loved giving presents."

Jack had left Hughes Aircraft and Rock was supporting him, which Jack liked and didn't like. "I had charge accounts and there was always cash on the table for me to take. Rock paid for my mother's divorce; I had to help support my mother and two sisters, so Rock gave me money for that. But I hated him for it, because it made me feel ball-less. I couldn't stand being dependent. If he did nice things for me, I was angry, and if he didn't do nice things and ignored me, I would be angrier. I was an angry young guy."

During the hours Rock was working, Jack took acting lessons, which Rock paid for. "Henry Willson would set up interviews, but I always felt he was doing it because of Rock." Mark Miller would call and say, "What are the movie stars' wives doing today? Shall we go to the Beverly Hills Hotel for lunch?" Jack and Mark began hanging out while Rock and George were on the set. Then the four would get together in the evening.

One night, Rock and Mark said they had a surprise. They went into the bedroom, asked George to turn on the record player, and when the music started, out came Rock and Mark with nothing on but two neckties tied around them like bikini tops and bottoms. Rosemary Clooney and Marlene Dietrich were singing a duet, and Rock and Mark did a dance and mouthed the words: "I want the name, age, height and size of you . . ." Rock played Marlene and Mark played Rosemary Clooney. George started laughing, but Jack yelled, "Stop! Turn it off. It's not funny!"

Recalling the incident, Jack says, "I didn't like anything to do with drag or camp. I didn't like homosexual humor." He was embarrassed, he says, if Rock wanted to hold his hand when they were driving, or if they were at a movie and Rock would call him "Baby." Jack says, "I was afraid that the people behind us might hear."

Shortly after Rock and Jack began living together, Rock was tested for the lead in his first major film, *Magnificent Obsession*. The director, Douglas Sirk, had already signed Jane Wyman, who was then married to Ronald Reagan. Universal didn't have many top male actors under contract, so Sirk felt he had to develop one. He watched Rock in *Iron Man* and said, later, "He was far inferior to Jeff Chandler, but I thought I saw something. So I arranged to meet him, and he seemed to be not too much to the eye, except very handsome. But the camera sees with its own eye. It sees things the human eye does not detect. You learn to trust your camera—it's the only thing in Hollywood which never let me down."

He asked Rock to do eight scenes—two days of extensive testing—then looked at the film with the producer, Ross Hunter. They decided Rock was ready to handle the starring role. *Magnificent Obsession* was a remake of a 1935 film that had starred Robert Taylor and Irene Dunne, based on a romantic novel by Lloyd C. Douglas. Rock played Bob Merrick, who, when the story begins, is a selfish, swaggering playboy. He takes a speedboat out on the lake, and when the mechanic warns him conditions aren't safe, he sneers, "You keep this engine tuned, that's all I want from you." Merrick cracks up the boat and nearly dies. He is saved by an emergency squad, but while he's being treated, on the other side of the lake, Dr. Wayne Phillips dies because the emergency equipment is unavailable.

Dr. Phillips was the opposite of Merrick—kind, humble, giving selfless service to humanity. Merrick meets his widow, played by Jane Wyman, and becomes infatuated with her. He also meets an offbeat painter, who was a friend of the doctor and tells Merrick, "He connected me to the infinite source of power." The method for attaining this power is simple: Find someone who needs help, help him, keep it secret and don't ever ask to be paid back.

Hudson tries the technique, and he also pursues Wyman, but she runs from him and, as a result, gets hit by a car and becomes blind. Secretly, Hudson pays her medical bills and arranges for her to go to Europe for surgery, which fails. He spends time with her, pretending to be someone else. They fall in love, but when she learns who he is, she vanishes.

Hudson goes to medical school and becomes, in essence, Dr. Phillips—performing selfless service. After many years, he's called to operate on Wyman to save her life. He is frightened, but the painter is there to inspire him with a fifties version of "May the force be with you." After the operation, Wyman lives, and she sees.

What's remarkable about the film is that Rock is converted, almost instantaneously, from sinner to saint, from rogue to gentle knight. He becomes completely wholesome, completely loving, and his face is simple and uncomplicated in its expression of that love. There are no shadows of doubt to follow to their forked and murky depths. At the beginning, he may have been rough and rude, but at the end, he is a sweet, good-hearted all-American man.

Douglas Sirk said that when he first read the script he thought, "This is a damned crazy story if ever there was one. The blindness of

---

69

the woman. The irony of it all . . . it is a combination of kitsch, and craziness, and trashiness. But craziness is very important, and it saves trashy stuff like *Magnificent Obsession*. This is the dialectic—there is a very short distance between high art and trash, and trash that contains the element of craziness is by this very quality nearer to art."

Two weeks before shooting began, in August of 1953, Rock and Jack went to Laguna for the day with Mark and George. They brought giant black inner tubes to ride the waves, but the surf was rough and Rock was picked up by a wave and thrown onto the rocks. His collarbone was broken and he fainted. George carried him up the steps to the promenade, while Mark ran to the bar of the Coast Inn. "We've had an accident, I need brandy!" He brought the brandy back and, to everyone's amusement, Jack took it and drank it down. They called an ambulance, then they called the Studio. Rock was in anguish and wanted Jack to ride in the ambulance. Jack said, "I don't think I should, I'll ride in the car with Mark and George," but Rock insisted. They were taken first to the Studio, where a doctor checked Rock and sent him on to St. Joseph's Hospital. When the fracture was confirmed, Rock was distraught. "How long will it take to heal? I have to start a picture in two weeks." He was terrified he would lose the part if they had to delay production because of him. The part was a breakthrough—he might not have another chance.

The doctors said he had two options: They could put a pin in the bone and immobilize his arm and shoulder in a cast for six weeks, or they could set the bone and wrap an Ace bandage around his arm and chest to hold his shoulders back. With the latter, he could work in two weeks, but he would have a large lump—a calcium deposit— on his shoulder and it would not heal perfectly. Without hesitating, Rock chose the Ace bandage.

After the accident, a faction at Universal did try to remove him from the film, but Rock had an ally who prevented it. Rock had started having an illicit affair with one of the most powerful executives at the Studio, a short, paunchy man who was married and had three children. Rock told his friends stories of how the executive would lock his office door, have his secretary hold the calls and come after Rock on his knees. Rock did not see him frequently, but it was enough to keep the executive hooked and eager to help Rock's cause. With this ally, it was easier for Rock to convince the Studio, later, to loan him to Warner Brothers to do *Giant* and to Twentieth Century-Fox to do *A Farewell to Arms*. Thirty years later, when the executive was retired and had dozens of grandchildren, he saw Rock at a cocktail party. He found a moment to take Rock aside and say, in a lowered voice, "I still love you."

Rock started *Magnificent Obsession* on schedule, with a broken shoulder. It was filmed at Lake Arrowhead and on the weekends, Rock would drive home to see Jack. They worked on scenes together, and got drunk to prepare for a drunken sequence in the film. "We read the lines and asked each other questions about how we felt and perceived things," Jack says. "We found that a drunk doesn't act drunk, he tries to act sober."

Rock wanted to do the best work he could, and received help from Sirk and Wyman.

I'm proud to say that Douglas Sirk took me under his wing. He was like ol' Dad to me, and I was like a son to him, I think. When you're scared and new and you're trying to figure out this thing, and suddenly an older man will reach out and say, "There, there, it's okay." That was Douglas Sirk.

Jane Wyman couldn't have been nicer. . . . Jane knew that I was new, anxious and nervous. And I'd go high; go over my lines at times, thirty or forty takes. She'd never say a word. "Fine, fine."

She said something interesting to me, many years later. I said, "You really went out of your way, Jane, to be nice to me when you didn't have to. I want you to know that I do know that and I appreciate it. And I love you for it. Thank you." She said, "Let me tell you something. It was handed to me by somebody. And I handed it to you. And now it's your turn to hand it to somebody else."

The studio held a sneak preview of *Magnificent Obsession* at the Four Star Theatre in the Valley to test the audience's response. Rock and Jack found out about it, slipped into the theater and sat in a back row, surrounded by unsuspecting moviegoers. When the film ended, Rock ran out of the theater. Jack got trapped in the crowd and when he found Rock, he was in the car in the parking lot, overcome with emotion. Rock was sitting with his head down on the steering wheel, crying. He knew, at that moment, he was a star. He had reached the peak, the exalted state he had dreamed of, the state that had seemed utterly beyond the grasp of a boy from the Midwest who had no training and no connections. Yet there he was, on the wide screen, with an Academy Award–winning actress and a chorus and orchestra playing the "Ode to Joy" from Beethoven's Ninth Symphony.

"You were really great," Jack said.

"Thank you, thank you," he sobbed.

"You know it too, don't you?" Jack said gently.

Rock laughed and still was crying.

"I'm proud of you."

Klieg lights swept the sky on May 11, 1954, as Rock Hudson arrived at the Westwood Theater for the premiere of *Magnificent Obsession*. His date was Betty Abbott; Jack Navaar came in a separate car, wearing George Nader's tuxedo and escorting a young actress, Claudia Boyer.

"Rock! Rock! Turn around! Look this way, please, just for a minute!" Rock's eyes were lit with brilliant sparks as the strobe lights flashed.

"What's your date's name, Rock? Are you engaged?"

As Rock walked up the red carpet, he spotted Jack Navaar's mother and two little sisters standing behind the rope barriers with the fans. He broke rank to go over and kiss them. Jack followed, and years later said, "Rock didn't have to do it—that's why I couldn't help but love him."

Rock had told Jack he wanted him to sit beside him for the film, but at the theater, they were shown to different sections. Rock and Betty sat with Ross Hunter and Jane Wyman, and Jack and Claudia had to sit in a less desirable area with Jacque Mapes and Ann Sheridan. Jack was furious and wouldn't speak to Rock for the rest of the evening. He refused to meet Rock's eyes at the party at La Rue's after the film. They took their dates home and met back at the house.

"You said we'd be sitting together," Jack said. "I felt like a fool. Like—you're the star and I'm the jerk!"

Rock said that Ross Hunter had changed the seating at the last minute. He had been surprised himself.

Magnificent Obsession grossed eight million dollars and turned Rock Hudson into Universal's most profitable star. His fan mail rose to three thousand pieces a week. A woman in Tacoma, Washington, wrote, "When you looked at Jane Wyman, I wanted to scream and deep down inside of me, I did." Rock broke out of B pictures to the top of the double bill, and was typecast as the romantic leading man. He would not be cast in works by Tennessee Williams, he would not play broken souls. He was heroic, handsome, square—Mr. Right.

Rock was treated differently by everyone after *Magnificent Obsession*. He told Mark and George, "A lot of folks say I've changed, but I haven't. Other people have changed to me. Before, I was considered a movie star, but now, people stare at me with their mouths open in . . . total awe." But Rock did change. Mark says, "Before, Rock would answer the phone, 'Hiya!' Now, it was a deep, 'Hello? This is Rock Hudson speaking.' He became an instant authority on everything. He could walk on water."

Jack Navaar watched as Rock lost his bashfulness and began to bask in the limelight. "If Rock burped, everyone laughed hysterically, as if it was the greatest burp they'd ever heard." Rock described the transition from insecurity to confidence in an interview with Hedda Hopper. "When you're very tall—I was six feet by the time I was fourteen—it gives you a sort of inferiority feeling. I guess I started coming out of it when people would recognize me. 'Why, you're Rock Hudson, aren't you?' Suddenly I began to feel, what the heck! I haven't anything to hide—so I stood up."

Rock was now being written about by national magazines. In a *Life* story in 1954 on the hottest male stars, Rock was pictured hanging on to the top of a ladder, with Tony Curtis and Robert Wagner below him. Rock was said to rate third at the box office with girls under twenty. *Life* said fans were undecided whether his appeal "lies primarily in his *basic honesty* or in his bare chest."

The fan magazines began to complain that Hudson was not married. They needed to keep presenting him to their readers as "eligible husband material." How to explain the fact that he was never coupled with any of the beautiful women he took to parties? How many times could they show him with Betty Abbott or Marilyn Maxwell and speculate "Friends say they may be getting serious"? They solved the problem by running headlines like SCARED OF MARRIAGE? and TOO BUSY FOR LOVE. They quoted Rock: "I'm looking for happiness, but I don't think I'm quite ready for marriage yet." The implication was, he just hasn't met the right girl.

Another magazine, *Confidential*, was taking an interest in Rock's single status. Unlike the fan magazines, *Confidential* ran scandalous articles, many of them fictionalized, about famous people. Its logo was: TELLS THE FACTS AND NAMES THE NAMES. The headlines promised more than the stories ever delivered, but they were enticing: WHY ROBERT WAGNER IS A FLAT TIRE IN A BOUDOIR and WHEN LANA TURNER SHARED A LOVER WITH AVA GARDNER.

Confidential wanted to do an exposé of Rock's homosexuality and offered Bob Preble money for information and pictures. Eventually, someone from the magazine would offer Jack Navaar $10,000—a large sum in 1954—to talk about living with Rock. Jack called Henry Willson and told him *Confidential* was after Rock. "We're aware of that," Willson said. "Thanks for your support."

No story was ever published, and the rumor at Universal was that the Studio had traded information about another of its stars—Rory Calhoun—to kill the piece on Rock. In the mid-fifties, articles were published that Calhoun had served time in jail for burglary and auto theft when he was younger. But whether there was a connection between the stories on Calhoun and the threatened exposé of Rock cannot be confirmed.

Recently, there was a rumor that the Studio traded a story about George Nader's sexuality to *Confidential*, sacrificing George's career to save Rock's. But this is not true. No article appeared in *Confidential* or any other publication about George Nader's sexuality, and he continued acting until he retired in 1972.

Nader says, "We lived in fear of an exposé, or even one small remark, a veiled suggestion that someone was homosexual. Such a remark would have caused an earthquake at the Studio. Every month, when *Confidential* came out, our stomachs began to turn. Which of us would be in it? The amazing thing is that Rock, as big as he became, was never nailed. It made me speculate that Rock had an angel on his shoulder, or that he'd made a pact with the devil, because he seemed under supernatural protection."

*   *   *

Rock and Jack began to quarrel more frequently during this period. "I couldn't go anywhere with Rock—even to dinner—without people watching him and trying to get near him," Jack says. "I was jealous of the acclaim and attention he was getting, but I also liked it. Thousands of people wanted him, but I was the one that Rock Hudson wanted."

Jack says he often provoked the fights, and gave Rock "every reason to throw me out. One night, I literally kicked him out of bed." Jack had been encouraging Rock to go out more socially because it was good for his career. Rock accepted a date to escort Joan Crawford to a party, but came home at three in the morning. "I'd been worried about him and he came home stinking drunk," Jack says. "I was angry he was with Joan Crawford and I wasn't. We got in bed, he started snoring, and I was so furious, I just rolled over and kicked him onto the floor. I told him to get his ass out of the house, I didn't care where he slept." Rock started walking down Grandview Drive, and Jack threw the keys to the car after him. "I told him to go sleep in his big fucking plush dressing room that the Studio had just built for him."

When tempers cooled, Rock asked Jack, "Would you be happy if I gave up all this shit, because I will. We'll move to the Midwest." Jack said no. "Rock didn't mean it, and besides, I didn't want to move to Chicago with Roy Fitzgerald and open a florist's shop. I wanted Rock to have his career, but I wanted one too."

Rock told Mark Miller about an incident with Jack that made him so angry he would use it through the years when he needed to call up rage for a film. Rock was working late at the Studio. He called home and Jack said he didn't believe Rock was working. If he wasn't home in thirty minutes, Jack was going to toss Rock's record collection over the hillside. Rock finished work, raced home and saw Jack hurling his 78 records of Ella Fitzgerald, Nat King Cole, Dinah Shore, Duke Ellington over the deck and hearing them shatter on the rocks below. Rock went crazy. He told Mark, "All I have to do to get insanely angry is to visualize those records flying down the hill." Jack Navaar says he has no memory of the incident.

In June of 1954, Rock left for Europe to make *Captain Lightfoot*. Jack drove Rock to the airport and walked him to the plane. When

Rock took his seat by the window, he used the overhead light to flash their code: 1-2-3. I love you.

Rock flew to Paris and met Betty Abbott, the script girl on the film, and Barbara Rush, his co-star. They had two weeks before shooting began, so they rented a big American car to give Rock plenty of leg room, and Rock drove the three of them through France and Italy. They stayed in small *pensiones*, and at midday they would stop in the countryside, spread a blanket and have a picnic of wine, cheese and fruit. Rock was learning about wine and European cuisine, about art and opera, architecture and history. He read constantly and wanted to absorb everything he saw. He particularly enjoyed Florence—the Uffizi Gallery and Michelangelo's statue of David.

While Rock was traveling through Europe, Jack Navaar was spending time with a young woman named Phyllis Gates, who worked as a secretary for Henry Willson. Jack had met Phyllis in Henry's office and they had started going out to lunch. "I had a tremendous crush on Phyllis," Jack says. "I could understand why Rock thought he could fall in love with her, because I could have. She knew how to make a guy feel fabulous. She would say, 'No, honey, you don't want to eat that for lunch, you should have this because it's better for you.' She was much more attractive in person than in her photographs, she had a marvelous laugh and an incredible personality— you'd meet her and in ten minutes, you'd feel you were the most important person in her life. It was a talent."

Jack says that on Sundays they would go to a bar in Santa Monica, the Tropical Village, which was frequented by gay men and lesbians. One weekend, when Rock and George Nader were on location, Jack and Mark took Phyllis to Laguna. The first night, they went to a bar called Camille's, Phyllis started talking to a woman and Jack and Mark say they did not see her the rest of the weekend. Mark says, "We'd call her room and ask her to come to dinner or the beach, and she'd say, 'You go on ahead, I'll catch up.'"

Phyllis had two weeks off in the summer, and Henry Willson called Jack and said, "Why don't you and Phyllis take a trip? Rock's away and you're just sitting there. Phyllis wants to visit her family." Jack agreed, and they drove Rock's new yellow Lincoln Continental convertible across the Rockies to Montevideo, Minnesota, where

Phyllis's family lived. "I enjoyed her company, and I felt secure doing this because Henry had proposed it," Jack says. "Later, I realized Henry had instigated the trip to alienate me from Rock."

To save money, they checked into motels as Mr. and Mrs. Navaar, shared a room but, Jack says, they did not sleep together. While they drove, they sang popular songs—their favorite was "Little Things Mean a Lot." As they were approaching Montevideo, Phyllis said they had to swear—they had to yell every dirty word they knew and get it out of their systems because in Montevideo, they wouldn't be able to do it at all. "So for ten minutes, we swore and shouted and cussed," Jack says.

They stayed with her family, and all her relatives and friends came to meet "Rock Hudson's roommate" and see "Rock Hudson's car." Then they drove to Kansas City, where Phyllis had worked as a stewardess before coming to California. Phyllis took Jack to gay parties, where women danced together and kissed. When they returned to Los Angeles, Jack found he was in trouble. Rock called from Venice, Italy, angry and accusatory. He had heard reports that Jack was using the house for drinking parties; that Jack had left the house unguarded and it had been robbed; that police had come to the house frequently; that Jack had been seen driving Rock's Lincoln convertible filled with unruly people yelling obscenities.

"I wasn't even in town!" Jack said. "You son of a bitch, how dare you ask me those questions."

The more Rock grilled him, the angrier Jack got, and the long-distance call ended badly. Jack's checks stopped coming, and when he called Rock's business manager, he was told there was no more money for him. Jack turned to Henry Willson, but Henry implied that Rock and Jack's relationship was threatening Rock's career, and it would be in Rock's best interest if it were ended. "The Studio is capable of taking extreme measures to protect a property," Willson said.

"Everyone turned on me, including Phyllis. She disappeared," Jack says. "Everyone treated me like I was dead meat. I felt like dead meat, and I didn't want to live like that. So I did exactly what they wanted me to do. I dumped the keys at Henry's office and moved out."

When Rock returned from Europe, he found the house on Grandview emptied of all traces of Jack Navaar. Rock had started living with Jack before he became a major celebrity. After Jack left, Rock became more cautious. "He went way into the closet, and didn't start coming out for fourteen years," Mark Miller says. Rock would not live with a man again until the late sixties, when social attitudes had loosened and his position as a star seemed safe.

CHAPTER 5

Phyllis was unbeatable. She was "family." She had the greatest sense of humor in the world—it wouldn't quit. She loved games, and she had to win. We had a ball together until we got married. From that day, it was all over. The white piece of paper changed everything. She became the movie star's wife. She had to have a new dress for everything and she had to have a mink, not a fox. She wanted to know where I was every minute. It didn't work.

Like Roy Fitzgerald, Phyllis Gates grew up in the Midwest and came to California to break into show business. She heard that a powerful agent, Henry Willson, was looking for a secretary and applied. She couldn't type, but Henry was charmed by her, hired her and paid for her to study typing at night. What Henry saw in Phyllis and felt he could use in his business was her gift for making people feel good. She could soothe tempers, soften bad news, and she could coax people into consenting to do things they had sworn they wouldn't do. In a short time, Phyllis had a warm acquaintance with all of Henry's clients.

When Rock Hudson returned from Europe in the fall of 1954, Henry started telling Phyllis, "You and Rock should go out to dinner." He called Rock and told him how much fun his secretary was and why didn't he take her out to dinner? Rock made several dates, which he broke. The next time Phyllis had to get Rock on the phone for Henry, Rock mentioned having dinner and Phyllis laughed. "Don't bother, you're just gonna break the date." He said he was serious this time, but she begged off.

Her resistance caught his attention; they had their dinner and afterward, as was true to Rock's pattern, he wanted to see her all the time. Phyllis was appealing and fresh-looking—she had reddish-brown hair which she wore swept up in a French twist, and she was slender, graceful, willowy. She possessed enormous confidence and spunk. She stood up to Rock and was not at all cowed by the fact that he was a star; she acted as if they both were stars. She had a melodious laugh that was infectious, and she loved to tease Rock and mimic him. "Who cares if you're a big movie star. Be quiet now."

At her suggestion, they started taking painting lessons together. Rock presented her to the "family"—Mark and George. Mark had already met her through Jack Navaar, and George remembers being enchanted. "Love at first sight," he says. "She was bright, down-to-earth, no phony manners or pretensions of glamour like some of the actresses we knew. We felt instinctively at ease with her. She accepted us immediately, which was unusual, because in that age, homosexuals were looked on as alien beings. People would feel nervous and avoid your eyes, but Phyllis met our gaze directly; there was no barrier."

The four started spending time together, fixing dinners, playing parlor games. One weekend, when George was away on location, Rock and Phyllis drove to Lake Arrowhead with Mark and Pat Devlin, a woman who sat across from Phyllis at the office and was her closest friend. They booked two rooms at the Arrowhead Springs Hotel, but men and women who were not married could not stay in a hotel together. Rock and Mark had to share a room, and Phyllis and Pat took the other. Mark says, "This was before king-size beds. We had one double bed for two big men. I slept on the edge of the mattress facing the wall, and Rock slept on the other edge. You could have driven a freight train between us. I was scared to death his foot might touch me in the night and I'd scream." The next morning, Phyllis kidded them, "How'd it go last night? Get much rest?"

They sat in the sun on the deck, rented a boat and water-skied, which was Rock's favorite sport. Rock taught Phyllis to water-ski, as he had taught George several years before. Mark did not ski because he'd had asthma as a child and never learned to swim. They took a drive through the pine forests to Big Bear Lake, with Rock driving and Mark taking home movies with a 16-mm camera. Rock had also started making 16-mm movies and staying up late at night to edit them.

In November of 1954, Rock bought his first house, a two-bedroom ranch house at 9151 Warbler Place, in the hills north of Sunset Boulevard. It was small but well built, with wood beams, peg-and-groove floors and a sunny country kitchen, all brick and wood. Rock fur-

Roy Fitzgerald and dog, 1929

At Grandmother Wood's

*At fifteen, with his cousin
Helen Wood Folkers, 1941*

Roy Fitzgerald and friends,
1944

With his father, Roy Harold
Scherer, Sr.

Kay in the 1930s

First professional photograph as Rock Hudson
to send to agents

Premiere of **Magnificent Obsession,** *with
Rock, Kay and friend Betty Abbott*

With Vivien Leigh

*"How to play solitaire, smile and hold my
stomach in at the same time"*

All That Heaven Allows, *with Jane Wyman*

nished the living room with redwood lawn chairs because he had put all his cash into the house. He asked Phyllis to move in with him, which she did, although she kept her own apartment and used it to receive mail. Mark and George remember being shocked at the arrangement. In the fifties, two men or two women could live together as roommates, but an unmarried man and woman living together was beyond the pale. It was "living in sin," and was practiced only in the most bohemian circles. "It would have been a scandal if the press had found out," Mark says. "Rock said, 'Fuck 'em.'"

For Rock, living with Phyllis helped to normalize his reputation in Hollywood. People could say behind his back, with a wink, "Did you hear—Rock Hudson's got a lady living with him." Rock and Phyllis did not have two phone lines on Warbler Place, they had one and Phyllis answered it. Rock told friends that being with Phyllis was a relief. He could do everything with her he had been unable to do with Jack Navaar: take her as his date to premieres, take her on the set to watch him work, take her to dinners given by people in the business.

Rock told three of the men he subsequently lived with that Phyllis was bisexual, and Mark Miller and Jack Navaar say that they saw her in lesbian situations. If both Rock and Phyllis were bisexual, that would have created a strong bond and been a source of mutual understanding. But when I asked Phyllis about reports that she was bisexual, she said, after a long silence, "No. You're hearing from the wrong people. That was part of the Henry Willson slander campaign. He started all that."

Phyllis was a good cook and made the kind of meals Rock loved— meat and potatoes. She fixed pork chops, meat loaf, and mashed potatoes with gravy, which was Rock's favorite dish up to the final days. Rock began to experiment with cooking himself, and he had two rules: No one could be around him while he cooked, and Phyllis had to do the dishes. His efforts came to flower in what would later be known as "Rock's gourmet dinner." He had called Mark and George and said, "I am going to cook a gourmet dinner Saturday night. You're invited, but I want no one in the house the entire day." So at ten in the morning, Saturday, Phyllis showed up at Mark and George's with her friend Pat Devlin. They all went out and bought Bermuda shorts, which were the newest fashion and which Rock hated. As soon as they got home, the phone rang—the first of thirty calls from Rock. "I'm starting my dinner," he said, "and you can't know what it is, but what is a roux?" None of them knew. George looked it up in the French-English dictionary but the definition was not helpful. The recipe Rock had chosen began, "First make a roux . . ." So Rock had to change his menu, find another recipe and go back to the market and re-shop. He called later to ask where various pots were and what does it mean when you heat butter and white foamy stuff comes to the top?

In the evening, Mark, George, Phyllis and Pat drove up to Warbler Place wearing Bermuda shorts and knee socks. "I'll kill you guys," Rock said when he opened the door. "You know I hate those faggot pants!" The dinner, to their surprise, was a sensation, and could serve today as an example of what was considered elegant cooking in the fifties. They began with cheese fondue, cooked in a chafing dish with Sterno, then coq au vin, potatoes Charlotte, salad with Robaire's roquefort dressing and for dessert, cherries jubilee, which Rock flambéed at the table.

"It tasted wonderful," Mark says, "and every pan, pot, dish and spoon in the house was filthy and it took Phyllis until five in the morning to clean up the mess. After that, Rock was banned from the kitchen."

After the success of *Magnificent Obsession*, Rock starred in five pictures for Universal, including a re-pairing with Jane Wyman in *All That Heaven Allows*, where he played a young gardener who defies social convention and woos an older widowed woman. In 1955, the director George Stevens asked to borrow Rock from Universal for the role of Jordan Benedict in *Giant*, being filmed at Warner Brothers. *Giant* was based on the best-selling novel by Edna Ferber, and promised to be the most prestigious film of the year. Clark Gable, Gary Cooper and William Holden wanted the role, but Stevens chose Rock after watching him in *The Lawless Breed*, where he had played a gunfighter from youth to old age.

The role of Jordan Benedict gave Rock a much-needed opportunity to expand his range. Benedict was not the pure, uncomplicated, goody-goody romantic Rock had been playing, but a racist who was pigheaded and insensitive. When his new wife, played by Elizabeth

Taylor, went into the Mexican slums to help the sick, Benedict yelled at her, "You're my wife, Mrs. Jordan Benedict, and I'm asking you right now—when are you going to settle down and behave like everybody else? It's none of your business, fixing the world. Why don't you join a club!"

Giant was an epic novel and the film would run three hours and eighteen minutes. It begins with Rock, as the owner of Reata, one of the largest ranches in Texas, falling in love with Elizabeth Taylor while in Virginia buying horses. They marry and he brings her home to what looks like a surreal vision: a Victorian mansion surrounded by nothing but flat, brown, dusty range. Rock and Elizabeth have a clash of personalities, and after a fight, she goes home to green Virginia, but Rock comes after her and brings her back to Texas. They have twins—a boy and girl—and a younger daughter, but none of the children grow up as the parents would have wished. Jordan Benedict III has no interest in running Reata; he becomes a doctor and marries a Mexican-American. His twin sister refuses to go to school in Switzerland, marries a local boy and starts a small, experimental ranch. The youngest daughter developes a crush on Rock's arch rival, Jett Rink, played by James Dean. At the end, Hudson gets in a fistfight to defend the right of Mexicans to eat in a local diner, and is knocked out by the owner. His wife says she's never been more proud of him, and they look to their grandchildren to carry on the tradition.

Rock had admired George Stevens's films—*Woman of the Year, The Talk of the Town, A Place in the Sun*—and was eager to work with him.

George Stevens—he's another one I fell in love with. He was like a god to me. I mean, I followed him around like a puppy. . . . Here was a man who had done, countless times, I felt, brilliant work.

Stevens had such a richness to him. . . . He read everything. He digested everything . . . so that when he prepared this film, he knew everything there was to know about Texas. His office had bulletin boards on rolling stands with articles, pictures, anything he could find was all Texas. Texas, Texas, Texas! He so inundated himself in Texas and Texanism that whatever decision he made was absolutely right. . . .

He did all the directing with me before the picture began, and hardly a word during shooting. . . . He had me so rich and so bigoted. I was Bick Benedict before we ever shot frame one. . . . He gave me so much power that I felt I could run the studio. "Off with their heads!"

I had lunch with him one day . . . he had kind of yellow eyes that would look right through you. You didn't dare lie to the man because he could just see right through to your core. I was having lunch with him and he said, "Would you like to go down and see your house?" Which was down at the carpentry shop, being built in sections. "Oh, yeah," I said, not giving a damn about the house. That's another department! I could walk out of a door of a modern house or a Victorian house and it didn't matter . . . wrong, but still that was my attitude. And I said, "Sure, sure, anything you say, sir." And there it was, in sections, the raw lumber. And he said, "What color do you want it?" And I said, "Oh . . ." And I realized he was serious. I was all set to make some flip joke. And I said, "Well, Victorian . . . I don't know. Tan with brown trim, I guess." "Okay, boys, paint it tan with a brown trim. Okay, let's go." Well, it was my house. It was mine from then on. Don't you see what he was doing? "Who would you like as your leading lady? Grace Kelly or Elizabeth Taylor?" Well! I can work with Elizabeth, I can work with Grace, you know. And he was serious. So I said, "Elizabeth." "Fine. We'll get Elizabeth." Well, I was eighteen feet tall.

Now, what isn't being said here is that they probably had Elizabeth signed. . . . If I had said Grace Kelly, he would have found a way to make me think that Elizabeth would be better. That was the wonderful way of his direction, of making me think that it was my idea.

And I was rich and strong and bigoted and powerful, so I didn't have to play it. I didn't have to go into a scene and say, "I'm rich and strong and bigoted and powerful, and I'll do this scene from that attitude." I was there. That's good direction.

George Stevens was able to draw from Rock the best performance he had ever given. Before they went into production, Stevens took Rock to matinees at the Wiltern Theater to watch films with Gary Cooper and Spencer Tracy. They sat in the balcony so they could talk. Stevens said, "Look at the way Cooper reacts—he doesn't move a muscle, but you can see what he feels."

They started shooting in Los Angeles in May of 1955, and Rock's first scene was at the dining table in Elizabeth's family home in Virginia. Rock was the stranger at the table, everyone was firing questions at him, and when Stevens shot Rock's reaction scenes, he put him in a chair behind a sawhorse with no one else around. Instead of shooting close-ups, Stevens stood with the camera far away from Rock, so that Rock felt isolated and distant. "He spoke quietly to me through a megaphone," Rock said. "I didn't have to act the scene because I felt strange and uneasy. He got just what he wanted on film."

Elizabeth Taylor invited Rock and Phyllis to dinner at her home with Michael Wilding. "Let's get acquainted," she said. "We're going to be playing husband and wife for the next six months." They ate and drank and when Rock was smashed, he said to Elizabeth, "How can you stand being so beautiful?"

"Beautiful? Beautiful! I'm Minnie Mouse." She went into her bedroom, pinned her hair back and put on a little red skirt and black pumps. When she came back into the living room, Rock said, "It was true! There stood Minnie Mouse."

They stayed up drinking and laughing until four in the morning, and Rock and Elizabeth had to be at the studio two hours later, at 6 A.M. They had to shoot the wedding scene, where Elizabeth has run home to Virginia and is matron of honor at her sister's wedding. Rock arrives, and without saying a word, goes and stands behind Elizabeth until she becomes aware of his presence, turns, and runs into his arms. It would become one of the most powerful scenes in the film. When Rock screened the movie for friends, he would stop the projector and explain: "In between takes, Elizabeth and I were running out and throwing up. We were both so hung over we couldn't speak. That's what made the scene."

Rock found he could joke and giggle with Elizabeth to the point where sometimes they could not look each other in the eye without breaking up. Elizabeth found Rock's laughter warm and cheering; his humor was never cruel or bitchy, it was usually directed at himself and based on a sense of the ridiculous. Rock called her Bessie and she called him Rockabye. They would clown, using Southern dialect:

"I daz," Elizabeth said.

"No you dazn't," Rock said.

"Oh I daz."

"No you dazn't."

They kept going, laughing harder, while everyone else looked on in puzzlement.

When it was time to shoot, however, all clowning stopped. Rock, throughout his career, was known as a consummate professional. He was always on time, always prepared, always willing to work as long as necessary without complaining. He never drank on the set and never held up production. Rock did not get on well with James Dean, and one of the reasons was that he regarded Dean as "unprofessional." Rock and Elizabeth once sat for a day, made up and in costume, waiting for Dean to return from Salinas where he was racing cars. "I didn't particularly like him, personally," Rock said. "But that didn't matter. Jimmy was certainly effective in the role, especially in the younger part. Mind you, he only made three films. He was a little guy and he thought little. . . . He was brilliant as the young man, but he didn't know what to do with the old man. As a matter of fact, he had a long monologue in an empty banquet room that was cut down to the nub because he couldn't sustain it. . . . Also, Jimmy was dead before the picture was over, and his dialogue had to be looped because Jimmy had played it too drunk and you couldn't hear it. So they got another actor to do it. Nick Adams."

After the initial shooting in Los Angeles, the company moved to Marfa, Texas. The Victorian mansion was shipped from California on a flat car, then assembled and lashed with cables to four telephone poles that kept it anchored. The heat was extreme during the day, but at night the air was balmy and the sky was so black that the stars stood out in brilliant patterns—a welcome contrast to the dull haze that covered the Los Angeles basin. Rock and Elizabeth stayed in rented houses across from each other, and it was in one of those houses on a Saturday night in 1955 that they invented the chocolate martini. They both loved chocolate and drank martinis. Why not put chocolate liqueur and chocolate syrup in a vodka martini? They thought it tasted terrific and they had made a great contribution to society until they began to suffer from indigestion. "We were really just kids, we could eat and drink anything and we never needed sleep," Rock said. One Sunday, it hailed and they ran outside with a bucket to gather hailstones to use in their Bloody Marys. "That was bright," Rock said. "The hail was so big it nearly knocked Elizabeth on her ass."

After *Giant*, Rock and Elizabeth remained close friends, although they did not work together again until *The Mirror Crack'd* in 1980. Rock was to become close with many of the women he starred with—Doris Day, Carol Burnett, Juliet Prowse—and almost none of the men. John Foreman, who was Rock's agent after Henry Willson and who later produced *Prizzi's Honor*, says, as a rule, major male stars are not friends. "They steer clear of each other in a room. It's almost like two male dogs that meet on the street—they'll fight or avoid each other. They rarely become pals. It has to do with the nature of the beast that becomes a star. They're intensely competitive, and they don't have close male friends who are also stars."

The shooting for *Giant* was completed in October of 1955, and that month, Rock appeared on the cover of *Life* magazine as "Hollywood's Most Handsome Bachelor." Rock felt triumphant—*Life* was the most popular magazine in the world, with a circulation of eight million. On the cover, Rock was pictured wearing jeans and a western shirt with a red bandanna around his neck. The story was titled "The Simple Life of a Busy Bachelor—Rock Hudson Gets Rich Alone." *Life* said that the fan magazines were "urging 29-year-old Hudson to get married or explain why not." But *Life* added, "Hardly anyone has noticed that Rock has been so busy making movies and money that he has barely had time to get a haircut, let alone a wife."

A month later, Rock eloped to Santa Barbara with Phyllis and got married. The only guests were Henry Willson, Pat Devlin, Jimmy Matteoni and his wife, Gloria. Rock had called Jimmy in Winnetka the night before at one in the morning and told him to be on a plane in five hours. "Don't tell *anyone*. We're getting married secretly. Henry Willson is making all the arrangements." Jimmy and Gloria managed to catch the plane but Jimmy forgot his cuff links. Rock and Phyllis met them at the airport, and they drove to the Santa Monica Courthouse to pick up the license, then to the Biltmore Hotel in Santa Barbara, where Henry had taken Rock to celebrate the signing of their contract. Rock was late, driving fast, and a policeman stopped the procession and gave him a ticket for speeding. "It cost me twenty-seven dollars," Rock said.

Henry had rented a cottage overlooking the ocean and filled it with roses and orchids. A minister performed the ceremony, and as soon as Rock and Phyllis had kissed, Rock went to the phone and called

Hedda Hopper and Phyllis called Louella Parsons. Then the group had supper in the dining room. "Phyllis looked radiant," Jimmy says. "She had that glow women have when they're getting married. She and Roy both seemed excited and happy." Phyllis Gates said, many years later, "I was very much in love, I couldn't help but look radiant. I thought he would be a wonderful husband. He was charming, his career was red hot, he was gorgeous, six foot six inches tall. How many women would have said no? If I had heard things about his being homosexual, I just put them in the back of my mind. So what if it was true? We were having an affair and he asked me to marry him."

Rock's mother, Kay, had not been informed of the wedding or invited to the ceremony, nor had Mark and George. After Rock left for his honeymoon, Kay called Rock's publicist, Roger Jones, in tears. "How could you let him do this! Why did you let him get married!" Mark and George were relieved when they heard the news. "Thank God they made it legal," Mark said. They were not surprised at the secrecy, or at not having been invited. "It was typical of Rock," George says. "He was always pulling something out of the hat. You just accepted it."

Jimmy and Gloria Matteoni drove Rock and Phyllis to the airport where they caught a plane for Florida. They spent a night in Miami, then flew on to Jamaica for a week. According to Phyllis, Rock had forgotten to make a hotel reservation in Miami, "and they put us in a room with a bare light bulb hanging from a socket. I said, 'Would you please go downstairs and say you're on your honeymoon and you want the honeymoon suite?' But Rock wouldn't, and I had to do it."

In Jamaica, they stayed at the Half Moon Hotel in Montego Bay and rented a Fiat that was so small Rock could stick his head out the top. They drove all over the island, swam and lay on the beach and came home tanned, rested and happy. Phyllis says, "It was wonderful. We never had an argument or a cross word on that trip."

Rock told friends that he and Phyllis had the worst fight on their honeymoon, and that it was a terrible week. He told Susan Saint James, his co-star on *McMillan and Wife*, that the honeymoon had been in Mexico and he had developed horrible stomach problems. "He said he had diarrhea and vomiting from the moment he was thrust into the marital situation," Susan says. "He was embarrassed—

it was supposed to be the most special week of his life and he was stuck in the can." (In fact, Rock and Phyllis did go to Mexico about a year after they were married, Rock had *turista* and they had to come home early.)

The marriage was to last two years, and afterward, the story that was told and retold until it became canon was that the marriage had been arranged to kill rumors that Rock was homosexual. The question of whether the marriage was real or phony is the central conundrum of Rock Hudson's life. It is still unresolved, and perhaps never can be, for one of the principals is dead and the other is not sure what happened.

There are two views: The first is that it was a set-up; Rock was married to his agent's secretary with lightning speed in order to ward off the threat of an exposé by *Confidential*. Rock told some of his friends, including Marilyn Maxwell and Armistead Maupin, that he had been forced to marry Phyllis and it was the one thing in his life he felt bitter about.

The second view is held by people who were close to Rock and Phyllis when they were married. They say the story about the arranged marriage was a rumor and had no basis in fact. In Roger Jones's words, "It was a lot of baloney. Phyllis and Rock were at our house constantly, and you get a feeling about people. They were happy together, they clicked. They were genuinely in love, and everything seemed okay for a while. Afterwards, who knows what happens between two people in a marriage?" Jack Navaar and many others who have known Rock intimately say he was not a man who could be pushed around. "Rock never did anything he didn't want to do. No studio could pressure him into marrying someone if he didn't want to." If the marriage had been arranged, others add, financial arrangements would have been covered, and there would have been no rancorous divorce negotiations over property and alimony. George Nader says, "I can spot an acting job and Rock wasn't acting. If that marriage was phony, I'll eat my left tit. We were with them three nights a week and they were all over each other, talking baby talk."

George says it's possible that Henry Willson may have said to Rock, "You have a chance to be a superstar now, but we've got to do something about your life-style. Find a girl, get married for a couple years and that will carry you into major star position. Then the rumors will stop." George says he himself was advised to do this by his publicist: "You're losing parts because you're thirty-five and you're not married." George had a long talk about it with Mark. They had a secretary who would have married George for that purpose. "She would have done it for Rock, too, and divorced him a few years later." But George decided he couldn't go through with it, and besides, Mark joked, "Where would I sleep?" But Rock's case was different, George says. Rock was in love with Phyllis, he was living with her, and Henry's advice or pressure from the Studio may have prompted him to do something he was already contemplating.

If the marriage was arranged, it was done without the knowledge of Phyllis Gates. When I talked with Phyllis, she was avoiding all publicity, keeping a low profile, working quietly as a decorator in Beverly Hills. She had been young, thirty-two, when she was divorced from Rock, but she had never married again. For almost thirty years, she had refused to talk to the press about Rock Hudson. She had put the experience behind her, but in the final months of 1985, when Rock was dying and the press was besieging her again, a tangle of buried emotions came to the surface.

Phyllis spoke fast, in breathy sentences, full of spirit and fire, with a tremulous quality that suggested tears or laughter might break through at any moment. "I never heard that my marriage was arranged until recently," she said. "I used to believe the marriage started with good intentions, but now I don't believe it was genuine. Rock charmed women. He acted from morning till night. I used to say he did better acting at home than at the Studio. He didn't love me, he wasn't even here! I'll bet you my marriage was arranged by Universal."

Phyllis said that if she had known Rock was marrying her to protect his career, "I wouldn't have gone through with it. You don't use people like that and toss them aside. I was set up—I believe that one hundred percent. Henry Willson was so evil, he may have set it up. Rock's reputation was getting out of hand. I was there, I was pretty, and we liked each other. I wish I could find out who did it. It's a puzzle—I wish I knew how to put the pieces together."

After evaluating the evidence and the sources, I have come to conclude that the truth lies somewhere in the gray area between opposing views. I would say that Rock did have genuine feelings of love for

Phyllis, and that concern for his career was one of the factors that led him to marry her. But I don't believe he acted with cold calculation; he was a romantic, he had romantic ideas about marriage and family, and he intended, when he married, for it to last.

After the marriage, Rock was absorbed in films and Phyllis. He and Phyllis called each other "bunting." If Phyllis was out, Rock would say, "I wonder where she is now? What do you suppose Phyllis is doing?" He stopped dropping by Mark and George's place for a drink after work and went straight home. When he walked in the door, he'd call, "I'm home, bunting."

"Oh, bunting is home. Would you like me to get you a drink?"

"Thank you, bunting."

They had private jokes and lapsed into baby talk in front of friends. Rock liked her to sit close beside him or on his lap. Phyllis stopped working for Henry Willson, and began redecorating the house. She threw out the redwood lawn chairs and replaced them with furniture from Sloane's, and she tried to throw out Rock's sloppy clothes and moccasins from Thom McAn's. She went to the set while Rock was shooting *Written on the Wind*, and she accompanied him to Kenya when he made *Something of Value* with Sidney Poitier.

In October of 1956, a year after shooting had been completed, *Giant* had its world premiere in New York and its Hollywood premiere at Grauman's Chinese Theatre. Mark, George and Phyllis decided to make a home movie recording all the events surrounding the opening and present it to Rock for his thirty-first birthday. They called it *Rock Goes A-Bunting!* The film opens on a red-velvet stage, which Mark and George had constructed in their living room. A placard reads: BITE SIZE PRODUCTIONS PRESENTS—ROCK GOES A-BUNTING! The curtain is drawn and there sits a champagne-colored poodle with ribbons and jewels in her fur. Another placard reads: MRS. HUDSON'S GOWNS BY DEMITASSE. The poodle was Phyllis's dog. Rock, Phyllis, Mark and George all had pets and they were presented as the production staff.

The film begins at Grauman's Chinese Theatre with FOOT-PRINT CEREMONIES, in which Rock's hand and footprints are being preserved on Hollywood Boulevard. We see Rock on his knees, dressed in a suit and tie. He writes his name with his finger in the wet cement, then plants his hands and holds them up, dripping and sticky. Someone brings a bowl of water to wash off his hands, and Elizabeth Taylor arrives to plant her hands in the square next to his. Rock then steps into the cement, and Elizabeth pounds on his shoes to plant them deeper.

"And now . . . we take you to New York." We see the marquee of the Roxy: WORLD PREMIERE—GEORGE STEVENS' PRODUCTION OF *GIANT*—ELIZABETH TAYLOR, ROCK HUDSON, JAMES DEAN. Rock arrives with Phyllis, who looks as glamorous as any actress, wearing a low-cut gown of iridescent material, a fur stole and diamond earrings. Phyllis winks at the camera and Rock seems oblivious.

"And now, back to Hollywood . . ." The movie shifts from black-and-white to color. There is a tracking shot down Hollywood Boulevard, showing what other films were playing: *War and Peace, High Society, 1984, Cinerama Holiday*. We arrive at Grauman's and stars sweep by: Clark Gable, Joan Crawford, Tab Hunter, Natalie Wood. Rock appears with Phyllis in a different gown and a different fur. Rock and Phyllis stand beside a platform, waiting to be introduced to the crowd; they look listless, nothing on their faces. Suddenly they come to life—radiant—as they're introduced and called into the spotlight.

When the film was screened for Rock, he roared with laughter at that shot. "See us turn on the charm? Charlie Movie Star!"

The home movie was a complete surprise to Rock. Mark had shot the footage at Grauman's, but Rock had not seen him because he was nearsighted and never wore his glasses in public. Phyllis kept trying to get Rock to look at the camera. "Isn't that Fred?" she'd say, pointing toward Mark, and Rock would squint and stare in his direction. Mark held the camera in front of his face, so Rock wouldn't recognize him. In New York, Phyllis arranged for a friend to shoot the footage, and Henry Willson obtained a press pass so he could stand up close with the other photographers.

Mark and George spent three weeks editing the film, hurrying to finish it by Rock's birthday, November 17. They asked Rock to bring his projector to the party, and after dinner, to run the film they handed him. "Why, what is it, what am I doing?" Rock said. When the credits began, he howled. "This is terrific. How'd you guys do this? I never saw a thing! What a documentary this is—won't it be great to have when I'm old?"

So began what Mark and George were to call the "Impossible Years" with Rock, when he became, in his own words, "Charlie Movie Star." His performance in *Giant* not only raised him to the level of superstar, but he was taken seriously as an actor for the first time. He was nominated for an Academy Award, and in 1957, he was voted the number-one box-office attraction—"Name Power Star"—by the Film Buyers of the Motion Picture Industry. He was voted number one for seven straight years. For seven years, no man in the world was considered more desirable, no star, male or female, was more popular or could bring more people to the theater than Rock Hudson.

F. Scott Fitzgerald told us that the rich are different, and it is equally true that movie stars are different from the rest of us. A movie star is like a king, surrounded by servants and ministers arranged about him in orbits, who guard and protect him from the hordes. Everyone watches him and caters to him as if he were a spoiled child who might throw a tantrum if not handled gently. Whatever he says is right, whatever he wants must be done.

Rock developed a slight swagger when he walked; he became more pompous, and everything was on his terms. If he wanted to see a friend, he would unilaterally set the time—"Come here at seven on Thursday." He would choose the restaurant and pay, he would never let anyone else pay. If he was invited to a party, he had to approve the guest list ahead of time. Mark and George began referring to Rock as "the movie star" or "the M.I."—the matinee idol. He was rude to waiters, and at home, when he had guests, he would take the seat nearest the phone. If it rang, he would say, "Hold it, nobody say a word." He would talk to the caller, then hang up and say, "Okay, you can go ahead now."

Rock often said he wanted to write a book called *How to Be a Movie Star*. There were rules:

1. Movie stars never make reservations; they walk into a restaurant and get a table.
2. Movie stars don't put money in parking meters; they never get tickets.

3. Movie stars never do bad things—it was somebody else's fault.

4. Movie stars never go to the door or answer the phone. (Rock violated this constantly.)

5. Movie stars never ask the price. This can have bizarre consequences, as when Rock was buying a birthday present for Nancy Walker and chose a blouse. As an afterthought, he picked up a scarf and told the saleswoman, "Throw this in too." When the bill came, he discovered that the scarf had been hand-painted by Salvador Dalí and cost a thousand dollars.

6. Movie stars have naturally perfect bodies, they don't work out.

7. Movie stars never carry money. Rock demonstrated the wisdom of this when he drove Princess Grace home from a party at Rupert Allan's in the late sixties. Her Serene Highness was staying at the home of Kitty and Mervyn LeRoy, but the LeRoys had left the party early and Grace and Rock had stayed on, drinking, until, Rock said, "We were ripped to the tits." Grace said, "I can't go back to the LeRoys' like this," and Rock said, "Let's go to Ollie Hammond's, they're open late." So Grace in her long gown and Rock in his tuxedo were shown to a booth at Ollie Hammond's. When the check came, Rock turned to Grace. "I'm sorry, I don't carry money."

"Princesses don't carry money. I guess we'll have to do the dishes," Grace said.

Rock called the manager. "Neither of us has any money. Could I leave my wallet?"

"No, no," the manager said. "We're honored to have you as our guests."

Rock developed an obsession with privacy; he disliked the press, interviews, publicity, and refused to give reporters any information about his affairs offscreen. He believed his private life was his own business, and that it was a mark of dignity not to speak about it. He acquired a reputation for being wooden, a poor interview, so colorless and ungiving that it was almost a waste of time to ask him questions. One writer described him as "a windup doll"; another said he was "the most difficult star to know in Hollywood—always pleasant but totally nonrevealing." If he consented to interviews, Rock amused himself by making up anecdotes, some of which he repeated so often that he forgot he had made them up.

I have given over a thousand interviews . . . and I've often wondered how an interviewer can come into somebody's home and ask all kinds of questions, brazen questions, about his personal life.

A favorite question among the fan magazines was whether or not I slept in the nude. I couldn't understand who could give a damn about my sleeping habits, but there were the questions. . . . As a matter of fact, I went through a great deal in learning to sleep in the nude. From my childhood, I remembered my mother saying, "Well, what if there's a fire?" and I thought, right, indeed, what if there's a fire—I'd have to run out naked and people would see my pee-pee.

Then when I was twenty-one, I thought, hell, if there's a fire you can just wrap a blanket around you, and I've slept in the nude ever since. But who in hell cares?

Rock had an aversion to giving autographs. Most of the pictures sent to fans through the years were signed by Mark Miller. When Rock appeared with Carol Burnett in *I Do! I Do!* he was startled to find that after the show, Carol would sit at a card table signing autographs. She said she felt she owed it to her fans, but Rock said, "You owe them the best performance you can give. You don't owe them this."

Rock's relationship with Phyllis began to deteriorate after *Giant*. In Rock's view, Phyllis changed when she became Mrs. Hudson. She went on buying sprees, and she fired Rock's housekeeper, a black woman named Truitt who had been with him since his first days at Universal and whom Rock considered "family." Phyllis became more possessive; she would call the Studio and monitor Rock's movements through the day. Most important, Rock felt, she was no longer warm and fun-loving, she was constantly picking on him.

Phyllis says Rock never thought about anything but his career. "He was out every night. He was always in a bad mood, and he'd pout for three days at a time. He would start an argument at the drop of a hat, then slam the door and not come back until morning. You couldn't talk to him. He froze people out—he just shut up and didn't talk. You'd say, 'Would you like some coffee?' and he wouldn't answer."

Phyllis said Rock never told her what he was thinking, never sat down with her for a heart-to-heart talk. "We talked about the business, about the pictures he was making, but not about personal things. I thought he talked to George." Phyllis became so depressed and unhappy with the marriage that she went to see a woman psychiatrist, who suggested that Rock come in for testing. "She gave him a number of personality profile tests, and said he had the emotional development of an eight-year-old." Rock laughed when he heard this. "What do they know?"

Phyllis gave Rock an ultimatum: Either he would go for psychiatric help or she would leave. "I thought maybe an analyst could break through the exterior and he would talk." Rock sat on the edge of the bed and cried. "I can never tell anyone what I do when I'm by myself."

Phyllis was puzzled. "No matter what you do, I'll be here with you."

Rock went to see the analyst twice and refused to go again. He said he did not believe in doctors or psychiatrists, and he also did not believe in germs, "because I can't see them."

It was about this time that Rock called up Mark Miller and said, "I have to have a boy. For a year, I've been faithful, I haven't had a boy and I'm going crazy. Can you fix me up with someone?" Mark called a friend in Laguna, who was interested, and Rock drove down to meet him one night before going home to Phyllis. The friend said later it had been an incredible encounter, because Rock was "so starved."

Usually, I can smell a failure as soon as I read the script. I can't smell a hit, though. If I could do that, I'd be a multimillionaire. But I can't. Nobody can.

In 1957, Rock was offered the lead in three major pictures being made at other studios: *Sayonara, Ben Hur,* and *A Farewell to Arms.* Rock liked *A Farewell to Arms* best, and prevailed upon Universal to release him for the project. He said, afterward, it was the "biggest mistake of my career." *Sayonara* with Marlon Brando and *Ben Hur* with Charlton Heston were both major hits, while A *Farewell to Arms* was a critical and commercial disappointment. Rock said he picked it because all the elements "smelled right." It was based on a novel by Ernest Hemingway, the screenplay was by Ben Hecht, the producer was David O. Selznick who had made *Gone With the Wind*. "You can't go wrong there," Rock said. The director was John Huston, "can't go wrong there," and the cast was outstanding: Jennifer Jones, Vittorio de Sica, Elaine Stritch, Mercedes McCambridge.

But Huston was fired the day before the picture began, to be replaced by Charles Vidor, who didn't get along with Jennifer Jones, who was married to the producer, Selznick. Hemingway's novels have never translated well to the screen, and the Hemingway hero is a hard-bitten romantic. Rock seemed soft, almost sappy in the role and entirely unbelievable as the adventurer-soldier drawn to war.

The six months spent on location in Italy were strained and difficult for everyone. David Selznick, Rock said, "had an air of confusion about him. There was nothing clear and set, as with George Stevens. This dynamo of a man was in constant confusion. He was so intense . . . always scribbling his memos. He wanted everything better than perfect. He never let up."

Selznick was concerned about Rock's Adam's apple, and insisted that it be shaded and camouflaged with makeup. "I'd say to him, 'Good morning, David,' and he'd never say good morning. He'd say, 'Your Adam's apple isn't made up.' He was such an intense man that it never occurred to him to say good morning. That's a waste of time. We've got work to do."

Phyllis had planned to join Rock in Italy, but in March, she developed hepatitis and was hospitalized. Rock called her in the hospital but wouldn't come home because he couldn't interrupt shooting. Phyllis felt hurt and abandoned, and had to rely on Pat Devlin for help. When she came home from the hospital, Phyllis discovered that the house next door on Warbler Place was being remodeled. To escape the constant pounding and drilling, she rented a house on the ocean in Malibu, where she could rest and recuperate.

The Oscar awards were presented in Hollywood at the end of March, while Rock was shooting in a small village in the Italian

Alps. He could not attend the ceremony, which was an additional source of frustration to Phyllis. Rock was nominated for *Giant* along with Kirk Douglas in *Lust for Life*, Yul Brynner in *The King and I*, Laurence Olivier in *Richard III*, and James Dean, his co-star in *Giant*. Kurt Kasznar, an Austrian actor who had a role in *A Farewell to Arms*, arranged for the Italian Army to carve a thirty-foot replica of the Oscar statue in the ice near Rock's hotel. "If you win, your Oscar will be there in the morning; if you lose, it'll be melted by sundown," Kasznar said. Rock came home from shooting and saw the Oscar melting—Yul Brynner had won. But Rock did not let on that he was disappointed or had even thought about winning.

In June of 1957, Mark Miller took his first trip to Europe with his brother, Philip. Rock had made a point of coordinating schedules with Mark so they could meet in Rome, where Rock would be shooting at Cinecittà. "Call me the minute you get in," Rock had said. "I'll show you everything!"

Mark and Philip arrived in Rome without reservations and found every hotel booked up because of a nurses' convention. The only place they could get a room was at the Atlantico, a seedy hotel by the railroad station. Their room was on the ground floor, and all night there was noise from streetcars going by. The room had a few pieces of dingy furniture, moldy wallpaper and threadbare paisley drapes on wooden rings. Mark called Rock at the Grand Hotel and left a message, waited around for a day but Rock did not call. Mark left messages for seven days and never heard from Rock. He and Philip decided to leave for Capri, packed their bags and went to sleep but were awakened at four in the morning by someone pounding on the door. "Open up, it's me!"

Rock Hudson swept into the drab little room like an apparition, wearing a tuxedo, grinning. "What on earth are you doing in this dreadful hotel?" he said, standing in front of the sagging twin beds where Mark and Philip were lying in their pajamas.

"There's a nurses' convention," Mark said. "We couldn't find a room. We were lucky to get this one."

"You should have called me. I could have gotten you into the Grand."

"We did," Philip said pointedly. "You didn't return our call."

"I'm sorry. I've been busy, working my tail off. I was out with

Sophia tonight." Rock said he had gone from work to the opera and a ball and was skipping sleep, he would go straight to work again at six. Mark and Philip had been fuming at Rock, but when he appeared, full of boyish charm and endearment, their anger dissolved.

"The picture's going great," Rock said. "They tell me the dailies look terrific. It's a hell of a part." He paused. "I'm seeing someone."

"Good for you," Mark said with irony.

Rock was having a romance with a young Italian actor, and had also had encounters with other men. "I'm having the time of my life." When he learned Mark and Philip were leaving for Capri in the morning, he said, "Come back here after Capri. I insist! I'm taking you to dinner—it'll be terrific. Call me the minute you get back."

Mark and Philip did return to Rome and did call, but they never heard from Rock. "He was Charlie Movie Star. He could do exactly as he pleased."

When the picture was finished and Rock returned to California, he joined Phyllis at the house in Malibu. Rock accidentally left the door open and her poodle, Demitasse, got loose and was run over and killed on the Pacific Coast Highway. Phyllis was distraught, she had had the dog for years, and she felt Rock was insensitive. "I'll buy you another dog," he said.

In October, Rock dropped in, unannounced, at Mark and George's house on Round Valley Drive in Sherman Oaks. George was alone, except for the Irish cleaning woman. "I've got to talk to you about something," Rock said. "Where can we go?" George suggested they climb up the cliff behind the house. He had dug steps into the hillside and built a small platform at the top, where he could sit and look out over the valley. He and Rock walked up the hill and sat down on the platform, side by side, legs dangling. George waited; he didn't want to stare at Rock so he looked straight ahead.

"I've got a real problem with Phyllis," Rock said. "I don't know what to do. I have tried everything. I have tried thinking of razor blades. I have tried thinking of black widow spiders. I have tried thinking of snakes. . . . It doesn't do any good. Nothing works. I can't go to a doctor about it."

George nodded, but he had no idea what Rock was talking about.

Black widow spiders? He didn't ask because Rock would clam up if questioned, and Rock implied that anyone should know what he meant.

"I'm sorry, I don't know what I can say," George said.

"You don't have to say anything. I just had to tell you," Rock said. "Now, I want you to promise me you won't tell anyone about this. And I mean *anyone*."

"Okay, I won't," George said, but he was uneasy. His understanding with Rock had always been that he and Mark did not keep secrets from each other. Was Rock trying to violate that now—asking George to exclude Mark from his confidence?

The next morning, Mark walked down the driveway to pick up the newspaper. Before he returned to the house, he had spotted a story: ROCK HUDSON LEAVES WIFE. Mark was flabbergasted, and showed the item to George, who then told him Rock had come by the day before, "and we had the damndest conversation I've ever had. I don't know what the fuck he was talking about." They speculated: Was it premature ejaculation? Was he telling George he couldn't satisfy her?

Rock had not told George he was going to leave Phyllis. "But he never goes all the way—he doesn't drop the other shoe." In fact, when Rock had left George's house, he had packed a bag and checked into the Beverly Hills Hotel, which is what movie stars do when they leave their wives. The next night, he called Mark and George from the hotel. Mark answered. "Rock, I'm sorry you left her. I thought it would work. I adore Phyllis; I think you didn't try hard enough."

Rock said, "I'm sorry you don't approve. Fuck you."

"Fuck you."

They hung up and did not speak again for a year. Part of the reason Mark had responded as he did was that he was still angry at Rock for giving him the runaround in Rome. "So it was easy to say, screw you, and not call. Rock had become unbearable." About a year later, Rock called Mark and said, "Let's have dinner," and they took up right where they had left off.

When Gail Gifford, one of the publicists at Universal, heard that Rock and Phyllis were splitting, she called his room at the Beverly Hills Hotel and Rock's mother answered the phone. She put her son on.

"Rock, I've heard . . . is it true?" Gail said.

"Yes."

"Is there anything I can do?"

"No, I'm fine. How 'bout you?"

Gail said, "It was so like Rock to say nothing further. He never burdened you with any of his problems. I don't think Rock and I ever mentioned the divorce after that."

On April 22, 1958, Phyllis Fitzgerald filed suit against Roy Fitzgerald for divorce, charging "extreme mental cruelty." The divorce negotiations were rancorous, with both sides charging the other with unscrupulous tactics. Phyllis said Rock hired a detective to follow her. She said she had to go stay with friends because "I was afraid I might be killed."

Rock moved into a furnished apartment on Crescent Heights, and suspected it was being bugged. His attorney, Greg Bautzer, ordered a sweep, and the investigators found evidence that induction equipment might have been used and removed just prior to the sweep. There were wires that had been freshly cut.

Rock did not answer his wife's complaint, nor did he appear in court. A settlement was reached by their attorneys, and on August 13, 1958, a hearing was held at Santa Monica Superior Court. Phyllis testified that Rock had been sullen and wouldn't speak to her, that he stayed out nights and when she asked where he had been, he struck her. Pat Devlin was her witness, testifying that she had seen Rock strike his wife, and that Rock had failed to visit Phyllis when she was in the hospital.

Phyllis was awarded alimony of $250 a week for ten years, plus the house on Warbler Place, which was valued at $35,000, and for which Rock agreed to make the payments, plus a newly acquired Ford Thunderbird. She also owned 5 percent of a corporation, 7 Pictures, formed to produce Rock Hudson films. At the time, Rock was earning $3,500 a week. The fan magazines turned against Phyllis, blaming her for the divorce and sympathizing with Rock. One columnist said, "Why did she get so much? She married Rock with her eyes open and gave him less than two years of marriage." In 1961, Phyllis went back to court, claiming Hudson had reduced the assets of 7 Pictures Corporation without advising her, and that her alimony was not sufficient. Friends of Rock say Phyllis told Rock she was considering writing a book about their marriage. She obtained an additional $130,000.

Rock was pained by the divorce, and he was particularly upset at losing the Warbler house—his first house, the tangible symbol of the success he had worked so hard for. On the surface, though, he kept up a sunny, carefree attitude. If someone asked why his marriage broke up, he said, with a disarming smile, "It didn't work." He refused to discuss the details with anyone, and his friends knew better than to probe. For Rock, Phyllis Gates did not exist.

CHAPTER 6

*S*hooting Pillow Talk *was like going to a party. It was a day's work of fun; it wasn't work at all. I was quite apprehensive, nervous and scared, because I'd never played comedy. And in Ross Hunter's office, I met the director, Michael Gordon. Michael Gordon is very intense . . . he belongs behind a big tome, blowing the dust. He has these enormous eyebrows. And I thought, that man is going to direct me in comedy? Light, airy-fairy comedy? Okay! So I said, "Mr. Gordon, I am nervous about one thing: How do you play comedy?"*

"Oh," he said, "just treat it like the very most tragic story you've ever portrayed." I thought about that for a minute. "That makes sense." Then he said, "If you think you're funny, nobody else will." And it's absolutely the truth. Of course, it's the most serious tragedy ever written.

Doris and I became terrific friends. She's a dynamo—a strong lady. And, boy, what a comedienne she is! The trouble we had was trying not to laugh. Doris and I couldn't look at each other. You know, that sweet agony of laughing when you're not supposed to? That's what we had.

The second film we made together, Lover Come Back, *was even worse. I think they added two weeks to the shooting schedule because of our laughter. We flat could not look at each other. I'd look at her forehead, her nose. And we did terrible things to each other; with our backs to the camera we'd make faces at each other. . . . It's perhaps acting rather juvenile in one sense, but in another, when you're shooting comedy, it isn't. What shows on the screen, I think, is what helped make those films successful. The twinkle shows in the eyes. And we had it.*

When Rock read the treatment for *Pillow Talk,* he thought it was "dreadful" and turned it down. When he read the finished script, he was impressed with its humor and cleverness, but he thought the material too racy. He was also nervous about comedy—a radical de-

111

parture from the roles he'd been playing—and the movie called for him to sing, which he'd always wanted to do but had not yet tried on screen.

Rock and Doris were brought together in the office of the producers, Ross Hunter and Marty Melcher, who was Doris's husband. "I felt he was shy and very sweet," Doris says. "I was aware of the chemistry between us. We looked good together, we looked like a couple should look."

Rock told them he wasn't sure he could be funny. Doris says, "I think it was fear of the unknown, but we thought he'd be perfect and tried to reassure him." Doris knew, and Rock suspected, that comedy was much more difficult to perform than drama. "It's harder because it's not real," Doris says. "Drama is real—that's life, and you react as in life and you don't have to think about timing so much. But in comedy, timing is everything. If you try to be funny, you will never be funny. I have to play comedy very real. If the situation is funny, you play it absolutely totally real." Doris says the audience demands more of a comedy. "People sit back and say, 'Make me laugh. Now make me laugh more. Now make me laugh really hard. Now make me laugh even harder,' and if they're not screaming when they go out, they say, that wasn't so hot. But with real-life drama, if they shed a few tears, that's okay. It's much easier."

Rock accepted the challenge, and *Pillow Talk* began shooting in February of 1959. Doris says, "It had a terrific feeling from the first day." Everyone thought the script by Stanley Shapiro and Maurice Richlin was exceptional. Tony Randall says, "It was brilliant. When you've tried all the lousy material I've had to do, you jump way in the air, your head hits the ceiling, when you get good material like this."

Rock and Doris found that they could make each other laugh off camera. "We had our own funny bits, our own craziness," Doris says. "We both loved the fact that Beverly Hills was trying so hard to be chic, and just a few miles away were places like Compton, Agoura and Bellflower. You leave Beverly Hills and you're in Bellflower." Rock would joke about spending the weekend in "Calabasas, the gateway to Agoura." Doris says, "There were only twelve families living there then, but they had a sign over the freeway that said CALABASAS, THE GATEWAY TO AGOURA." Rock would tell her how he was going to spend his summer in Bakersfield, which may be the hottest and most miserable town in California in the summer. "He had me rolling on the floor, yelling 'Stop!'"

Rock gave Doris the name Eunice Blotter, and she called him Roy Harold. "I think he liked saying that name, Eunice. You-nis. It sounds funny. He loved calling me up and saying, 'Eunice? Is that you? It's me, Roy Harold. What's doin' up there?'"

In this atmosphere of clowning and giggling, Rock was working hard and learning a great deal. He studied Doris, "her sense of timing, her instincts. I just kept my eyes open and copied her," Rock said. "Doris was an Actors Studio all by herself. When she cried, she cried funny, which is something I couldn't even try to explain; and when she laughed, her laughter came boiling up from her kneecaps."

From the opening credits of *Pillow Talk*, the audience gets a sense of the freshness and sauciness of the piece. On a split screen, a man and woman wearing white silk nightclothes are lying on beds, tossing and kicking pillows toward each other as Doris sings the title song.

Doris plays a "career girl," Jan Morrow, who lives alone in a glamorous apartment in Manhattan and works as an interior decorator. She shares a party line with Rock, who plays Brad Allen, a songwriter who hogs the line, singing love songs to different women while Doris, unable to use the phone for business calls, listens in and fumes. Rock is suave, relaxed, a charmer who seduces women by passive manipulation. The cooler and more disinterested he pretends to be, the more desperate the women are to cook him dinner, wash his clothes, jump into his bed. He is the perfect playboy and lives in a playboy "pad." He has a control box by the couch, so that when a woman is with him, he pushes button one and a record drops onto the turntable. He pushes button two and the front door locks. He pushes button three and the couch unfolds into a bed with baby-blue sheets.

Doris and Rock fight over who gets to use the phone. He insults her and she complains to the phone company. He calls her and we see them on a split screen:

"Miss Morrow . . . why are you so fascinated with my personal affairs? . . . You don't see me going down to the phone company and complaining about your affairs."

"I have none to complain about," Doris says.

"It figures . . ."

"What do you mean?"

"Obviously, you're a woman who lives alone and doesn't like it."

"I happen to like living alone."

"Look, I don't know what's bothering you, but don't take your bedroom problems out on me."

"I have no bedroom problems. There's nothing in my bedroom that bothers me."

"Oh, that's too bad."

She hangs up in a snit. "Bedroom problems!"

Doris is pursued by a millionaire producer, played by Tony Randall, who wants to marry her, but Doris says she's not in love with him. Tony tells his best friend, who happens to be Rock, about his unrequited love for Doris, and Rock realizes she's the woman on his party line. Tony advises Rock to get married, and they have an exchange that mirrors, in wittier form, a debate that, in 1959, was being waged in bedrooms and parked cars across the country.

Tony says, "You ought to quit all this chasing around. . . . Believe me, there is nothing in the world so wonderful, so fulfilling as coming home to the same woman every night."

"Why?"

"Because that's what it means to be an adult. A wife, a family, a house. A mature man wants those responsibilities. What have you got against marriage anyway?"

Rock answers: "Before a man gets married, he's like a tree in the forest. He stands there, independent, an entity unto himself. And then he's chopped down. His branches are cut off, he's stripped of his bark and thrown into the river with the rest of the logs. Then this tree is taken to the mill, and when it comes out, it's no longer a tree. It's a vanity table, the breakfast nook, the baby crib, and the newspaper that lines the family garbage can."

Rock meets Doris in a nightclub, but he pretends to be a wealthy Texan named Rex Stetson. You hear their thoughts as they ride together in a cab. She says to herself, "What a marvelous-looking man. He's so sincere." Rock smiles and thinks, "I'd say, five or six dates oughta do it."

The struggle between the playboy and the virgin thus begins. She wants to get married, and he wants to go to bed. Viewed today, it all looks so primitive, and yet, so much clearer and cleaner than our vague rumblings about ambivalence and commitment. In 1959, men were trees fighting against being domesticated, and women were honest trappers or they were sluts. The women Rock takes to bed in his baby-blue sheets are strippers and dancers at the Copa. When he's with Doris, playing the Texan, he acts the perfect gentleman and doesn't even try to kiss her. By being passive, he forces her to take the initiative. She begs him, finally, to kiss her, and agrees to go away with him for the weekend. "I certainly should be able to trust you now." She sings what she feels, "Possess me," and they sit before the fire and drink champagne. The furniture is massive, oversized, which makes Rock look huge and manly and Doris look dwarfed and vulnerable. Just at the moment of truth, Doris discovers his real identity and runs away.

Rock is surprised at his reaction. He feels guilty and can't write songs. "You're in love," Tony Randall exults. "The mighty tree has been toppled! For years, I've been waiting to hear them yell 'timber' over you. You love her and she can't stand the sight of you. What a beautiful sight. The great Brad Allen, chopped down to size, floating down the river with the rest of us guys."

Rock hires Doris to decorate his apartment, giving her free rein to "make it the type of place you'd feel comfortable in." She redoes it like a bordello, and when he sees it, he carries her kicking and screaming from her apartment to his, where he tells her he wants to get married. The movie ends, three months later, with Rock emerging from a doctor's office, victorious. "I'm gonna have a baby!"

Delbert Mann, who directed Rock and Doris in their next film, *Lover Come Back*, says they were keenly aware of the social conventions they were playing with. "The films were not intended as morality tales, but to poke fun at social mores," Mann says. "The assault on Doris's fiercely guarded virginity was where the humor came from." Yet large numbers of people listened quite attentively to the message behind the laughs. I remember, as a high school student in the late fifties, watching *Pillow Talk* and identifying with Doris. I wanted to be a career girl, I thought I would like to work in advertising and wear designer clothes and live in a beautiful apartment—all my own—with a maid to look after me. And this was what I could expect from my romantic life: If I stuck to my principles, as Doris did, if I did not become "damaged goods," if I played very carefully and cleverly, I could land a Rock Hudson. The man could be transformed from playboy to perfect husband, and the woman could pass from virgin to multi-orgasmic partner in one night. Three months later, we would see the fruit: the husband, happy in his domesticated state, crowing, "I'm gonna have a baby."

I was astonished, when I interviewed Doris Day twenty-six years later, to learn that she did not feel she was playing a virgin. "I was a businesswoman. I don't think I was a virgin. I went off to the country with him and I probably would have succumbed, except I found out he was a phony and ran away. The audience—*you* thought I was a virgin. *You* thought, when I went off with him, oh, she'll think of some way to wiggle out." (Actually, what I thought in 1959 was that Doris could neck and sleep in the same bed with Rock but not go *all the way*.)

The film hit a social nerve. No two stars were more suited to play the contenders in the American sexual battle than Rock Hudson and Doris Day. Sparks flew—you could feel the charge between them. She was so blond, he was so dark, and both were such clean, wholesome products of the heartland. *Time* magazine, which was famous then for its comically bitchy reviews, said they looked like two shiny Cadillacs "parked in a suggestive position."

Few teams in movie history have so captured the imagination of the public. Rock and Doris had a special chemistry on screen that neither had with anyone else. Rock said, "I don't really know what makes a movie team. First of all, the two people have to truly like each other, as Doris and I did, for that shines through. Then, too, both parties have to be strong personalities—very important to comedy—so that there's a tug-of-war over who's going to put it over on the other, who's going to get the last word, a fencing match between two adroit opponents of the opposite sex who in the end are going to fall into bed together."

There was a third member of the team, who served as a foil, Tony Randall. Rock did not become close with Tony as he did with Doris. Tony says, "He was not a warm man. He wouldn't tell you much about himself. Off camera, we weren't friends, but that didn't mean anything. At work, on camera, we had glorious rapport." Tony says he had heard Rock was gay, "but I found it difficult to believe. He always had girls around. He told me he liked the starlets who were about because they didn't expect you to marry them and he was certain of getting laid." Tony says that if Rock had come out, "that would have been death to the romantic image. All the women in America were crazy about him. He was the idealized all-American boy. He really looked like a truck driver who'd gotten some class."

Doris Day says when people asked her if it was true that Rock was gay, she said, "I really don't know. He seems very straight to me. He doesn't seem any different than James Garner."

As a team, Tony says, the three worked wonderfully together. "Acting is fun when everyone works hard and is good—it's such a joy! Rock was a hard worker, and I like that. Rock did not have acting genius, as Doris did on occasion. Rock's great strength was his romantic quality. He could play romantic parts because he really believed in romance. He really believed in love. He had romantic notions. He told me once that he'd never performed the act of cunnilingus."

I told Tony I was not surprised.

Tony went on. "Rock said, 'It's too beautiful.'" Tony paused. "I think that's romantic."

By the time *Pillow Talk* was released, in October of 1959, Rock had patched things up with Mark Miller and George Nader. He sent Mark to a sneak preview at the Encino Theater. "Meet me at my house afterward. I want a full report." Mark came back and said, "You got a hit, kid. I was surprised how good you were in comedy. The audience laughed at all the right places and came out just bubbling."

"Is it too racy?" Rock said.

"It is racy. The audience didn't seem offended, though."

The audience was not offended because the film was, in Marty Melcher's words, "a clean sex comedy." All the sex took place in words, not action. It was one long tease, with no actual lovemaking, just a few kisses. It was "enticing but legal," in the same way the Playboy Clubs were enticing but legal—like a brothel where no one ever goes upstairs. *Pillow Talk* captured the fancy of the critics and the public. The film grossed more than $7.5 million in this country, and Doris was nominated for an Academy Award. Doris and Rock were exhilarated. Doris recalls, "Right away, we said, we have to do another one."

While he was shooting *Pillow Talk*, Rock was living in Malibu in a house built on stilts over the rocks. At high tide, the waves would come up under the house, and seabirds would perch on the deck. It was like living on a boat. Rock had moved there after the divorce, and fallen in with a group of actors and stuntmen who lived along the beach. Among them were Rod Taylor, Don Burnett, an actor under contract at M.G.M., George Robotham, who did stunts for Rock, and Paul Stader, a veteran stuntman who had done the diving scenes in *Hurricane* for Jon Hall. When Rock met Stader, he said, "You son of a bitch. It's your fault that I wanted to be an actor. I thought all along it had been Jon Hall."

Don Burnett describes their life as "macho and physical. We went swimming in the ocean without wetsuits all year round. We did a lot of running in the Malibu hills, then we'd come down to the beach and jump in the ocean. We went sailing and scuba diving—we taught Rock. In those days, you could pick up lobsters just beyond the surf line." He said Rock hadn't done much running, but was strong and pressed himself to compete with the group. "One night, we had an arm-wrestling contest and Rock won, which was impressive, because there were some tough guys there. Some of the guys had to get in fights now and then, and would go to bars in rough neighborhoods and empty them out." There was heavy drinking, but "the sexual stuff was private," Burnett says. "People didn't brag about their conquests." Rock never had a woman or a man with him when he was with the group. He kept his life in airtight compartments, never mixing gay friends with straight friends or business associates.

Rock told Jack Coates, whom he lived with in the sixties, that when he first went to Malibu, it was to retreat and lick his wounds. He felt strapped financially, and angry that he'd been "taken" by Phyllis Gates. He was worried his career might be over; the divorce would hurt his standing with the public. After a month, though, he found that living on the ocean was restorative: the constant rolling of the waves, the movement of the tides, the brilliant streaks of orange and pink at sunset that illumined the clouds like a painting. Rock knew, once again, that all would be right. The divorce from Phyllis would not hurt him, and he would cease to worry about things over which he had no control.

Rock was developing a mental discipline that would allow him to control his thoughts and feelings. He did not call it "positive thinking," he never showed any interest in psychology or religion, but he had an extraordinary ability to wipe from his mind any matter that disturbed him. He could will a problem out of his thoughts so that it no longer existed. George Nader says, "That was how he handled problems—he tuned them out. He had a marvelous way of deciding that something simply had not happened." If a friend gave Rock unpleasant news, a veil would drop over his face. He would fall silent, or change the subject, or go on talking as if he had heard nothing. Rock was able to maintain a calm assurance that whatever was happening was right.

I have had the best summer of my life at Newport Beach with my boat and my house. I enjoy being alone. Boats and the sea are the greatest things in the world for relaxation and peace of mind, when the only thing that really matters is: Are the sails right? I am going to live at Newport all the year round. I can get to the studio in an hour.

In the summer of 1959, Rock moved from Malibu to Newport Beach and bought a sailboat, a Newporter, from the actress Claire Trevor and her husband, Milton Bren. He changed the name of the boat from *The Lady Claire* to *Khairuzan*, after the character he had played in *The Golden Blade*. He spent a great deal of time with Claire and Milton, who became a surrogate father and taught him to sail.

These were halcyon days for Rock. He was the number-one star in the world, he had just embarked on a new phase of his career—comedy—and he threw himself into sailing with a passion and zeal for perfection. He bought a book called *The Proper Yacht*, and developed his own ritual for weekend trips. He liked to sail to Catalina

Island, twenty-six miles off the coast. On the way out, no one was allowed to drink, but the minute they dropped anchor, Rock would go to the galley and fix the "perfect martini," from a recipe Claire had developed. He called the drink a Claire Trevor, or "C.T." It was made with Tanqueray gin, a twist of orange and an eyedropper of vermouth. Claire would use an atomizer to spray vermouth into the drink. The twist of orange was critical—it took the bite off the gin and made it smooth. After rounds of C.T.s, Rock would barbecue "the perfect steak."

Rock's favorite crew for sailing were Lynn Bowers and Pat Fitzgerald, a lesbian couple who both worked as publicists. Lynn was smart and funny and heavyset, and she sat with her legs apart and talked dirty. Pat was slender and fluttery and liked word games and wordplay. Rock called them, respectively, Bullets and Fitznigger, and by the time the summer was over, they were part of his inner circle.

Rock was seeing numerous men, but he discovered that as a major movie star, it was increasingly difficult to get laid. People were awe-struck, afraid to make the first move. They assumed that Rock was deluged with partners and wouldn't be interested. It was true that Rock could have his pick of the most beautiful young men in the country, and he used this to full advantage. But when a liaison was arranged, many young men were so self-conscious they couldn't per-form. They may have had fantasies about Rock Hudson, but when they were face to face with the real person, all they could think was "I'm in bed with Rock Hudson!" Rock told a friend, Jon Epstein, "I wish I could go to bed with a bag over my head, because when peo-ple go to bed with Rock Hudson, they're so nervous they can't do anything. It's a waste." It would take a special person with a strong ego to be a match for Rock, and in 1959, Rock had not found that person.

Rock went to Mexico in 1960 to make *The Last Sunset* with Kirk Douglas, then to Italy to make *Come September* with Gina Lollobrigida, Sandra Dee and Bobby Darin. In January of 1961, he was back on the set with Doris Day and Tony Randall, shooting *Lover Come Back*, written by a team that included Stanley Shapiro, who had done *Pillow Talk*. The film was just as clever and racy as *Pillow Talk,* and it had the same plot structure, the same characters with different names, and the same outcome—the lady wins. Rock felt it was the best of the comedies, as did Tony, but Doris liked *Pillow Talk* better.

Those were both playable roles. The advertising man in Lover Come Back, *like the composer in* Pillow Talk, *was a ne'er-do-well. And playing a ne'er-do-well is terrific. I mean, you automatically like a ne'er-do-well, don't you? I guess it's because it's what we all wish we were, but don't have the guts to be. The advertising executive who played around all the time, and who was bored with it until he met Miss Day and said to himself, "That would be rather interesting to toss in the hay. But I think I'll see if I can get her to go on the make for me"—now that's fun. And it's very playable.*

In *Lover Come Back*, Rock plays an advertising man, Jerry Webster, and Doris plays Carol Templeton, an account executive with a rival agency. She tries to land a new account by hard work and original ideas, but Rock steals the account by staging an orgy for the company president, with his favorite booze and his favorite type of girl popping out of a bass fiddle. Rock states his philosophy to his boss, Tony Randall: "Give me a well-stacked dame in a bathing suit and I'll sell aftershave lotion to beatniks."

Doris calls Rock to complain about his unscrupulous tactics, and they wage the same witty sexual warfare that they did in *Pillow Talk*, on a split screen.

"I don't use sex to land an account," Doris says.

"When do you use sex?"

"I don't!"

"My condolences to your husband."

"I'm not married."

"That figures."

"What do you mean?" she says, getting flummoxed.

"A husband would be competitive. There's only room for one man in a family."

"Oooh. I wish I were a man right now," she says.

"Keep trying. I think you'll make it."

The same plot device of mistaken identity is used, as it was in *Pillow Talk*. Rock asks a scientist to invent a product, called Vip, for him to sell. Doris tries to steal the account from Rock by wooing the scientist, but she mistakes Rock for the scientist. She tells him she'll do anything to get his account. He rises to the game, pretending to be a sheltered academic who is completely inexperienced with women. He asks her to teach him how to kiss, and says he's afraid to get married, he's afraid he'll be a failure. Just at the moment she's about to give herself, or rather, take him as he lies limp on the bed, she discovers the hoax and leaves him stranded.

They meet again at the unveiling of Vip—a candy wafer that has the impact of three martinis. They end up in bed together in a motel, married. "I don't know how it happened," Rock says, "but apparently I did the decent thing." Doris flees and has the marriage annulled, but nine months later she has a baby and they get married again on the way to the delivery room.

During the shooting, there was the same atmosphere of hilarity and juvenile pranks that had made *Pillow Talk* so much fun. Delbert Mann, the director, says, "Sometimes we went ten or twelve takes because Rock and Doris would keep breaking up." There was a scene on the beach—shot in a sandbox on the set—where they had to kiss and could not because they were laughing so hard. Doris says, "Our teeth bumped one time, and after that, we got hysterical every time we tried to kiss." Rock said that as he was about to do the scene, lying on the sand in his trunks, one of the crew yelled, "Your balls are hanging out!" Whatever it was, they laughed so long and uncontrollably that it got out of hand. Mann says, "The laughter would subside and they'd say, 'Okay, we're ready, we'll be serious.' We'd start rolling and they'd break up again. I finally blew my top. 'Cut it out now!' I said, and they did."

Except for this incident, the playful atmosphere made everyone look forward to coming to work. "Rock was always bubbly and filled with jokes," Mann says. "When the set is loose like that and everyone's having a good time, the work gets done better and quicker because there's not a lot of tension." He says Rock was easy to direct. "He had a natural instinctive response in playing a role, and he would modify it with the slightest verbal communication. There was no need to argue or discuss a scene in detail. He instinctively understood what to do."

Lover Come Back was an even greater success than its predecessor.

It grossed $8.5 million in this country, and Bosley Crowther, the dean of critics, wrote in *The New York Times*, "Mr. Hudson and Miss Day are delicious, he in his big sprawling way and she in her wide-eyed, pert, pugnacious and eventually melting vein." Rock and Doris wanted to do more films together, and were constantly looking for material. In 1963, they made *Send Me No Flowers*, which was based on the play by Norman Barasch and Carroll Moore. In it, Rock and Doris did not play the sparring virgin and playboy but a married couple in the suburbs. He was a hypochondriac who mistakenly thought he was going to die, and she was the wife who mistakenly thought he was having an affair. The film lacked the spice and magic of the previous two comedies, and it underscored, for Rock, the importance of having the right script. He and Doris continued to search for another film for twenty years. At one point, they discussed a *Movie of the Week* with Delbert Mann, but he says, "We couldn't come up with a story that would have the same sexual innuendos that had made those comedies fun—in a way that would be valid in modern terms." Rock felt, if he was going to act with Doris, the material had to be special.

While Rock was commuting from Newport Beach to Burbank to make *Lover Come Back*, he overslept one morning. The executive producer, Robert Arthur, reached him at home and thirty minutes later, Rock walked onto the set. Arthur was alarmed; the trip should have taken at least an hour. Arthur told Rock the Studio had too much invested in him for Rock to be racing back and forth on the freeways every day. "We'll rent you a house in town." Arthur learned that Sam Jaffe, the agent and producer, was moving to London and wanted to rent his house at 9402 Beverly Crest Drive. Universal leased it for Rock for a year.

It was a classic Spanish house on the outside, with thick stucco walls, dark beams and a red-tile roof, but inside, it had been redone in pink and black Japanese-modern style. Rock fell in love with the setting and the view, and saw the potential of the house if it could be remodeled. It sat like a fortress on its own peninsula—three and a half acres with cliffs on three sides. There were two massive gates in front and no other way to gain access to the grounds. The cliffs ensured privacy. On a clear day, the view from the deck gave one the

giddy sense that one gets in an airplane as it comes in for a landing—
the sense of being able to grasp the entire form and shape of a town
as it lies spread below you. The longer Rock lived in the house, the
more he wanted to own it.

In June of 1961, Rock left for Surinam to shoot *The Spiral
Road*. Marion Wagner, who was Robert Wagner's wife between his
two marriages to Natalie Wood, was returning from Rome and
needed a place to stay. Rock asked her to house-sit. Marion took the
liberty of firing Rock's housekeeper and began looking for a replace-
ment. A woman who had worked for her before recommended a
friend, Leatrice Lowe, who was called Joy. Marion hired Joy on a
trial basis, and told her that when Rock came back from Surinam,
"We'll see."

Joy was thirty-seven, a handsome black woman who had been Miss
Cleveland in a beauty pageant. She wore her hair pulled back tight,
and at various times, she was slender and overweight. Joy was a diamond in the rough, funny, sharp-eyed, with a theatrical way of expressing herself. She had never worked as a housekeeper, she had
worked as a clerk in the post office and was raising a son by herself.
When her friend asked, "How'd you like to work as a housekeeper for
a movie star?" Joy says, "It came out of left field. Just like the finger
of fate. I thought, gee, I'd like to see how the other half lives, even if
it's just for two weeks. That's how I went, not intending to stay.
I thought, once I get a little peek into the big life, I'll go back to
work."

She moved into the servants' quarters—two rooms, a patio and two
baths—and when Rock came home, she says, "I was so nervous I
almost fainted. He came in the kitchen and jumped up on the sink
and said: 'So you're Joy.'"

She wanted to say, "So you're Roy," but held her tongue. "If you
want your other housekeeper back, that's okay," she said.

Rock fixed his eyes on her. "What would you do if I said, we'll
have four for lunch?"

"I'll call my mother."

Rock laughed—the marvelous baritone laugh that shook his elon-
gated frame. "The job is yours."

"I don't know what the procedure is around here," Joy said.

"You'll do fine."

Joy was to stay with him for fourteen years, and they would develop an intimacy that few people understood. She was paid $60 a week; it never occurred to Rock to give her a raise. But they ate together, drank together, read scripts together, and in many ways, she became Mrs. Hudson, the mistress of the Castle. They were like an old married couple who bickered and made up and had little private jokes and fought over the crossword puzzle. "One time we didn't speak for a week," Joy says.

"At first I was awed. He'd stand over me, so good lookin', healthy and tall and with that deep deep voice. But then we got to calling each other Roy and Joy, we got to be more like a family." Joy says they laughed all day. "Everything was a joke. Two things you never said in the house were 'What do I do with this?' and 'Guess what I got?' He'd give you funny answers—syphilis, gonorrhea." One night, Rock was dressed in a tuxedo, waiting for a limousine to take him to the Academy Awards. The floors were buffed, the house was shining. Joy studied him and said, "Gee, you look good." Rock smiled and with a flourish, dropped his cigarette ash on the floor. "How dare you," Joy said. "You little dickens! I'll get you for that." She chased him around the living room, grabbed his cummerbund which gave way and his formal pants dropped. "We laughed so hard, he had to go back upstairs and get dressed again."

Rock adored Joy's cooking. She made Southern-fried chicken and mashed potatoes with gravy and homemade biscuits and pecan pie. Rock loved the way she fixed chicken gizzards—he called them "gizzies"—and deviled eggs and beef burgundy and chili pie. Mark Miller says, "She'd pull out a plate of deviled eggs and gizzards and Rock was in hog heaven. She cooked exactly what he wanted and when she left, he never got it again." After she'd been working there a while, Joy told Rock, "I love to cook but I hate cleaning the house." He went to the phone and hired a cleaning service. "After that," Joy says, "I'd stand and point—the living room's that way, the bathroom's that way."

Rock was addicted to doing crossword puzzles, and got Joy started. They became competitive. She'd pick up his *New York Times* on Sunday and start on the puzzle before Rock got up, but if she filled it in too much, he'd get mad.

"Buy your own *New York Times*. Leave mine alone!"

"Okay," Joy said. "If you get in trouble, call me."

Joy says, "Rock was too lazy to look things up, he liked to do it in his head or call George Nader for the answer. But I would research everything. On Sundays, nothing happened in that house until we got the puzzle done."

Joy found Rock easy to get along with. "He was even keel most of the time. It was always a happy day. If it wasn't, we'd go back in and start over again. If something was wrong, I'd know it. There was such a closeness, I could feel his feelings. I lived there, slept there, raised my son there and I was happy, I didn't need anything."

Joy was paid a low salary but Rock gave her gifts—pearls, furniture, a trip to Hawaii, "an intricate TV system that could get everything except Japan. He was a very loving man. When he had screenings at the house, I sat beside him. If I went to the Studio, I got special treatment. At parties, I wouldn't stand in the back in the kitchen. He'd grab me and introduce me. We had Leonard Bernstein, Princess Grace and Prince Rainier, Jack Benny, and I was right out front. He bought me nice clothes, so I could go out dressed as nice as anyone. I'd socialize and mingle. If the party was gettin' dull, I'd help it out. I'd get hors d'oeuvres and pass 'em, or I'd introduce people. It was a knack. You need a woman's touch some time."

For most of the years, Rock and Joy were alone in the house with Rock's seven dogs—Fritz, Wee Wee, Sally, Nicky, Murphy, Jack and Jill. If Rock had men stay overnight, he would try to have them leave before Joy woke up, but she always knew. "The most marvelous thing about us was, he knew that I knew, and he never said a word. We never discussed his love life. He just knew I knew." Joy was discreet, and knew when she could walk through the house and when to stay in her quarters. One night there was a blackout, all the lights went off and Joy went out to the patio to investigate. "The door to the theater opened," she says, "and out came a group of young guys, just as the lights flashed back on. I thought, uh-oh, you came out at the wrong time. I turned around and didn't say a thing. I felt, if that makes you happy, it makes me happy."

Joy says there was never a woman staying over at the house, with the exception of Marilyn Maxwell. Rock and Marilyn had met in the early fifties and had been instantly attracted to each other, but they did not become romantically involved until 1961, when she broke up with her husband, Jerry Davis, and started spending time with Rock. People who saw them together said they laughed and played "like little kids." Rock had an aversion to Jell-O, and Marilyn would chase him through the house with a bowl of green Jell-O. She'd get him on the floor and tickle him, and they'd wrestle like bear cubs, laughing until tears were streaming down their cheeks. Rock would put on Marilyn's favorite forties big-band records and say, "Show me the shimmy one more time." He called her Max and she called him Big Sam. They would sit down at the piano, put on their glasses and play Beethoven four-handed, fracturing the "Moonlight Sonata" or the "Pathétique." The tempo would change, they'd try to speed up but they'd never make it and would fall to the ground in hysterics.

Rock became close to Marilyn's son, Matthew, and for his sixth birthday, gave him a party at the Castle with a real merry-go-round and clowns on the lawn. In 1963, Marilyn had an ovarian cyst that burst and she came close to dying. She went to her brother's house in Armonk, New York, to recuperate, but she felt awkward there, and Rock flew to New York and brought her back to his house, where he cared for her until she was better. Marilyn said, "He left a picture to bring me home with my son. He really, literally, saved my life. He is without question the best friend I've ever had."

At Christmas, Rock called Jean Greenberg, who was Marilyn's secretary for twenty-six years, and asked for all of Marilyn's clothing sizes. Rock ordered a mannequin made up to look like her and dressed it from head to toe with presents: a white knit suit, a hat, gloves, stockings and shoes, a purse with money in it, jewelry, even underwear. On Christmas Eve, he left clues and notes around the house and Marilyn had to hunt until she found the image of herself, fully outfitted.

Jean Greenberg says, "I know for a fact they were having an affair. Marilyn confided everything in me, and she talked about it in detail. She was in love with him. She said he always told her he loved her but he wasn't *in* love with her."

When Rock was making *The Spiral Road*, he called Marilyn from Surinam and she told him how much she was missing him. "Why don't we get married?"

"Sure, I'll marry you," Rock said. "But you have to let me have my other life too. If you can put up with that . . ."

Marilyn brooded about it for months. At times, she thought it could work and they would be happy. She and Rock talked about having a child, and building a nursery over the garage. But on reflection, she knew it would make her miserable if Rock was also seeing men. She told him she was jealous and couldn't handle the situation. But they continued to be lovers, on and off, and devoted friends.

CHAPTER 7

My house is the only place I really have any privacy. Outside the house, everything I do is watched and talked about, but once I come in those gates, I can relax and let go. I love to work on my house; to tear down walls and lay bricks. And for real relaxation, there's nothing like gardening. When I'm thinking about career decisions and working out new roles in my head, I like to go out in the garden and sweat! Where're my nippers? Where're my pruners? I'll prune and water and plant, sometimes I'll just pull weeds for hours and be totally lost in my thoughts. If I had it all to do over again, I'd probably be a landscape architect.

Rock decided he had to own the house on Beverly Crest Drive, but he did not have the cash to buy it. Universal used it as a bargaining tool when his contract expired in 1962: If he renewed the contract, they would get him the house. Don Morgan, a publicist and friend of Rock's, lectured him that he was selling his career down the river for $150,000. But later, Don recanted. "I was wrong. Some things can't be measured in money, and Rock loved that house and had to have it." Universal bought the house from Sam Jaffe for $167,000, and transferred the title to Rock five years later. (In 1985, it was appraised at $3 million.) Rock sold his boat and turned the Newport Beach house over to his mother and Joe Olson.

Rock embarked on a restoration and construction project that would continue for twenty-three years and cost more than half a million dollars. It was not until the final months of his life that Rock pronounced the house completed. "When the house was done, so was the man," Mark Miller says.

When he began the project, Rock hired a designer and bought books on Mexican colonial architecture, which he nicknamed "the Bibles." He copied many designs from homes in Mexico and the Southwest: stone archways, hand-painted tiles and ceilings made of whole tree limbs placed together on the diagonal. Rock liked everything dark, heavy and massive. He filled the house with zebra skins and African masks, Spanish wooden doors, pewter candlesticks that were four feet tall, marble fireplaces and wrought-iron candelabra. He loved giant statues of eagles, lions and horses, and his favorite color was red. A friend once described his taste as "early Butch." It was so determinedly masculine that Mark Miller asked Rock, "Do you ever worry about the gay part of you showing?"

Rock said, "There's a little girl in me that I just trample to death." He made a squashing motion with his foot. "You will not come out!"

Rock created an atmosphere, a world all his own, where he alone would star. By day, the house feels dark and gloomy, like a medieval Spanish castle where heavy presences reside. But at night, the house turns into a wonderland. It's warm and welcoming, with roaring fires in every room and giant candles flickering in parchment shades. The red rugs and candle flames are reflected in the ceiling and bring out the rosy tones of the wood. Rock wanted the house to be called "Whiskey Hill," but it exerted a will of its own and became known, almost immediately, as "the Castle" or "the Crest."

Visitors to the Castle drive through the gates and park in a circular holding area. The first front door, made of carved wood with a border of Mexican tile, opens not to the house but to an enormous red-tile patio. The house is built in a U, with all the rooms opening out to the patio. There are metal sculptures of naked boys playing—one is throwing another into the pool—by the Mexican artist Victor Salmones. The pool is forty feet long, with a Jacuzzi and a lion's-head fountain. Behind it, a wide deck looks out over the city. On one side of the patio, Rock built a twenty-foot barbecue where he could cook whole turkeys and steaks to feed a hundred, and an outdoor fireplace so that on winter nights, he could take a steam bath, fix a martini and sit in the moonlight beside a crackling fire.

Rock gave nicknames to the rooms and every corner of the grounds. There was "Assignation Lane," a walkway that zigzagged down the cliff through dense ferns and flowering trees. The path could be lit, but during a party, Rock would leave it unlit so that people could have "assignations" there. He called the theater "the playroom," and the guest bedroom "Tijuana," because it was all red, like a Mexican whorehouse. There was a cabinet he called "Texas" and a table he called "Portugal." In an area called "Panama," there were tropical plants and ginger, and in "Ferndell," behind the pool, there was a plant that Rock made the outdoor urinal. "Every good garden should have one," Rock said. He built a greenhouse and filled it with orchids; in other spaces he grew mint for mint juleps, limes for frozen daiquiris and peaches for fresh peach ice cream, which he made ritualistically every summer. There were terraces for corn, squash and tomatoes, and cutting beds for tulips, zinnias and roses of every color.

Rock's favorite recreational activity was working in the garden with Clarence Morimoto, the full-time gardener he'd inherited from Sam Jaffe. Rock called Clarence "the inscrutable one," for he had a haiku-like way of expressing himself. Clarence's favorite flower was the iris, which he called "pieces of star on earth." Rock did not pay Clarence much, but he counted him, as he did Joy, part of the "family." Clarence had free run of the house and grounds, moving quietly in his old tan pants and work boots with a green cap on his head. On Monday nights, Clarence would stay after work to watch football with Rock, and sometimes Rock would barbecue steaks for the two of them. "It was unusual—you don't get that close to an employer," Clarence says. "How often does a man have a big star cook for you?" Clarence went to the opening night of Rock's plays and movies, and was invited to the tree-trimming party at Christmas. When Rock wasn't working, he was outside with Clarence, pruning, weeding, germinating seeds to plant. Rock filled every square inch of the property until Clarence said, "Please, no more planting. Already full."

From the first front door, it was a long walk across the patio to the second front door, which led to the two living rooms and stairs going up to the two bedrooms. Rock's bedroom was called "the blue room," because it was carpeted in royal blue. The scale of the room made people feel like Gulliver in the land of the Brobdingnagians. The sofas and chairs were extra deep and extra long, and the bed was an immense wooden four-poster. Carved on the headboard was a nude male figure adapted from Spanish mythology—a man with a crown, the wings of an eagle and legs of leaves. There were no doors between the bedroom and the bathroom and dressing areas, just dark wooden closets and mirrors that served as dividers. The bathroom had two sinks, a shower with a marble seat and an enormous tile tub, raised so that Rock could look out on the city. On the wall, brass elephant heads were mounted, with towels hanging from their trunks.

Rock spent most of his time in the bedroom, the kitchen and the "playroom," which he built out of what was originally the garage. He outfitted the playroom with the latest technological toys: a juke box, a player piano, four VCRs, stereo equipment, a large-screen television, film projector and a film vault with a vast library of films. He had a record collection that covered an entire wall and included rare 78s, all numbered and catalogued. There was a full bar with stools, and a wooden stage with footlights, where Rock rehearsed roles and where he and his friends sometimes performed shows.

One Halloween, Rock gave a party where all the guests had to perform—in costumes and wigs—numbers in a vaudeville show, with Joy dressed up as the card girl who announced the acts. Mark Miller was Sylvia Casablancas, who sang in her own tongue and wore balloons in her brassiere. Rock and three friends were the dancehall girls from *Sweet Charity*, and sang "Hey, Big Spender." They had rehearsed their dance for weeks and been fitted for costumes at Universal. Rock had called Tom Clark, who was playing one of the dancers, and said, "You have to be at Universal today at two P.M."

Tom said he had a press luncheon at one. Rock said, "This is a *call*. This is an official call. If you didn't get your call sheet, I'm notifying you by phone—you *have* to be there at two."

Tom rescheduled the lunch and "drove a hundred miles an hour to the Studio." He went to the wardrobe department and said, "Where's Rock?" He was told, "You're in men's wardrobe. You want women's." Tom went next door to Edith Head's private dressing room and there were Rock and the others, in fat suits, being stuffed and pinned into flouncy dresses. "They had to open up the backs of the costumes to make 'em fit," Tom says. The men were outfitted completely, from wigs with fancy curls to fishnet hose and high-heel shoes. "We were the hit of the show," Tom says.

Despite Rock's claims about wanting privacy at home, he refused to lock the doors or shut the gates to the Castle. If a staff member locked the front door, Rock would shout, "Who locked the goddamn door? I want it open!" George Nader says, "There was always the chance of an encounter that way. He wanted the world to enter. He liked the excitement of the unknown." When Rock came home from work, he would ask, "Any calls? Anything juicy in the mail?" He wanted to see letters from fans who included photographs of themselves. When the door bell rang, Joy says, "He'd be at the door faster than the dogs. When the phone rang, he'd grab it. I used to say, that cat will answer the phone from the casket." Rock laughed at this vision—which in some ways was prophetic—of his hand reaching up from the coffin and lifting the phone off its hook.

In 1962, the year Rock acquired his house, a young man named Lee Garlington was working as an extra on a TV show, *The Virginian*, being shot at Universal. Lee had come to California the year before from Atlanta, where he had been raised in a wealthy, conservative family. He had gone into the army and come out with a flattop and a desire to be an actor. "Once I hit town, that was it," Lee says. "No way I was going to be anywhere else but right in the middle of Hollywood. It was so gay! There were bars, and people walking up and down the street and it was very exciting. I thought, all you had to do was be pretty and you could be discovered like I heard Rock Hudson was." Lee found work as an extra at Universal, where he heard Rock was shooting *Man's Favorite Sport*. "I'd heard about this man so much. In the gay subculture, he was talked about all the time— how he was gay and very handsome and a kind person, well liked. So I decided, by golly, I'm gonna see this man."

Lee was twenty-five, tall and blond, and he had no gay mannerisms—the exact type Rock was most attracted to. On one of his lunch breaks, Lee went to the cottage that had been pointed out to him as Rock's private quarters. He stood outside the cottage, pretending to read *Variety*. Lee recalls, "My God, it just so happened that he walked past me, walked into his cottage and I got a chance to see him." Lee stood vigil until Rock came out a half hour later. Rock walked by again but did not look at him. "I thought, man, I really made an impression. I was too shy to say anything. I practically had the *Variety* in front of my nose." Rock walked about fifty yards down the street, stopped, turned and looked back at Lee over his shoulder. Then he walked on. That was the only acknowledgment Rock gave Lee that he had noticed him, and for months Lee kicked himself for not having seized the opportunity.

In 1963, Lee gave up on acting and took a job with a stock-brokerage firm in Beverly Hills. He had been living with another young man, but they broke up, and as soon as Lee had moved out and found his own apartment, he received a call from an acquaintance. "There's somebody who would like to meet you."

"What are you talking about?" Lee said.

"Someone well known."

"Who is it?"

"Rock Hudson."

Lee was flabbergasted. It had been six months since that brief passing look at the Studio. How had Rock found out who he was and where he lived? Lee learned, later, that Rock had wanted to make contact sooner, but had heard Lee was "involved" and had waited until he was on his own. The mutual acquaintance invited Lee to go up to Rock's house and meet him. "I was scared to death," Lee says. "We talked, and had a couple drinks, and then we tried to play around but I was so intimidated that nothing happened. I mean, zero. I thought, oh, well, he'll never want to see me again. But he was patient. He understood I was nervous and it wasn't that big a deal to him that we couldn't have sex."

Rock began seeing Lee several times a week, and Lee overcame his shyness. Lee would drive up to the Castle after work in his 1963 Chevy Nova, sleep there, and at six in the morning, he'd get in his car and let it roll down the hill so Joy and the neighbors wouldn't find out he'd spent the night. But Joy knew. Years later, she told Lee, "You wasn't pullin' any wool over my eyes."

Rock and Lee became the major person in each other's life. Lee wanted to live with Rock, but "that was out of the question. He was concerned about his image, but I would have moved in in a second." Rock admired Lee's independence. He was working hard to become a broker, he never asked Rock for anything, and when they traveled together, he insisted on paying his way. They rarely went out to parties or dinners; they stayed at the Castle, talking, watching movies, and Rock drank what Lee considered an excessive number of martinis while Lee struggled to keep up. "Rock was fun, he was always in a good humor, I never saw him get angry at anyone," Lee says. Six months after they met, Rock gave Lee a gold keyring with the key to his house. It was inscribed: "At the end of the first quarter the home team was ahead and at the end of the half the visitor is ahead damn it. R.H."

In 1964, Rock and Lee went on a trip through the South. Rock thought the Studio might object if they knew he was going off traveling with another man, and in a drunken moment, he said he would go to the head of the Studio and tell him, "I'm gay, I have a lover and if you don't like it, shove it up your ass."

"No way are you going to do that!" Lee said. When Rock had cooled, he decided simply to leave quietly with Lee and tell no one. They flew to New Orleans, tourist class, because Lee was paying his way. Lee told Rock, "I can't afford first class. I know that's what you're used to, but all I've got is tourist class and I barely have that." Rock said, "Okay, fine," and sat with Lee in the tourist section.

In New Orleans, Lee's family had arranged to have a Lincoln Continental convertible waiting at the airport. Rock and Lee drove through the plantation country, stopping at small motels, where Lee would check in and Rock would sneak into the room. "We couldn't go anywhere slowly, we had to go fast or he'd be recognized and mobbed." In New Orleans, they went to Pat O'Brian's and were sampling the famous hurricane drinks that came in hurricane glasses when a fan came up and asked Rock for an autograph. The fan turned to Lee. "Are you somebody?" Lee gave a flip answer, "but it pissed me off. It made me feel like nobody."

Lee says he was overwhelmed by Rock—his fame, money and power—and struggled to maintain his own identity. "It was hard to handle. Since the fifties, I'd gone to the movies and seen him as this hero, larger than life. After I met him, I would watch him do love scenes and know exactly what moves he was going to make, because he did the same things with me." Lee expected Rock to be strong and heroic in real life. "He was so big and towered over me, I wanted him to be a father figure, but he wasn't. He was shy—when the phone rang, he'd grab a cigarette. He could not speak on the phone unless he had a cigarette in his hand. He drank too much and was really sort of passive. He was easily controlled by the people around him, by his hangers-on, and I found myself dominating him."

Disappointed that Rock did not match his image of a strong paternal figure, Lee began to seek out men younger than himself, where he could be the father. "Also, I was attracted to people who were smaller than me, so I was not that attracted to Rock sexually." On the sly, Lee had affairs with men in their early twenties, but he felt guilty and began developing an ulcer. One night, Rock called Lee at his apartment, wanting to come by, and Lee had a young man with him. "Rock was devastated. I tried to hide it, but I couldn't, he knew what was going on." Lee went up to the house and told Rock they would have to break up. Rock got drunk and cried. "I think it was the first time anybody dared break up with him, a huge movie star," Lee says. "It was all my fault, not his."

Lee was to drift in and out of Rock's life for nine years. Perhaps it was because Lee was elusive, but Rock became obsessed with him and was always eager to start up again. It became one of those back-and-forth relationships that was never resolved. Lee would go off and have an affair, then break up and Rock was "waiting in the wings. We'd have lunch or dinner and decide to take a trip, but then I'd split again." They went to Puerto Vallarta, Mexico, and in 1971, to Banff and Lake Louise in Canada. Lee worked as a stockbroker for many years, then started a medical-electronics company that he built into a successful enterprise, sold it and invested his profits in real estate. He went back to college for a Ph.D. in psychology, and at present, he is counseling coordinator at a community clinic.

Before Rock died, he told Mark Miller that Lee Garlington was one of the people in his life he had truly loved. I told this to Lee, and tears came to his eyes. He had to cover his face. He had not seen Rock since 1973, and had been unable to make contact with him after he learned he had AIDS. "After Rock and Tom Clark got together, I was frozen out. I never got a hostile word from Rock, but I was given the feeling from Tom that I was not welcome. I was told Rock had been so hurt by me that I had no right to be his friend anymore. Since it had been my fault, I was embarrassed, and I just sort of drifted out of the picture." Lee said he wished he had been more mature when he had known Rock. "I didn't have enough sense to realize what a wonderful man he was and to hang in there. If I'd been older and had more sense, we probably would be living together today."

In 1962, after fourteen years with Henry Willson, Rock gathered the nerve to extricate himself and change agents. He had been disgruntled with Henry for many years, but had stayed because of loyalty and fear of Henry's response. Henry was not developing projects for Rock or aggressively seeking good roles. "He sat back and waited for the phone to ring," Rock said. Rock signed with John Foreman at C.M.A., who said Rock was "virtually unexposed around town. No one knew him, casting directors weren't thinking of him. He didn't go out much or entertain. Henry Willson wasn't interested in hustling and I was."

Rock began to socialize with John and his wife, Linda, a gracious and articulate woman who grew up in a small California town, Fontana. They had a glittering circle of friends who saw each other constantly. "Hollywood was much more social in those days. The community was smaller and more intimate," Linda says. "John and I gave two or three parties a month." At one of their dinner parties, the group, which included Rock, created a fantasy about a small town called Newton that was somewhere "mid-USA." They gave each other names, invented jobs and private histories. Rock was Russell Burgess, a dirt farmer. Linda and John were Vi and Art Wilkins, who sold ladies' shoes. Steve and Neile McQueen were Leon and Rosita Brown, Jr. (he was the town mechanic). Henry Fonda was Lloyd Potts, a mailman. Princess Grace was Olga Brooker, who taught ballet, adagio and tap-toe. Natalie Wood was Mary Frances Peterman, an usherette at the local movie house, where Paul Newman was the projectionist. Faye Dunaway was Helen Smeader, a beautician. Roddy McDowall was Homer Box, a CPA who lived with his mother over the theater and was madly in love with Mary Frances Peterman.

At dinner, they'd laugh and make up stories about the people and what they were doing and who was sleeping with whom. Linda told the group, "We don't have a mayor. I think it should be Lloyd Potts." Henry Fonda was spooning his soup and, without missing a beat, said, "No, no, no. I can't do that. I'm much too busy with my Christian Endeavor." Everyone roared.

It was bizarre: movie stars fantasizing about being simple folk, leading dull little lives. But they would talk about these characters for hours, and they even considered making a movie about Newton and using themselves as the all-star cast.

As they sat spinning tales, Hollywood was undergoing profound changes that would affect all of them. The studios were declining, and there were fewer and fewer contract players. Everyone wanted to be independent; power was shifting from the studios to the directors and independent producers. As the studios fell, so did much of the apparatus that had sustained them. The fan magazines went out of business, there were no more gala premieres, and stars did not attend the Academy Awards unless they were nominated. The studios could no longer require their stars to attend.

In the sixties, the trend in entertainment shifted from glamour to realism. Television had reduced the stature of stars: They were no longer mythical and larger than life, but tiny figures who appeared in a box in the living room. The new male stars were referred to as "the little uglies"—Dustin Hoffman, Al Pacino, Robert De Niro, Richard Dreyfuss—who were excellent actors but not knights. "You couldn't put them on a white charger," Rock protested. "They'd tumble off and make a mess." They were ordinary guys who performed in ordinary stories.

Rock was one of a dying breed—a movie star built by the studio, promoted by fan magazines, whose looks had been more important, initially, than his acting ability. There was nothing lifelike about him. "How could he suddenly play a smaller than life, utterly realistic figure?" John Foreman said. "You can't imagine Rock Hudson and Al Pacino on the same planet, let alone in the same film."

These were the years of social and political upheaval in the country, and Rock actively disliked politics. He thought of himself as a patriotic American, and voted Republican. But he would never take part in a political discussion, let alone a movement. He did not endorse candidates or attend functions, and he never gave money to a campaign. He watched the Vietnam protests and civil unrest on television with bewilderment. The closest he came to any direct involvement was during the Watts riots of 1965.

On that summer night in 1965, Rock stood on the deck with Joy and watched the smoke rise up over the ghetto, where blacks were looting and setting fires and there were gun battles between police and residents. Joy was worried about her best friend, Peggy, who lived in Watts. She called Peggy and found she had no electricity and little food in the house and had barricaded herself in. Rock said, "Tell her we're coming." Joy thought it was a crazy idea, she was scared a sniper might pick them off. But Rock put Fritz, the German shepherd, in back of his new Chrysler Town and Country station wagon and started the engine. Joy and her son, Gil, got in, "and we hit the freeway," Joy says.

Rock drove through police barricades, past blocks that looked like bombed-out ruins. "We passed policemen in riot gear and kids with rocks and Molotov cocktails in their hands, and I kept expecting one to fly through the window. There we were in a big shiny car—a white man with a black woman and child and a German shepherd that could have been an attack dog. If that didn't look funny on Central Avenue."

By the time they pulled up to Peggy's house, Joy was sweating and her teeth were clenched. They honked, Peggy ran out, got in the car and said, "Let's get out of here." Rock sped back to Beverly Hills. Joy told him, "If the Studio knew where you were just now, they'd have flipped." When the group reached the Castle, they went straight to the bar. Joy recalls, "I said, Roy, fill 'em up, please. We drank a lot that night, and laughed. When you finish something like that, you feel your nerves."

Rock continued to make comedies that were less and less successful: *Strange Bedfellows*, *A Very Special Favor*, *Blindfold*. He had a tight group of crew members that he had worked with for years and whom he now insisted be hired for every picture he made. They were called "the bridge group," because they played bridge with Rock between setups. After the fiasco in 1951, when Rock had tried to learn bridge from Mark Miller and collapsed with laughter, he had become an accomplished player. He played constantly with Mark Reedall, his makeup man, Pete Saldutti, his wardrobe man, and George Robotham, his stuntman and double. The group ate their meals together, went drinking together and took trips and were constantly trying to "hang each other" with gags and practical jokes.

Mark Reedall, a tall, angular man with sandy hair, used to make up Rock in his dressing room, a large mobile home that Rock called "Big Irene." It had a kitchenette and a sitting room with a makeup table and closets. One morning, Rock told Mark, "I'm gonna pull a gag on Pete. When we wrap tonight, I'll take my clothes, stuff them in the freezer and Pete'll go nuts because he won't be able to find them." Pete Saldutti designed Rock's clothes, and was responsible for making sure they were cleaned every day and that continuity was maintained from scene to scene. Mark Reedall finished making Rock up and immediately told Pete what Rock was planning. He suggested that Pete hide in Rock's closet. When Rock came in and put his wardrobe in the freezer, he would have to go to the closet to get his own clothes. "That night," Mark says, "they yelled 'wrap,' and Rock flew to the trailer like a gazelle. He ripped off his coat and tie, his beautiful slacks, balled them up, shoved them in the freezer and ran to the closet, but when he opened the door, Pete went 'Boo.'" Reedall laughed, recalling the incident. "Rock's hair literally went straight up. His instinct was to run, but he was in his shorts and there were people outside."

Mark said he could often hang Rock, but Rock could also hang him and Pete and it became a game of one-upmanship. When Rock was making *McMillan and Wife,* he had a driver, Bernie Hellerstein, who drove Big Irene to San Francisco when they were shooting on location. Rock was asked one year to throw out the first ball at the World Series in San Francisco, but he had had a car accident and was worried he wouldn't have the strength and would disgrace himself before the crowds. Bernie said, "Hey, Rock, I'll throw it out for ya."

"Sure, good idea," Rock said.

Outside the trailer, Mark took Bernie aside and whispered to him. Shortly afterward, Bernie went back in the trailer and told Rock, "Great news! The Studio says it's okay for me to throw out the ball for you. I called my folks back in Brooklyn and they're all excited. The whole neighborhood's gonna watch!"

Rock looked at him. "Jesus, Bernie. I was only kidding."

Bernie's face fell. "Kidding. What'll I tell my folks?"

Bernie slumped out of the trailer, and Rock felt awful. He had taken up needlepoint and was working on a pillow when Mark came in to touch up his makeup. Rock told him what had happened with Bernie.

"Yeah, Rock," Mark said. "I put him up to it."

For the longest time, Rock kept on stitching, saying nothing. Mark watched him. "I knew I had him." Rock suddenly looked up and banged his work on the table. "Fuck you fuck you fuck you!"

The gags began to get more elaborate and more serious until they all realized the game was "getting too strong" and they stopped.

In 1964, after seven years in the number-one position, Rock dropped to number-two "Name Power Star" in the Motion Picture Film Buyers' poll. In 1965, he dropped to the top ten, where he remained in 1966. Then in 1967, he fell off the chart completely.

The irony was that Rock was hitting his stride as an actor just as he was losing his popular standing. In 1966, he appeared in *Seconds*, which showed a depth and brilliance to his acting that he'd never had the opportunity to display. It was neither a romance nor a comedy, but a dark, cautionary tale.

The last picture I'm high on is Seconds, *just being released. Controversial as hell—a horror film that is bizarre . . . frightening. I play a sixty-year-old man, a "reborn." I've had a facelift, and there's a before and after, and for most of the picture I'm the "after." At the Cannes Film Festival, they compared it to the Faust story.*

In *Seconds*, Rock plays a banker in the eastern suburbs, trapped in a loveless marriage and a stultifying life. He goes to a mysterious "clinic," which sells him a new life. They operate on him, give him a new face and body, even a new voice, arrange a phony "death" for his old self, and set him down in Malibu as a painter with a house and studio on the ocean and new friends, even a mistress. "You've got what every middle-aged man in America would like," the clinic director tells him. "Freedom." Rock does not take well to the new life; the destruction of his past and all its associations leaves him feeling unmoored. When he discovers that his new friends and mistress are fellow "reborns," he revolts, goes back to the clinic and demands his old life back.

The film gave Rock the most challenging role of his career. He had to change from an uptight businessman who was timid and dour to a free spirit who could tear off his clothes and stomp naked in a vat of grapes, laughing and losing himself in Dionysian abandon. Then he had to become a soul filled with rage, desperate to grasp for a frail and impossible chance to live his life over again, on his own terms.

The film was directed by John Frankenheimer and photographed

141

by James Wong Howe in black-and-white. It had an eerie visual style, with many of the shots distorted, as seen through a fish-eye lens. *Seconds* was the only time Rock drank on the job. He had a long drunken scene at a party, where he had to have an emotional outburst and collapse. He wasn't sure how to play it, so, with Frankenheimer's permission, he stayed drunk for three days while they shot the sequence. Jimmy Dobson, Rock's dialogue coach, argued against it. "I think the best drunk scenes are played by people who don't drink," Dobson says. "But the scene came out beautifully, so I had a hard time convincing Rock that this was not the way to do it."

The film was shown at the Cannes Film Festival in the spring of 1966. Rock stopped in Hamburg to visit Mark Miller and George Nader, who had moved to Germany in 1964 when George signed a contract to make eleven pictures in which he played Jerry Cotton, an FBI agent who was a kind of German James Bond. Mark and George met Rock at the airport, and as they drove back to town, Rock said, "I want to tell you something, right off. I am now a world-famous star."

They looked at him quizzically. "Good. Good."

"I mean it, you guys. I'm a world star."

"Wonderful," George said. "How was your flight?"

Later, when Mark and George were alone, they wondered what had gotten into Rock. "We knew he was a world star. He delivered the news as if it was the word of God come down from the mountain, etched in stone. It was hard to take. This was the guy we used to buy dinner for from tips Mark earned at the drive-in. We went back too far and had seen too much to have him pull this."

Mark flew with Rock to Cannes, while George stayed in Germany to work. Paramount arranged for Rock to take Pamela Tiffin and for Mark to take another actress, Edra Gayle, to the screening of *Seconds*. They drove to the Palace of Fine Arts in separate limousines, and sat in separate sections. When the film ended, the audience booed. The M.C. came on stage and said, "Mesdames et messieurs, we have a surprise: in the balcony, Monsieur Rock Hudson." It was an awkward moment for Rock, but the booing changed instantly to cheers and applause as people rose to their feet. It was disconcerting, but later Mark realized, "They were applauding him for his previous films."

Rock and Mark went to different parties, and met back at the Carlton Hotel at four in the morning.

"Shit," Rock said. "I thought I had a hit."

Mark told him the first half hour of the film, before Rock appeared, was slow and dull. "It's gonna kill you. Can't you get them to reshoot it?" No, Rock said, that was not possible. The film was released in America and quickly disappeared. Over the years, however, it began to acquire a cult following, and Rock started receiving awards and praise from film societies and universities. In time, Rock came to like it again, and to count it among his best work.

In the summer of 1966, Rock terminated his contract at Universal and became, at last, a free agent, free to make pictures anywhere and to choose the roles he wanted, not those dictated by the Studio. But his latest films had not been hits, and he found himself dressed up with nowhere to go. The phone did not ring with offers. Rock grew despondent; he had been accustomed to working all the time. Was the wild ride over?

It was about this time that Rock came out of the "impossible stage" and returned to being the Rock Hudson his old friends had known. "He came down off his high horse," George Nader says, "just in time to jump into the bottle." Rock started drinking heavily every night. He would not eat until ten or eleven, because he wanted another Scotch and soda and would not drink after eating. When he invited friends for dinner, they'd start dropping hints and then ask outright to be fed, but Rock would say, "Oh, let's have another drink." Joy told people, "If you're invited here for dinner, you better eat first." When Tom Clark was asked why Rock was drinking so much, he said, "He can't stand it that he's no longer number one."

Rock was becoming close to Tom Clark, who worked as a publicist at M.G.M. They had met in 1964 at a bridge game, and Rock had begun to have dinners with Tom and his longtime companion, Pete De Palma. Shortly after leaving Universal, Rock went to the Far East with De Palma, and while in Hong Kong, Rock received a disturbing call from his business manager, Andy Maree. Rock did not understand finance and had no interest in understanding it—he left the handling of his money completely to Maree. He was taken unaware, then, when Maree told him, "You're down to fifteen hundred dollars in the bank. You better come home and get to work."

Tom Clark told Rock that Martin Ransohoff was producing a picture at M.G.M. called *Ice Station Zebra*.

"God, I'd love to do that," Rock said.

"Why don't you come out to the studio and have lunch with me, then walk into Marty's office and say, 'Hi, I'm Rock Hudson and I would like to do *Ice Station Zebra*.'" Rock took Tom's advice, his agent also lobbied, and when Laurence Harvey backed out of the starring role, Rock got the part.

The picture gave Rock a lift—he was still a star—and he exhibited a boyish excitement about the technical aspects of the production: the icebergs, the snowstorms, the nuclear submarine constructed on the sound stage. Tom Clark was assigned to do publicity for the film, and it was the first time he and Rock worked together.

While Rock was shooting the picture, in 1967, he met an unusual young man who would prove Rock's match for silliness and giggling. He would be the first man to live with Rock since 1954, and the Castle would come alive with laughter and play.

CHAPTER 8

I love to smoke. I keep hoping someone will discover it's a healthy habit because the smoke kills all the germs in your system.

I love to drink, and I hate exercise. I don't mind going out on the side of a hill and chopping down a tree, but I hate organized exercise. I built a gym in my house but I never use it. I don't even like to walk through it.

I'm a night person. When I'm not working, I never want to go to sleep. I'd much rather stay up and talk or read and play music. Music is real important in my life, like air. I need it to breathe. I like being surrounded by music all the time, and I like all kinds.

Rock had an acquaintance, Frank Shea, who owned the old Dick Powell and Joan Blondell estate in Beverly Hills, and had a tennis court that was always open to friends. Rock stopped by one afternoon in the summer of 1967 to hit balls and socialize. He left his racket there by mistake, and when he came back to retrieve it, a new group was playing on the court. Rock was introduced to a young man named Jack Coates, who was twenty-three and exceptionally attractive: tanned, blond, sun-washed. But he possessed more than superficial good looks. He had a sparkle in his eye and a restless energy that made him seem charged and full of life. Rock shook hands and walked off the court, but stopped outside the fence, which was covered with ivy. There were a few holes in the ivy, and Rock placed himself near one so he could watch the game unobserved.

Jack Coates knew he was being observed. He could see Rock's tennis shoes through the bottom of the fence, and this made him run faster, serve harder and catch the ball in the sweet spot. He had wanted to meet Rock Hudson since he was thirteen and had gone to see *Giant* in his neighborhood movie house in Phoenix. "When I came out of the movie," Jack recalls, "it was three hours later and my life had changed. I knew then and there that Rock

Hudson was special, and that some day I would meet him and get to know him. Something about the role he played—the transformation of the man on screen—touched me personally, and I never forgot it."

When Jack finished high school, he became involved with an older man, a real-estate developer who brought him to California where he was building homes in a luxurious section of Los Angeles. Jack and his friend lived in one of the luxury homes, and in the summer of 1967, Jack was taking courses in anthropology at UCLA, working part time at a gas station and part time at a hamburger stand at the beach, the Sorrento Grill. He had a red Corvette convertible, a motorcycle and a '47 Mercury woody station wagon that he used when he went surfing. He loved living in Beverly Hills, loved his red Corvette, "the most perfect car I ever had," and loved playing tennis with stars. "I was encouraged to play tennis because it was very social at that time. I could play a decent game, and I would not drive a ball down Dinah Shore's throat. I would go, one, two, cha cha cha, and hit it right to her."

The only star he really wanted to meet was Rock Hudson. After the day at the tennis court, when, he said, "I noticed I was noticed," he started to drive by Rock's house on his way to or from classes. The Corvette broke down one day right in front of the house. Jack opened the hood and was fixing the problem when Rock happened to come out with one of his dogs. He said, "Hi! Need some help?" Jack says, "The strongest impression I have of Rock is the way he said, 'Hi!' It was so deep and hearty, it would go out and lasso you with warm good feeling. 'Hi!'" Jack had hoped something like this would happen, but when he saw Rock walking toward him, he got scared, closed the hood and drove away. A few days later, he was driving on a narrow, winding road in the hills when he realized Rock was in front of him, in a blue Cadillac convertible. Rock saw the Corvette— now familiar to him—in the rearview mirror, stopped his car and blocked the street. "Hi! Want to go to lunch?"

"I can't, I have to get to work," Jack said.

"Where?"

"Standard Oil, corner of Wilshire and La Cienega."

That afternoon, Rock pulled into the gas station in the blue Cadillac and stopped beside Jack. "Fill her up." The car took a gallon and a half. An hour later, Rock came back with the Chrysler station wagon. "Fill her up," he said, and that took three gallons. He asked Jack what time he got off work.

"Tonight I get off early—ten."

"Why don't you come by for a steam or a swim?"

Jack agreed, and at ten he presented himself at the Castle. "It was a complete disaster," Jack says. "I couldn't get over the fact that I was with Rock Hudson. For ten years, I'd been a fan. I was much too nervous to do anything except have a beer and get out of there quick." Rock invited him back on Sunday afternoon for a small gathering, and Jack brought a new Mamas and Papas album, *The Mamas and Papas Deliver*. Rock had never heard of the group, but he put on the record and played it several times. "Let's get some limes from the lime tree and make frozen daiquiris from scratch," Rock said. "Race ya!" They ran to the tree and picked limes, then Rock got out his ice crusher and fixed the drinks in special glasses. He made a ceremony of it, putting on the right music for lime daiquiris on a summer afternoon, and opening the windows of the bar so the scent of jasmine floated through the house. "That's when I started to relax, when we really started to have fun," Jack says. "We just clicked—the way we talked together and laughed. He could get me to crack up with a word, or a look, and I could do the same with him. I'd wanted to meet the man, but I didn't know there would be so much fire."

They started playing what Jack called "a cat and mouse game," where Rock pursued Jack and Jack would let himself be caught and then spring off. He would sneak out to see Rock, then retreat to his home with the developer and decide not to take Rock's calls. Mark Miller flew in from Europe that summer to do his taxes, and when he came to the Castle, Rock said, "I've found *him!*" He pinched his shirt over the heart and made it flutter, while he rolled his eyes upward. "He's dynamite, but somebody else has got him so it's gonna take time." Rock gave a party for Mark with thirty people, and Mark spotted a blond in tennis clothes, with mischievous blue eyes and "gorgeous legs. His whole person seemed to give off a glow." Mark walked up to him and smiled. "You're new."

Jack Coates had been with the developer for five years, and was not eager to make a change. People told him Rock would use him and discard him. Jack told Rock, "I can't see you anymore, I'm happy where I am." But Rock kept calling, sometimes from the phone in his Cadillac parked on the hill above Jack's house.

"Look, I like you more than I ever liked anybody," Jack said.

"Let's go to Will Wright's and have double-vanilla ice cream with extra hot-fudge sauce," Rock said.

"People say you are not sincere," Jack said.

"Let's go to Bob's Big Boy and get outside trays and order cheese-burgers with extra catsup."

Jack gave in, and then withdrew again until one day Rock had his agent call Jack and tell him Rock was refusing to appear on a Bob Hope special unless Jack agreed to see him that afternoon. Jack stopped by after class. Rock picked mint from the garden and made mint juleps in silver goblets. "I'd never had a mint julep in my life. That afternoon was a turning point—I felt he *was* sincere, that his feelings were genuine." Rock drove Jack down to the developer's house, packed his belongings in the woody, including Jack's teddy bear—a faded koala with a yellow ribbon—drove him back to the Castle and moved him in.

The next weekend was Labor Day, and Rock proposed they take a trip to celebrate, a kind of "honeymoon." They threw a few things in the Cadillac, put the top down and started driving north on Highway 1. "Everything went wrong, everything you can imagine," Jack says. Rock was trying out new contact lenses, but on the free-way, dust blew in his eyes, which made them tear and he couldn't see. They stopped at Solvang, a mock Danish town, and were served warm beer and stale sandwiches, and Rock got recognized and people shrieked and pressed around him. Jack was spooked and ran for the car. When they reached Monterey, it was the week-end of the Monterey Jazz Festival and there wasn't a vacant room in town. They drove to San Jose, where they had inedible rubbery steaks in a diner, and finally found a room in a Holiday Inn. "But Rock could take a disaster, where everything went wrong, and make it into the best time you ever had, just by seeing the humor and making you laugh hysterically. How can anything be bad when you're laughing?"

Jack had never ordered room service, so the next morning, at the Holiday Inn, Rock announced, "*I* am going to order room service for you." He ordered a huge breakfast, but it arrived an hour later, cold. They drove to the Napa Valley wine country, "and from then on, everything was perfect." They had lunch at an inn, on a terrace overlooking the vineyards, and were sampling a local Chablis and talking about all the problems they'd had in getting together and how wonderful it was now going to be. They fell silent, looking into each other's eyes, when they heard a rustling in the hedge nearby. Two girls had sneaked up behind the bushes and were eavesdropping on the movie star. Rock rose and walked toward them and the girls scampered away. "That was our first romantic trip," Jack says.

Rock's friends took an instant liking to Jack. Tom Clark and Pete De Palma taught him to play bridge, and if Rock was away on location, Jack would go out with Tom and Pete. Mark and George thought Jack was a free spirit with whom Rock could regain his childlike sense of delight in the ridiculous. "People loved Jack on sight," Mark says. "He's outgoing and bright, and his eyes dance with amusement. He makes you want to giggle." Jack was perpetually in motion, he could not stay in a chair and when he talked, he used his whole body, bending his knees, gesturing with his arms and throwing his head back. Joy said, "Can that cat dance! Every muscle in his body is loose." He ran by his own time clock and was difficult to pin down. One of his friends said, "You have to nail him when you get him—two spikes to the ground." He was young in the sixties and was influenced by the youth culture. He wore jeans and a belt with a Navajo Indian buckle, became a vegetarian and smoked pot, which Rock tried and did not like. Rock thought cocaine was "terrible—sobered me right up," and asked that no one smoke or use illegal drugs in the house.

Jack had no interest in the gossip and plots that circulated around the Castle. He was guileless, and found something to like in everyone. What he liked most about Rock was his gift for celebrating life, for making a festive occasion out of small moments. Jack recalls: "Rock would say, 'Let's go to the Valley and go to Builders Emporium!' That was one of his favorite afternoons. He'd put on baggy cords and comfortable old shoes and a shirt with a pocket for his cigarettes, then he'd have to find his glasses. I told him, movie stars should have twenty pairs of glasses. But Rock had one pair, they were plain with black rims, and we'd always have to race through the house hunting for them. When he was dressed in his baggy clothes and glasses, he hardly ever got recognized. We'd get in the station wagon and drive to Builders Emporium, which has everything in the world for the house. Rock could spend four hours in garden hoses, having more fun than kids do at Disneyland."

Jack enjoyed the wordplay and games Rock engaged in. Rock was constantly looking up derivations of words and making puns. Rock once asked Jack, "Why do people say, 'There, there,' when consoling someone, and 'Here, here!' when reprimanding someone?" Rock called Jack "bad doggie." Jack says, "What's the worst thing on the planet? A bad dog." When something went wrong in the house, Rock would point at Jack and say, "Bad doggie." Rock could invent nicknames for everything: Tijuana for the guest bedroom, and "the Narrows" for the back road down to Sunset, whose curves and bumps reminded Rock of a treacherous strait.

After Jack moved in, he had to decide what to do about his studies. He had acquired two years' credits at Arizona State and was considering transferring to UCLA for the fall term, but he would lose ground if he transferred. Rock was scheduled to be away on location for many months, so Jack decided to finish his degree at Arizona State. For the next several years, he flew back and forth between Phoenix and Los Angeles. He arranged his schedule so that he had no Friday classes and he could spend Thursday night through Monday morning with Rock. He duplicated his wardrobe—mostly T-shirts and jeans—so he never had to pack, and Rock always picked him up at the airport. Rock supported Jack while he studied, which made Jack uncomfortable. "I told him I had my job and my savings account, but Rock said, 'Look, I wanted to go to college. I never did, and it makes me feel good to see you get your education.'"

They did not discuss how Jack's moving in might affect Rock's career, but Jack assumed he should be circumspect in public. If they went to a concert or a large affair, they went separately, and Jack kept out of photographs. "It wasn't so much a deception," Jack says, "it was a role. Rock was an actor and he played two roles—one in public and one at home. In public, he was guarded, but at home, he could be what he called 'a secret libertine.'"

Rock and Jack had the house to themselves, except for Joy and the seven dogs and Clarence. "The dogs ran wild and went in the pool with us and ate out of the same dish," Jack says. Rock had stories and nicknames for all the dogs. His first and most beloved was Fritz, or "Fritz the Nitz," a German shepherd. Miss Sally was a big, white Belgian shepherd, and her daughter, Wee Wee, was the runt of the litter that Rock, wearing a tuxedo after a premiere, had helped Sally deliver in the rain outside the kitchen. Nick the Dumb was another German shepherd. Mr. Murphy was a schnauzer sent to Rock by fans; and Jack and Jill were Irish setters who had come to Rock with the names Rhett and Scarlett from *Gone With the Wind*.

In the summer, Rock and Jack liked to lie by the pool and swim. The pool had no diving board, so Rock invented a game called "underwater slow-motion diving." He would try to do a four and a half gainer under water before running out of breath, but one of the dogs would usually go down and try to pull him up by his trunks, while the other dogs ran along the sides and barked.

Rock and Jack also played hide-and-seek. Jack would climb one of the trees, and if it took Rock too long to find him, he'd send the dogs to hunt him down, and Jack would yell, "Unfair!" They both liked to work in the garden with Clarence. They'd take the radio and stools into the greenhouse and sit for hours, potting and repotting. "Our favorite tree was the star pine," Jack says. It was a Norfolk Island pine with five branches on each tier, like a star. They had a running game to see who could spot the most star pines. Rock once sent Jack a telegram: "Saw a star pine yesterday, in Rome."

Jack helped Rock remodel the house. "Let's go down to Meade Wrecking in Pasadena," Rock would say, "see if they have anything interesting." They took the wagon down to the wrecking yard, and Rock found a set of imitation Greek columns that had once stood in front of a bank. He had the columns transported to the Castle and placed around the pool. He also found a gigantic marble fireplace that he installed in the formal living room. "People told him it was too big and wouldn't draw—it had been an ornamental piece in the ballroom of an old mansion, but Rock bought it and it worked beautifully."

On weekends, they liked to plan barbecues. They'd rent a dozen old movies to be screened continuously in the playroom, and they'd buy two-inch-thick steaks and marinate them in bourbon and teriyaki sauce. Rock still liked to barbecue the steaks himself, and still failed to deliver a piece of meat that was edible. Jack found Rock's eating habits eccentric. "His favorite sandwich for a late-night snack was peanut butter and jelly, ham and cheese and Miracle Whip on white bread. He would eat raw hamburger with his fingers from the package, and he was always asking for gizzards. 'Joy, would you do up a pot of gizzies?'"

The years Rock spent with Jack were a happy period, years of good times and stability and very little friction. Jack says he and Rock never argued or had a disagreement. "If something bothered him, he wouldn't talk about it, he would get silent, but his silence was more devastating than anyone's anger because you could feel it all through the house." Joy would ask Jack, "What's wrong. Did you do something?"

"No, did you?" Jack said.

"Maybe it's something at the studio," Joy said, and they would sit down in the kitchen and try to figure it out. "But the silence never lasted more than a day," Jack says.

"Rock was not introspective, he wouldn't talk about feelings, but we could communicate in a very unusual way." Sometimes they sat and stared into each other's eyes without speaking. "It made other people nervous if they were around, but for me, it was bliss."

In the spring of 1968, Rock went to Europe to shoot *Darling Lili* with Julie Andrews. When Rock arrived, the film was behind schedule and over budget, and the atmosphere was chaotic. Rock told Jack that he had met Julie before, and when he did his first scene with her, she told him, "You realize, I'm a big star now." Rock lit a cigarette and smiled. "Thanks for joining us."

Rock sent for Jack Coates, who had never been to Europe. It was the first time Rock had had a lover visit him on location, and he gave Jack two airline tickets so he could travel with another man, an international banker who was gay. It would appear that Jack was the banker's friend and not Rock's. "I was so excited about going to Paris, France, Europe, that I stayed up all night on the plane," Jack says. For Rock, it was exciting to bring someone he loved to a place he'd never been. He met Jack with a limousine and took him straight to the Café Foch for wild raspberries and heavy cream, then to the

Eiffel Tower, where Rock had a special permit to go up on a private observation deck. Jack says, "I tried to be cool. I leaned against the rail and said, 'So this is Paris.'"

Jack slept all the following day, and when he woke up, found Rock dressed and ready for dinner. "Why'd you let me sleep in!"

"*We* know what's best for you," Rock said with a wink. "This is Paris."

Jack stayed for three weeks, and when the film was finished, Rock rejoined him at the Castle for the summer. "Let's have fun in the sun with Dick and Jane," Rock said.

That summer, 1968, was the most tumultuous of the decade, with two recent assassinations, violent demonstrations against the Vietnam War and a Democratic National Convention that had to be held behind barbed wire. Rock watched the news on television and said, "What is this crap? Let's celebrate America." He did not understand the demonstrations, just as, a few years later, he would not understand the movement for gay rights, "where you march with a jar of Vaseline." He could not fathom why people would impose their beliefs or sexual practices on the public. But he did not brood on the news. "He was too busy showing old movies and barbecuing," Jack says.

Rock gave what many people have called "the last great Hollywood party"—for Carol Burnett. Rock had appeared on Carol Burnett's television shows, and they had become fast friends. John and Linda Foreman had been encouraging Rock to entertain because his house was ideal for parties and few people in the Hollywood community had been there. When he gave the party for Carol, "everyone came." Rock and his staff spent weeks preparing for it. They drained the swimming pool, built scaffolding over it and laid down a parquet dance floor. Clarence wrapped chains of flowers around the outdoor columns, and placed hundreds of flowering plants throughout the patio. A band of mariachis was engaged to stroll the grounds and play Mexican songs, and an orchestra was hired to play by the dance floor.

On the night of the party, Joy stationed herself by the front door and did not budge, "so I could look at everyone. I never saw so many movie stars in my life!" In addition to Rock and Carol, there were Frank Sinatra, Lauren Bacall, Judy Garland, Elizabeth Taylor, Dean

Martin, Paul Newman and Joanne Woodward, Steve McQueen, Debbie Reynolds, Princess Grace and Prince Rainier, Steve Allen, Janet Leigh, Eva Gabor, Sandra Dee, Henry Fonda, Jane Fonda and Roger Vadim, James Garner, Rex Harrison, Doris Day, Robert Mitchum, Lucille Ball, Jason Robards, Jennifer Jones, Peter Lawford and Andy Williams, who brought Senator Robert F. Kennedy.

Jack Coates was sitting with Jack Benny when Barbra Streisand walked in. She had just made her film debut in *Funny Girl*, and everyone craned their necks to see her. "Look, there's Barbra Streisand," Jack Benny said.

"But you're Jack Benny," Jack Coates said.

It was six in the morning when the last guests had left. Rock stood at the bar with Jack Coates and Joy, holding a Scotch and soda in one hand, a cigarette in the other.

"Isn't it beautiful?" Rock said.

"It's gorgeous," Joy said.

"What are we gonna do with all the flowers?" Jack said.

Joy suggested they go to bed.

"Good idea," Rock said. But they all stood motionless, savoring the after impressions of a long and dazzling night. Snips of conversation, unforgettable faces, funny actions and exchanges and shimmering hair and the sound of trumpets whirled through their minds.

Jack thought, how did I get here? Why am I so fortunate?

In October of 1968, there was a premiere for *Ice Station Zebra* at the Cinerama Dome in Hollywood. Rock took Flo Allen, a striking woman who'd become his agent when John Foreman had begun producing films. As Rock stepped out of the limousine, someone in the crowd yelled, "Faggot!" Rock turned white, and wanted to plow into the crowd and find the heckler. Tom Clark, who was close by, grabbed Rock's arm and guided him to the spot where Army Archerd, a columnist, was conducting live television interviews. After the interview, Rock went into the theater and out a side door. "That's it! I'm never going to another premiere," he said.

In 1969, Rock went to Durango, Mexico, to make a western, *The Undefeated*, with John Wayne. He had never worked with Wayne and was nervous about meeting the man who symbolized America's ideal of masculine strength. When Rock first saw him on the set,

154

Wayne was looking in a small mirror, applying natural lipstick. They were introduced, and Wayne narrowed his eyes on Rock. "Well," he said slowly, "I hear you're a good bridge player."

The first day of shooting, Wayne started giving me suggestions. "Why don't you turn your head this way . . . ?" and "Why don't you hold your gun like that for the close shot?" They sounded like good ideas, so I tried them, but that night I started thinking, am I going to be directed by this guy? Is he trying to establish dominance or something? So the next day, I said to him, "Why don't you turn your head this way . . . ?"

Wayne pointed his finger at me. "I like you," he said. And we became great friends.

The phone connections from Mexico to the United States were poor, and it was difficult for Rock to stay in touch with Jack Coates. They made plans to meet for a week when Rock had a break, but through a miscommunication, Rock went to Mazatlán and Jack went to Puerto Peñasco, and they never connected until Jack was back in Arizona.

Rock came home for a few months and then went to Italy to make an action adventure picture, *The Hornet's Nest*, with Sylva Koscina. He had been told Sophia Loren would be his co-star; Koscina had been substituted at the last minute. Rock wrote Jack funny letters. "This is my new Italian secretary (actually she is a portable Olivetti). She doesn't spell very well and you have to press her kind of hard, but she's a faithful girl." Rock wrote that he had a good feeling about the film and that one of the young boys in the cast was a "great natural talent." Rock was never able to tell, while shooting a picture, whether it was working, but in the process of investing himself in the character, he became emotionally involved, and inevitably he was infused with hope.

More often than not, he was disappointed, as he was with *The Hornet's Nest*. Rock returned to the Castle in time for Christmas, and his concerns with career and business fell away.

Rock had always made it a condition of his contracts that he have the last weeks in December free, so he could give himself over to Christmas. Christmas was the high point of the year for Rock, when

music and laughter and food and drink and the joy of surprising people with ingenious and welcome gifts came together in one magnificent celebration. Roger Jones, when asked by a reporter for a
one-word description of Rock, said: "Christmas. Think of the music,
the color, the lights, everything that Christmas might mean to people—this was Rock."

Rock and Jack went down to the railroad yard to watch the first
Christmas trees being taken off the boxcars. They waited until Rock
saw "the perfect tree." It was a Scotch pine, almost twelve feet tall,
and they set it up in the stairwell between the formal living room and
the "red room," which had a red rug and the oversized couches from
the set of *Pillow Talk*. Rock's next excursion with Jack was to the
downtown flower market, where they bought pine boughs, mistletoe,
wreaths and pots of scarlet poinsettias, which Rock called "apointaset-
tas." The scent of pine would permeate the house.

Rock personally shopped for gifts for every person on his list,
wrapped them and delivered them himself. He had worked as a gift
wrapper one Christmas in Chicago, and he turned the playroom into
a wrapping station. He would sit for hours, surrounded by skeins of
different-colored ribbons, rolls of paper, pinecones and baubles.

During the years at Universal, Rock would walk around the Studio
with a giant burlap sack, delivering presents. Each gift showed planning and thought. When Gail Gifford admired a set of stools in
Rock's house, she received them for Christmas. Jack Coates had said,
in passing, he wanted to learn to ski, so his gift was a complete ski
outfit: metal skis, boots and poles, pants, sweaters, jackets, socks,
long underwear, hats, gloves and goggles, plus a ski trip and lessons.
Rock gave his mother a diamond necklace, an organ and, one year, a
cruise around the world.

Joy spent a week preparing for the feast on Christmas Day. She
ordered a fresh-killed turkey and two pounds of extra gizzards.
She polished the silver and turned the red room into a dining hall.
The couches were moved aside and, in their place, a large table was
set, with a linen cloth and silver candelabra with giant red candles.
There were crystal goblets and silver goblets, and boughs and berries
in the centerpiece. When it was finished, Joy took photographs,
which she would show years later with pride. "That was my table."

Around 5 P.M. on Christmas Day, Rock put on the Christmas

UNIVERSAL INTERNATIONAL

Kay and Rock during filming of **The Golden Blade**

*"Always well done—no one ever had a rare
steak when Rock was cooking."*

"That was the most nervous I ever was!"
Meeting Queen Elizabeth II, 1954

The Golden Blade, *1954*

Phyllis telling her parents in Minnesota that
she was married today, 1955

*Rock Hudson with dogs. From left: Fritz,
Murphy, Wee-Wee, Sally*

1955

Rock and Phyllis in the 1950s

With George Stevens, Sr., and Elizabeth Taylor on location in Texas in the fifties

With Mae West, rehearsing **Baby, It's Cold Outside** *for 1958 Academy Awards*

With Doris Day in Pillow Talk, 1959

music he had selected and made his traditional eggnog. "What a mess in the kitchen," Joy says. "That eggnog was so strong, it could have walked out there on its own feet. Rock would say, 'Joy, want a glass?' I'd say, 'You want dinner?'"

The guests included Rock's mother, Kay, who drove up from Newport Beach with homemade pies, Mark and George, who flew in from Europe, Lynn Bowers and Pat Fitzgerald, Tom Clark and Pete De Palma, and Peter Shore, the decorator who worked with Rock on the house. Rock usually wore his corduroy pants and a bright red shirt. One Christmas, Jim Nabors came by in a candy-apple-red Rolls-Royce convertible, wearing a Blackglama mink coat. Rock leaned toward Jack Coates and whispered, "Do you think Jim has gone Hollywood?"

Joy carved the meats and set up the buffet: turkey with dressing and cranberries, ham, corn pudding, homemade relishes and rolls, three vegetables and at least three kinds of pie. Rock raved about his mother's pumpkin pie, and how she made it from scratch, picking the pumpkins and boiling them. After he'd eaten it, Kay went to the kitchen and came out with a box from a bakery chain, Marie Callender's. Rock's face fell. Everyone roared with laughter, but Kay tossed the box in the fireplace and said, with a wink, "I just had that box from an old bridge party."

After dinner, Rock presented his gifts. He did not like receiving gifts and often gave the items away, but he was excited to watch his friends open their gifts from him. Rock put on more music, people played bridge and gathered around the Steinway grand piano and sang. Late at night, when everyone had gone, Rock would go back to the kitchen and eat a plate of gizzards with Joy's turkey gravy. No one who spent a Christmas with Rock ever experienced another like it, not because the elements were unique, but because it had such meaning to Rock.

In 1970, Rock was given his first chance to play a villain in *Pretty Maids All in a Row*, an X-rated black comedy directed by Roger Vadim, a legendary sensualist who was then married to Jane Fonda. "I'm a murderer and a stud! I get to do everything," Rock told Mark Miller. Rock played Tiger, a high-school counselor who screws the prettiest girls in school and murders them when they become troublesome. As Tiger, Rock has a mustache, wears hip-hugger pants and likes to balance on a bongo board. He seems to have a perennial hard-on, and has to shoo the girls off him. The film captures the spirit of a time when sex was in the air and everyone wanted to try it with everyone else. The girls wear miniskirts and see-through blouses, presenting themselves with bouncing breasts and wiggling rears and long, bare legs. Angie Dickinson plays a sex-starved teacher, and in one scene, Rock lifts up her blouse and grabs her breasts with both hands, forces her down on the table, gets on top of her and, just as she's about to come, he stops and leaves her lying there, clawing. The film is a jumble of spoof and murder mystery that doesn't work, but the sexual excitement Rock gives off is palpable, and leaves the viewer in a state of arousal. Roger Ebert, the critic for the Chicago *Sun Times*, wrote, "Rock Hudson sex comedies sure have changed since *Pillow Talk.*"

Rock was entering a period when sex would be his first concern. He told friends he had to have sex every day, and that he was constantly thinking about it. At business meetings, while driving in the car, he was thinking about having sex that night. He told Mark Miller there were three things he cared about, in this order: sex, career and people. Jack Coates says that when Rock walked into a party, "the whole room filled with sexual heat. Everyone could feel it— women and men. He was that strong. His favorite expression was 'Wanna have some fun?' You knew what that meant."

Jack says Rock liked his bed made up with blue or white sheets and down pillows. He was a "champion cuddler." He once sent Jack a letter from Europe saying, "They're having cuddling championships this year in Davos, Switzerland. You can ski from Davos to Klosters and stay at inns on the way, and it's very cold. Let's enter it, I think we can win."

It was at this time that the first doubts about Rock's sexual identity were voiced in public. In the summer of 1971, a group of gay men in Manhattan Beach, California, who held a party every year with funny themes, sent out invitations to a party celebrating the wedding of Rock Hudson and Jim Nabors. One of the cards fell into the hands of a gossip columnist, who wrote an item in which he did not mention names but said that two male Hollywood stars had been married. "One is like the rock of Gibraltar; the other is like your neighbor."

The rumor spread—Rock Hudson had been secretly married to Jim Nabors. It was repeated on television and radio shows and in more columns, and the phone at the Castle rang constantly with reporters asking for comments. There was no truth to it; Rock had done a guest spot on Jim Nabors's variety show, and they had become casual friends. Rock liked to sing with Jim, and Rock and Jack Coates had gone to Lake Tahoe to ski and see Jim's show. When Jim's house had burned, Rock had called and said, "You can stay here, you can wear our underwear," but Jim had never stayed at the Castle. Joy said to Rock, when she heard the rumor, "Of course it's not true. He's not even blond."

At first Rock ignored it, with his usual attitude that if he refused to deal with an unpleasant matter, he could will it out of existence. When he did comment, he made a joke of it, telling Joyce Haber, "It's over. I've returned all the emeralds and diamonds Jim gave me." Finally, both Rock and Jim had to make public statements that the wedding had not happened. In July, Rona Barrett said on her TV show *Rona Reports*: "We've received thousands of calls and letters from all over the country, asking us about the validity of perhaps the most vicious rumor to come from Hollywood in the last fifty years. We emphatically state the wedding never occurred! This vicious rumor is totally false."

But rumors take on a life of their own, and gossip is harder to retract than to spread. People came forward and swore they had attended the ceremony, which they placed, variously, in Las Vegas, Carmel, Tijuana, New York and Vancouver. Many people still insist that the marriage took place. Last year, my aunt, who sells real estate in Beverly Hills, told me, "I *know* they were married. You ask Carol Burnett, she gave the wedding in her home."

Rock became furious; how could he defend himself when people were swearing that something untrue had happened? Jim Nabors's variety show on CBS was canceled, and he and Rock could not be seen together again. Rock was even reluctant to go to Hawaii because he knew Jim had a house there. They did not speak for the rest of Rock's life.

By 1971, Jack Coates had finished college and was in full-time residence at the Castle, but he was growing restless. He did not want to spend his life as the consort of a movie star, with no identity of his own. He did not want to be, as his friends put it, "Rock Hudson's wife." He decided he would leave and go to graduate school in anthropology.

Years later, Jack would say he left because of "my own ego. It's not because there wasn't great love. I wish I had been stronger, and I wish I'd been more sophisticated at chess playing, because I couldn't take the intrigue in that house. It was brutal." Jack did not know how to handle the gossip and infighting around Rock. "Everyone wanted to be the movie star's best friend, and because I had pillow talk, they tried to get to the throne through me." Someone would start a campaign to oust Mark Miller from favor, spreading rumors and telling Jack, who was supposed to tell Rock, that Mark had said or done something, and then Mark would have to defend himself and launch a counterattack against his rivals. Or, friends who had been welcome at the Castle for years would suddenly find that their calls would not be returned. There was no explanation, they were out and new friends were in, so they would seek Jack's help in breaking through the barriers and regaining their place.

"When I learned to play chess, I understood what was going on," Jack says. "Rock was the King. Tom, after I left, was the Queen, who had the most power on the board. Mark and George were the Bishops. I was the Knight and I could always do a jump straight to the throne if I needed to. The problem was, I liked everyone and I didn't care what they said about each other or who was in what position."

Two days before Christmas, 1971, Jack told Rock he had decided to go back to Arizona. "Rock would not show any emotion," Jack says, "he was silent." Jack walked down the stairs in tears, got in his truck and drove away. Joy looked at Mark Miller and said, "What happened?"

If Rock had wanted to, he could have prevented Jack from going, but he said nothing and let him walk out. They spoke on the phone, and Jack came back frequently for visits and holidays. "Jack *was* like a knight," Mark says. "Whenever he wanted to, he could snatch up the movie star and take him away and nobody could do a damn thing about it."

Jack wandered through the Southwest, living out of his pickup truck, visiting Indian reservations and meditation centers. Rock never spoke with Jack about their relationship until many years later, after Rock's mother had died, and Rock saw Jack in Santa Fe, New Mexico. They wanted to be alone, so they hiked up a trail in the Sangre de Cristo Mountains, and as they stood in a clearing, talking softly, Rock said to Jack, "What went wrong?"

CHAPTER 9

There's a tremendous difference between television and movies, and nobody told me. In television, the enemy is time. Everything is done so hurriedly, there is no time to do good work. You have to exist in mediocrity. On a film, you may shoot two or three pages a day. On a TV series, you do twelve pages a day. When I made Seconds, with John Frankenheimer, we took four months to shoot the picture. On McMillan and Wife, we had three weeks to shoot a segment, and they were both the same amount of screen time.

In television, you have to remember that what you're doing will come out of a little box. So you have to exaggerate and play everything bigger than life. You can't be subtle, or your character will get lost. In a movie, on the big screen, the slightest move—the lifting of an eyebrow, the curling of a lip—comes across like a blasting horn, because it's magnified twenty times. The same thing would register zero on TV.

It was a difficult adjustment for me when I started McMillan and Wife. We had a different director on every show, and he would say, "Now, come in the door and I want you to go over to the fireplace and put a log on. . . ." And I wanted to say, "Well, I can't do that. I just did that on the last show with the other director."

So I went down to the office and told the producer, "The director's doing stuff that I don't think is any good." And he said to me, "You don't understand. You have to direct." I said, "That's not my training. . . ." Well, ultimately, it became necessary for me to say, "Look, you can't do it that way. It has to be done another way. Put the camera over there. . . ."

The scripts became progressively worse as the seasons wore on. They weren't particularly funny, and we had to ad lib a lot of them. But that's dangerous. Comedy should be proven, well worked out, not done off the cuff. It's grounds for alcoholism.

Rock had been approached to do television for many years, but he had never given it serious thought. He felt television was beneath him, a lesser form, a refuge for sinking ships who could no longer float in the big sea. He had criticized George Nader for doing television in the fifties, and he did not even watch television. He wanted to work in films all his life.

But Rock was a romantic leading man, not a character actor, and in 1971, there were fewer romantic leads for him. He was forty-six, he was gaining weight and losing his skin tone because he was drinking so heavily. It became necessary for him to have his wardrobe specially cut to camouflage the extra flesh around his waist. Friends and advisers began telling him, "There's a whole other career out there for you on television, a new generation you could reach." The young people who had been Rock Hudson's fans in the fifties were now at home, raising families, watching television.

NBC ultimately made Rock an offer that, he decided, "I'd be an idiot to turn down." He would star in a ninety-minute series, *McMillan and Wife*, that would be part of NBC's *Mystery Movie* cycle, and would alternate every three weeks with *Columbo* and *McCloud*. He would be paid $120,000 per episode, the highest fee that had yet been paid in television. He would have approval of scripts and his leading lady, and he would still be able to make films during the yearly hiatus.

The series was modeled loosely on the old *Thin Man* movies with William Powell and Myrna Loy. Stewart McMillan was police commissioner of San Francisco, and his wife, Sally, was a naïve, adoring young woman who managed, often unwittingly, to help solve the cases her husband worked on. When it came time to cast his wife, Rock told the producer, Leonard Stern, that he wanted to have dinner with the candidates. They took seven women to seven restaurants, and the last was Susan Saint James, whom they met at Tail o' the Cock in the Valley. Susan was twenty-five, and, like Rock, she had come to Hollywood from a small town in Illinois with a different name, Susan Miller, no training and no connections but an absolute determination to be a star. She was awestruck at the idea of working with Rock Hudson. She remembers sitting in the darkened booth of the restaurant with him, "talking a mile a minute" and feeling warm and happy. "He was as big as he looked on screen. Nobody else I'd worked with had been anywhere near the size I'd imagined. He was so relaxed and natural. I got a complete crush on him. I thought he was incredibly sexy."

After the dinner, Rock called Leonard Stern at home and said, "Well, it has to be Susan. I've gained seven pounds." After Susan, they hired Nancy Walker to play the family maid, and John Schuck to play Rock's sidekick, Sergeant Enright.

The pilot, "Once Upon a Dead Man," was shot in Rock's home, using the red room as the set for Rock and Susan's living room. On the first day of rehearsals, Susan, whose straight black hair was parted in the center and fell halfway down her back, was wearing a short slip called a "teddy." Rock was sitting on the couch, and she came up behind him and put her arms around him, then jumped over the couch and sat in his lap. She kept her arms around him all the while they were discussing the scene. "He never flinched. He was totally receptive to that physicality," she recalls. "He was cuddly, you couldn't help but want to sit in his lap."

Rock and Susan had terrific chemistry on screen, despite the twenty-year gap in their ages. But for Rock, the relationship was awkward at the start. He saw Susan as a flower child, a member of the antiwar generation, who ate brown rice and was having babies at home and nursing them on the set. She was relatively new at the craft and could be temperamental. To Susan, Rock was "Mr. Meat. All he wanted to eat was steak. He had grown a mustache and wore jackets with big lapels and wide ties that I thought looked on the way out." He drank and smoked and would say, "Fuck the ecology. Let's get more oil out of the ground." He was an old-guard movie star with a protective staff around him. Susan was green, "a baby," who was creating an acting style as she went, a loose, natural style that was different from the stiffer acting practiced on television at that time. Rock told Tom Clark, "If Susan put on film what she puts into the rehearsal, she'd be an enormous star. But the minute the camera's rolling, she gets tight and doesn't show her real talent."

The show was a hit and stayed on the air for six years. Rock and Susan gradually became good friends, despite their surface differences. "We were together twelve hours a day," Susan says. "That's more time than you spend with your spouse. You can't help but fall in love with someone when you're working together so intimately and giving each other the energy and spark that makes it work on screen."

Susan and her husband would go to Rock's on Sunday night to watch the show and have dinner, and they were always invited there for Christmas.

Susan says Rock never talked to her about his personal life, and she didn't ask, because "I worshiped that man." He held her babies when she brought them on the set, and told her anecdotes about his past, and they laughed together and played pranks. Once they were rehearsing a scene at the end of a long week when everyone was exhausted, and they decided to wake up the crew. Susan came down the stairs and said, "Mac, be careful, take your gun." Rock said, "Oh, shut up!" slapped her and sent her sprawling, and the entire crew broke up.

She says she never saw Rock have a tantrum or throw his weight around. He had a clause in his contract that stipulated that he couldn't work late on Friday, and everyone envied him for it, but if he was asked to work late, he always did without complaint. "He bought the crew drinks on Friday night, and I've done that ever since," Susan says. "He had class." She says Rock loved "normal American things. He loved to make ice cream, he loved to eat candy." Rock told Susan he loved martinis but saved them for the weekend and drank only Scotch during the week. "If he ever had a martini on a work night, he'd come in the next morning groaning, 'Why, why, why did I do this!'"

When Susan was told, early in the first season, that Rock was gay, she says, "I couldn't believe it. My feeling was, if I used my complete feminine wiles, I could disprove it." When she began making appearances to publicize *McMillan and Wife*, people would ask her about Rock's sexuality. "Everyone—women at the May Company, friends, hippies making peace posters—would say, 'You can tell me, is he gay?' I always answered, 'You could never tell by me.' I never felt shut out from him physically. I could hug Rock and get goosebumps. I got the same readings from him I'd get from Bob Wagner or Peter Fonda. If I hadn't been married, there was nothing to tell me I couldn't get all the way to home plate with him."

Rock was never satisfied with *McMillan and Wife*. He maintained his professional attitude, was always prepared and on time, was courteous and helpful to everyone but he never put his all into the role. At home, he drank every night, partly because he was unhappy with what he was doing. Susan was nominated for an Emmy award four out of the five years she did the show, but Rock was not nominated. In 1974, a new producer came on, Jon Epstein, who worked hard to improve the segments. He said he found Rock a "pro," who was underrated as an actor. "Because he did it with such ease, nobody thought he was acting. The show wasn't award-winning material, it was fluff, and therefore, harder to do than meaningful material. What Rock did was hard, and he pulled it off so effortlessly that people didn't realize what an actor he was."

Many fans of the show had never seen Rock's films. They came to know him as the character on television, and liked him because they saw the softness under the macho detective. One young woman said, "He was beautiful and strong, but he also seemed like a man who could be a real friend. You could talk to him."

At the end of the fifth season, Susan's contract expired and she asked for more money than the company was willing to pay. She was tired of playing the same character; she was ready to move on. "I didn't realize how good I had it," she said years later. She left the show, and it continued for a season with Rock alone as *McMillan*.

Susan never had a chance to tell Rock personally she was leaving, or to say good-bye, and she did not see him again for nine years. It was a shock to her to have been so close and then not speak. She had not yet grasped the nature of show-business friendships, where you go on location with someone for four months and fall in love and come to feel you know and understand each other better than anyone else in the world and then the show ends and you never see each other. "The closeness is terribly real and sincere, but the minute you don't get a work call, you're off in separate directions," Susan says. "People say, let's get together, let's have lunch, but it isn't gonna happen." She says that Peter Fonda told her to think of it as the circus coming to town. She worked with Fonda on a movie, *Outlaw Blues*, and had an intense friendship that dissolved when the picture wrapped. "He taught me it's okay for that to happen. It's like the circus—you have the best time of your life when it's there and then the circus moves on."

Susan moved to the East Coast, worked on other shows, divorced her first husband and married Dick Ebersol, who was producing *Saturday Night Live* and who had known Rock through his first wife,

Susan Stafford. Over the years, Susan Saint James thought about Rock with aching fondness and a growing sense of unease. She read interviews with Rock where he freely described how much he had detested doing *McMillan and Wife*. Had he also detested her? Was he bitter about the way she had left? She longed to see him in private, so she could ask him: "Did you like working with me? Didn't we have a great time? Didn't we do a good job on that series?" They were not questions she could ask on the phone or at a show-business party, and Susan says, "I thought I would take those questions to my grave."

In the spring of 1984, she got a call out of the blue from a publicist, asking if she would speak at a dinner for Rock—the only dinner he had ever allowed to be given in his honor—at the Sands Hotel in Atlantic City. The dinner was a benefit for the Actors' Fund, one of the few charities Rock had contributed to over the years. Susan jumped at the chance. She was doing a new series, *Kate & Allie*, and living with Dick and their children in Litchfield, Connecticut. They set off for Atlantic City with trepidation. Susan wanted to know if Rock had liked or hated working with her. Dick Ebersol was nervous because a joke about the Rock Hudson—Jim Nabors wedding had been used on *Saturday Night Live*, and Dick was worried Rock would be angry at him for permitting it.

They flew in a rainstorm to Philadelphia, where they were met by a limousine and driven to Atlantic City. Carol Burnett, Morgan Fairchild and other celebrities had been scheduled to appear at the dinner, but the storm had hit New Jersey that morning and many of the celebrities had canceled at the last minute. It turned out Susan was the biggest star to attend, and the only speaker.

When they reached the Sands, Susan went to their room, put on makeup and a new dress she'd bought for the occasion. With trembling step, she walked downstairs to the lobby where she saw Rock Hudson, surrounded by photographers. Rock spotted her and came toward her, tailed by the press who were eager to catch the reunion between McMillan and wife. "I saw him and completely busted into tears," Susan says. "Right away, I knew, I'm home. We ran to each other across the crowded lobby, put out our arms and just enveloped each other and there was that same old feeling. It was one of the great moments of my life."

They sat together at the head table during dinner, and when it was time for the speeches, they both reached into their pockets, took out glasses and put them on. They looked at each other, bespectacled, and burst out laughing. "It felt like we were veterans now, like we'd been in a foxhole together years before." Rock asked Susan and Dick what they were doing after the dinner. "Going home to Connecticut," Dick said.

"Come with me," Rock said. "The Sands is flying me in a helicopter to New York. We'll go to my apartment and catch up."

They took off from the roof in a jet-black helicopter, flew up along the Hudson River and over the World Trade Center. Because of the noise of the chopper, they could not talk, but Susan remembers looking across at Rock, who was wearing tan slacks, a tan sweater with brown stripes and a Burberry raincoat, and thinking, "That is the most beautiful man." It was just a few months before Rock would be diagnosed as having AIDS. "He looked stunning to us that night. Later, though, we looked at pictures taken and realized he'd been sick. The camera had seen what we couldn't."

When they landed at the Thirty-fourth Street Heliport, it was 2 A.M. and the limousine that had been ordered wasn't there. Dale Olson, Rock's publicist, got on the phone trying to round up cars and finally secured a gypsy cab, which took them to Rock's apartment at the Beresford on Central Park West. Dale went home, and Rock gave Susan and Dick a tour of the apartment, which he had bought and remodeled a few years before. It had two bedrooms, a living room, a den and terrace, but Rock's favorite spot was the master bathroom. With boyish enthusiasm, he showed them the sinks, built extra high for him, and the shower, which was also a steam bath and had a window looking out on Central Park. "I can be naked, taking a steam, and look out on all of New York!" Rock said.

He fixed himself the first drink of the day—a watered-down Scotch. He had been told he must stop drinking and smoking after he had had a quintuple heart-bypass operation in 1981. "The doctors say I'm not supposed to have this," Rock said. "Fuck the doctors, I hope they die."

Rock, Susan and Dick sat down in the den, which had a safari motif, with a sisal rug, white canvas furniture, African drums and spears and a painting of a zebra. Susan's first words were: "I couldn't

---

176

believe you would kiss another woman on *McMillan*, three months after I died in a plane crash. For five years, you worshiped your wife. You had sex every night of your married life." Rock laughed. "Life goes on." Susan felt the old longing to cuddle in his arms. "I kind of wished Dick wasn't there, because I wanted to sit in Rock's lap. I wished the world would go away and I could say, 'Aren't you my best friend?'"

They reminisced about the shows, and how they never made sense and Rock always had to give a long speech at the end explaining the mystery. The speech was usually the first scene they shot, so Rock had no idea what he was talking about. "Remember the show with the bag?" Rock said. At the end of one season, the production company had run out of money and couldn't afford sets and extras, so they came up with an episode where there was a bag over the house where Rock and Susan lived. "More people tell me they remember that show," Susan said. "It turned out to be one of the most popular episodes."

It was six in the morning and the sky was lighting up with streaks of pink when Susan and Dick left the Beresford. "We didn't want the night to end, and Rock didn't want it to end. It was so warm and important to me," Susan says. "It was a validation of those twelve hours a day for five years." When she learned Rock was sick and dying of AIDS, she sent flowers to the hospital and called once, but he was sleeping. "I never got my courage back to call him again. But I feel comfortable, because we had that chance in Atlantic City to tie up loose ends, and to say, yes, we really were friends."

Rock went back to California after the dinner at the Sands and told people how marvelous it had been to see Susan, what a fine actress she'd become and what an endearing friend she was. He looked at reruns of *McMillan and Wife*, and was surprised to see that they weren't as bad as he'd remembered. "It was better than I thought," he told Mark Miller. "Why didn't I put more into it?"

CHAPTER 10

One Sunday afternoon, I was out in the swimming pool when Carol Burnett called. She said, "Want to do I Do! I Do! with me?" I said, "It's a musical. I've never sung, and I've never been on stage."

Carol said, "Oh, come on, do it."

So I said, "Okay." I went outside and told Tom, "I've just agreed to do a two-character play, here, in this town, and it's not funny." We played the record from the New York production, and then I read the script and I said, "Jesus Christ, every page has three laughs. It's excellent writing. They didn't see it when they did the show in New York."

I was nervous about the singing, but everything happens by degrees. I've studied singing a lot, not that that matters. I love singing, and I worked with David Craig, who teaches actors how to present a song. You learn what's behind the lyrics, what the humor is, and how to make the story of the song come across.

We had four weeks of rehearsal, and Gower Champion told me, in four weeks, you'll do it. Four weeks is forever when you're rehearsing. It was only a four-week run, and usually you'd do two weeks of rehearsal. We opened the show out of town, in San Bernardino, so by opening night at the Huntington Hartford, I was ready.

In March of 1972, Marilyn Maxwell died of a heart attack, and Rock was one of the first people called. Marilyn's son, Matthew Davis, who was fifteen, had come home from school and found her slumped on the floor of the closet. He called the paramedics, who arrived and told him, "Your mother's gone." Matthew went into shock. He walked into the maid's room at the back of the house and sat down in a big red chair. The house began to fill with people, but Matthew refused to leave the chair. People were talking to him, but he didn't hear the words and looked about in confusion. Suddenly, a face swam into focus. It was Rock Hudson, who picked Matthew up in his arms, carried him out to his car and brought him up to the

178

Castle, along with Marilyn's secretary, Jean Greenberg. Rock called a doctor, who gave Matthew a sedative, and Rock put him to bed in the guest bedroom he called Tijuana.

All night, Rock sat on the floor of the red room with Jean, drinking vodka straight up, manning the phones, making plans for the funeral. Rock was a pallbearer, and during the service, he sat with Tom Clark and Jimmy Dobson. Rock and Jimmy were weeping and trying not to. Rock said, under his breath, "Jimmy, tell me about the next picture I'm doing. What'll it be like?"

"You'll be in beautiful country. Red mountains and tall green trees. Clean air that makes you feel good to breathe."

"That's right. I'm gonna like it," Rock said.

On his way out, Rock turned to Tom and said he didn't want a funeral. "Please, please, don't ever let them do this to me."

A few days later, Rock went through Marilyn's things and found old, 78 recordings of every radio show she had done. He had them transferred to tape, and gave it to Matthew. Matthew says, "I didn't realize, until later, how important it was to preserve those recordings. Rock just knew what to do. He was the best friend my mother had."

The next picture Rock did, which he had fixed his thoughts on to take his mind off the loss of Marilyn Maxwell, was *Showdown*, filmed in New Mexico in 1972. There was a sequence where Rock had to drive an antique car, borrowed from Laurence Rockefeller's collection of antique cars. As Rock was rehearsing, the brakes failed and the car ran full speed into a concrete wall. Rock suffered a concussion, a cracked rib, fractures in one leg and both arms. The production was halted and he flew home where he spent six weeks in bed, recuperating.

Mark Miller and George Nader had moved back to the States from Europe, and George had had an accident with even more serious consequences than Rock's. He suffered a detached retina and became blind in one eye. He had surgery to repair the retina, but he developed glaucoma, which brought an abrupt and unexpected end to his career. He could not work in films because the strong lights made him lose vision. Rock was upset when he heard about the illness. Rock had a phobia about blindness, and often said, "I could live with anything but that." He contributed every year to eye clinics and institutes for the blind.

Mark and George came to dinner at the Castle, and Rock said, "What are you gonna do now, if George can't work?" Mark said, "I'm gonna sell real estate." He had obtained his license and a position as a salesman with Larry O'Rourke Realty.

"No, you're not," Rock said. "You're gonna work for me."

"But . . . what will I do?"

"Run my affairs. I need a secretary."

"There's nothing to do," Mark said.

The line would become a running joke. "There's nothing to do." Mark says, "It was a full-time job, it took seven days a week if I let it." Mark set up an office in Tijuana with a desk and files, and took over the running of Rock's house. He answered mail and phone calls, paid all the bills, kept records and straightened out the crises that swirled around Rock. Mark called the house "Castle Chaos," because there was always a brush fire raging and Rock sat placidly while others got their hands burned trying to put it out. Rock was nine months behind in cashing checks, and had years of fan mail piled in boxes. "The cars were a mess," Mark says. "Rock had six cars and none had gas or oil. Rock would drive them until they ran out of gas or broke down, and then he'd switch to another car."

Rock paid Mark $100 a week. Joy was still getting $60 a week, and Clarence had been getting $600 a month since 1962. Mark referred to Rock as "cheap chicken. He was the most generous cheap person I ever knew." Rock would never ask the price of things when he shopped, but he wouldn't give raises, and he asked the staff to clip coupons and shop for groceries on Thursdays, when the markets had specials. For Christmas, Rock gave Mark and George a trip to Europe, but said, "I can't afford to send you first class. I hope you don't mind going tourist."

Mark says, "I took the job because it was fun. Where else could I find anything like this? I worked from nine to four, there were trips to Hawaii and New York and Europe, and I got to spend all day with my best friend sitting there, telling jokes and giggling." Rock liked to sit in the office in a wooden chair with lions' heads carved in the arms, a chair that had once belonged to George Nader's mother. While Mark typed, and messengers and workmen and barbers came

and went, Rock did needlepoint. He'd taken up the craft while re-
covering from a foot operation. Tom Clark had bought him a starter
kit when Rock complained that he was bored. "Rock fell in love with
it because it was mathematical and precise," Tom says. Rock started
Mark needlepointing. "You gotta try this, it's fun." Rock worked on
pillows, then a large rug with American Indian patterns, which he
carried in a special suitcase whenever he went on location.

Every day at noon, Rock and Mark would go to the kitchen and
have lunch with Joy, the cleaning staff and whoever else was around.
Rock liked what he called a "casual house," where the staff were
treated as family and they all ate together with Rock at the table.
Mark called it "the People's Republic of Hudson."

Late in the day, if things were slow and Rock and Mark were
alone, they would clown. Mark would call Rock "Trixie," a nickname George had invented and which Rock liked because of its
meanings: he played tricks; he was a benefactrix; and "tricks" was
slang for sexual partners. Rock called Mark "treasured bird," a phrase
from a W. C. Fields movie.

"Treasured bird," Rock would say, "it's time to practice our bows."
Rock would give Mark his arm, Mark would take it, and they would
strut through the house and grounds, making fun of the way opera
singers and grand actors of the stage take their bows. Sometimes they
would start at the top of the grand staircase and come down smiling,
their arms extended and their heads held high. They pretended they
were in full costume and there was an audience cheering. "It's not
easy to go down stairs," Mark says. "You have to make a turn on the
landing without ever looking down, and maintain eye contact with
the audience." When they reached the foot of the stairs, they would
bow. Whoever was playing the lady would curtsy, and the man
would bend low. The game was to see who would break down and
laugh first. Then they'd both howl and roll on the carpet.

Tom Clark often stopped by for a drink on his way home from
work. Tom had left M.G.M. and was working for Rupert Allan, who
had a private public-relations firm and represented Rock. One evening, Mark was working late on correspondence. Tom came by for
his drink and left. Mark left shortly after, drove a few blocks and
realized he'd forgotten his wallet at the house. He drove back to get it

and saw Tom Clark's car back at the house. Mark continued out the gate and drove home.

The relationship between Rock and Tom had been developing gradually over the years. Tom was tall and imposing, with blue eyes and fair hair that was turning steadily to white. He spoke with an Oklahoma accent (he was raised in Oklahoma City, a Bible Belt Methodist) and had a mellifluous voice that could carry through a stadium. He was a colorful presence, emotional and tempestuous, a great storyteller and a crack bridge player.

He and Rock had met in 1964, at the home of Pat Fitzgerald, when Rock had stopped by unannounced and usurped Tom's place at the bridge table. Tom had thought Rock was "another self-involved actor," but they met at other parties and gatherings and discovered they shared the same humor. Over the years, they became close friends, and they became lovers while both were still with other people.

In 1972, Rock was invited to Australia to receive a "Logie," the equivalent of an Emmy award. He asked Tom to accompany him as his publicist, and they stopped in Tahiti to break up the trip. Tom had never been to the South Pacific, and Rock told him the sunsets were the most spectacular in the world. "Tonight, we are going to see a sunset," Rock said. "We must have martinis to toast this sunset. *I* will go and get them." There was no room service, so Rock went for the drinks and came back with a plastic dishpan filled with peculiar-looking liquid and strange little olives. "These are our martinis," Rock said. They showered and put on white trousers, went out to the deck and raised their martinis and the sun set into a cloud bank.

The next night, they tried again. They were staying on a different island in the penthouse of a tall, new hotel. There was room service, so they ordered martinis, which arrived in proper stem glasses. They took showers and Rock said, "Let's just sit on the balcony in our towels and toast the sunset." They settled themselves in their towels, with their martinis, "and it was the most glorious sunset you have ever seen," Tom says. He went into the room for refills, and on the way back, the door accidentally slammed shut behind him and locked. They had to climb down a fire escape, holding skimpy towels over their privates, and knock on windows until they got a cleaning lady to open a door. "That was Rock's perfect sunset. But we had a great time on that trip to Australia," Tom says. "We found we really worked well together. I organized everything and took care of what Rock needed, and I was a buffer. Rock could never say no to people, and I could and did."

The following year, 1973, Rock was invited to Buenos Aires by a television station that wanted to do a special on his career. Ordinarily, Rock would not have considered going, but the show coincided with Mardi Gras, and Rock had always wanted to see Carnaval in Rio. *McMillan and Wife* had just been sold in South America, and Rock persuaded Universal to send him on a three-week publicity trip. He asked Tom to accompany him again, and Tom had to take a vacation from his job with Rupert Allan to go.

They had what Tom calls "another spectacular trip." Hollywood celebrities rarely appeared in Buenos Aires, and Rock was nearly trampled by fans. Rock and Tom sampled the world-famous Argentinian steaks, flew in military helicopters all over the countryside and listened to gaucho music in a small club, where they sat on couches and sipped Scotch while the gauchos sang to them until early morning.

In Rio de Janeiro, they had a penthouse overlooking Copacabana Beach. They went to formal balls and costume balls, where Rock was asked to be a judge, and were invited to sit in the governor's box for the Samba Parade, which is the central event of Mardi Gras. All year, the samba clubs, which are formed mostly in poor neighborhoods, work on their dances, raise money and prepare their costumes. Each club has a theme and colors—one is all in yellow, another all in blue—and as they dance past the governor's box, they stop to perform special numbers. Rock and Tom went out in the street and danced with the clubs. "We got in samba lines, and people passed us bottles of beer and we drank from them." It started to rain and the samba clubs kept dancing. Rock and Tom stayed in the box, drinking rum, eating and dancing out in the streets until daylight.

It was one of those trips where people feel a heightened sense of adventure and abandon, and a special attachment to those who've shared it with them. When it was time to leave Rio, Rock and Tom were rushing to pack, taking their clothes out of the huge closet in the suite, and Rock felt a wave of sadness: The trip was ending, and they would be going back to their separate lives. He took hold of some clothes and Tom stopped him. "Those are *mah* fine things.

Don't you touch *mah* fine things." Rock burst out laughing, tickled at the way Tom expressed himself. He looked at him and said, "Why don't you move in?"

When they returned to California, Tom called Mark and George. "Can I come down? I have the most wonderful news." George says Tom walked into their apartment "filled with fire and music, throwing handfuls of glitter dust." Tom said he had never been so happy. "Rock has asked me to move in." George did not think it was a match made in heaven, but he said he and Mark would accept it because "Rock is our friend." Tom said Rock wanted him to quit his job, and Mark and George argued against it. "You've seen people come and go in that house. Rock wants them all to quit work and stay home, but the minute they do, Rock can't stand it."

"This is different," Tom said. "He wants me to work for him and be an officer of the company."

Rock and Tom called Jack Coates to tell him the news. Jack's response was: "What took you so long? You've got my blessing."

It seemed, in the beginning, that Rock and Tom were an ideal fit. They liked the same things: bridge, dogs, drinking, football, traveling, dressing casually, reading, listening to music. "Everything was just right on. There was not one thing that was discordant," Tom says. Tom had worked in the movie business all his adult life, and he knew and was respected by everyone Rock knew. "I can take him anywhere," Rock said. "I can introduce him to Princess Margaret." They traveled together and went out socially without subterfuge. They had a legitimate connection: Tom was Rock's publicist, and later, his personal manager.

Tom was completely unlike the men Rock had been with before. He was not a young blond hunk with a mustache. He was nearly Rock's age, and he was an equal match. He stood up to Rock and, more often than not, got what he wanted. Rock told Mark and George, "I've always been looking for a Mark," by which he meant a person who was loyal and supportive, who would do everything to help his career, and yet would have substance and intelligence. "I've never found it, and I hope I can with Tom."

In the early period, Rock and Tom seemed happy. When Rock came home from work, the first thing he said was, "Where's Tom?"

"Upstairs," Mark said.

"Thank you," Rock said and went off to find him.

The two men took a steam bath around six, then put on floor-length robes, fixed drinks and built a fire in the outdoor fireplace. "How was your day?" Tom would say, and they'd catch up. If they weren't going out, they might go into the playroom for a long record session. "First Rock got to pick something and then I got to pick something," Tom says. "We played big-band albums and Broadway musicals and opera, and by the time we were through, there'd be records all over the playroom and poor Mark would have to come in the next day and sort them out." They drank through the night and ate late, sometimes not until midnight, so Joy would cook dinner and leave it on the stove.

Everyone in the house was drinking more. Joy had started drinking heavily, and Tom told Rock, "We've got to get rid of that woman," but Rock refused. Rock was drinking more because he had company. Tom could match Rock drink for drink, and some nights, they both passed out. In the morning, one of them would tiptoe into Mark's office and say, "Could you go downstairs and find out from staff what happened last night? Because something happened and we don't know what. See if there's anyone we need to apologize to."

In the morning, Tom watched a game show, *The $25,000 Pyramid,* and could not be disturbed between nine and nine-thirty. The staff called him "Lana Lump-up, our lovely lady of Lullabye Lane," because he would say, "I'm gonna go upstairs and lump up," meaning he would get comfortable in his robe on the bed and watch television or read. Rock told him, when he moved in, "Make the house yours," and, Tom says, "I did, I absolutely did." He rearranged furniture, planted roses and kept after the staff to keep the house immaculate. When he learned how little the staff members were being paid, he immediately gave them raises and made sure they received a generous bonus at Christmas—something Rock had not thought to do. "There was no question in anybody's mind that came here: The house belonged to both of us," Tom says.

Tom began to use the collective "we." He would say, "When *we* did *McMillan* . . ." and he would talk about "our dogs," "our car," "our performance." He took over Rock's career and business affairs, as well as the house. He kept track of "our engagements," made reservations and appointments and carried the money. "Rock was not

185

organized. He never put a date down. He could never fire help or raise a fuss if things weren't going right at work. 'Who cares?' he would say. I used to tell him, 'You're a movie star, goddammit! Will you act like one?'"

Tom read scripts submitted to Rock, listened to proposals and presented them with his recommendation as to what Rock should do. People asked, "By what right does he do that?" Mark Miller would shrug and say, "He just does."

Rock became dependent on Tom and Tom wanted him to be dependent, but Rock resented it. Tom was the keeper of the gate. "Our worst fights were over that," Tom says. "Rock kept saying, 'Why do you do this?' I said, 'Rock, because, A, you shouldn't, and, B, you can't.' I wanted to keep unpleasant things from him. If there was a rumor, I tried to prevent him from hearing it. If he found out about it anyway and learned I knew, he was angry. He said I should have been the one to tell him."

Rock's life-style began to change after Tom moved in. Tom liked "fine things" and the society of people of achievement. They bought a Rolls-Royce, but Rock wouldn't drive it because he thought it was ostentatious. "It didn't bother me at all," Tom says, tongue in cheek, "but I was to the manner born."

Tom went into Mark's office one day and said, "Rock and I have decided to get rid of all the losers in Rock's life. We're going to clean 'em all out and get a fresh start." Old friends who had been welcome for ten years were suddenly dropped from the guest list. They would call Mark and say, "I can't get Rock on the phone, and Tom was very cold. Why, what've I done wrong?" Mark would try to let them down gently. "It's nothing you've done. Give it time."

The new circle included Ross Hunter and Jacque Mapes, Nancy Walker and her husband, David Craig, Roddy McDowall, Sylvia and Danny Kaye and Olive Behrendt, a wealthy socialite. Ross Hunter had produced eleven of Rock's films, but Rock had maintained his distance; he didn't quite trust him. Tom told Rock, "Come on, let's have him over, we'll have fun," and he set up a dinner with Ross and Jacque. With Tom's prompting, Rock came to enjoy Ross Hunter. He had a merciless wit and would liven up a gathering. The four became fast friends, constantly playing bridge, taking trips and going back and forth for dinners.

In the years Tom lived on Beverly Crest, he made the house sing. He was a master at planning parties, and he gathered the Hollywood community around Rock, to pump up his career at a moment when it was beginning to sink. Tom says Rock had been reluctant, before, to ask Joy to cook for parties. "I can't tell you how many times I was invited here for bridge and Rock would say, 'Could you stop and pick up Kentucky Fried on the way?' So I said, 'Let's use this house. Let's entertain in it. We have entrées to some of the most fascinating people in the world. Let's have them in for dinner.'"

They started having small dinners for eight to twelve people, where everyone could sit at the same table and talk. They had Fred Astaire and Gene Kelly one night, Elizabeth Taylor and Carol Burnett on another. Pat and Michael York. William Holden and Stephanie Powers. Bette Davis. Then there were the larger "career parties." Tom says, "Movie stars have to keep up a front. You have to invite the president of NBC and M.G.M. to your house, when you'd rather have your good friends." On Sundays, they had brunches. Rock liked to make a soufflé with fresh Parmesan cheese, and Tom's job was to put the collar on the soufflé dish and then to mix bull shots: vodka, beef bouillon, Tabasco and lime. There were lunches and bridge parties and swimming parties. When Rock was not filming, he and Tom were out or entertaining seven nights a week.

In March of 1973, Carol Burnett called with her proposal that Rock appear with her in a summer revival of *I Do! I Do!* The show was a period piece, a musical comedy based on the play *The Four-Poster*. There was an old-fashioned bed in the center of the stage, and in and out of and around the bed, a husband and wife sang and danced through fifty years of marriage.

Rock had seventeen songs and a solo dance. It was a challenge that many actors in his place would have rejected as foolhardy. Tony Randall says, "He had guts. It took nerve for someone with no stage experience at all to go out with a high-powered performer like Carol Burnett. Rock didn't fool around; he went to work."

The stage, even more than television, was a world apart from film acting. In the theater, the actor has to project to the last row of the house, and to enunciate so clearly that every final *t* can be heard. Subtlety and underplaying, which had been Rock's trademark on film, do not work. Rock had four weeks to prepare himself, and during that period, he shut out everything from his life but the play. He worked in the mornings with Jimmy Dobson and in the afternoons with Gower Champion. He gave instructions to his staff that the front doorbell was not to chime, the phones were not to ring and he was never to be disturbed. If someone accidentally made noise on the patio, Rock would get furious.

"He absorbed every word of Gower Champion's," Mark says. For Rock's dance, Gower gave him a little routine to do with a cane. It looked effortless, but Rock worked and worked at it. He could not get his arms and legs and head all moving the way he wanted. He struggled in frustration, until finally, one day, he emerged from rehearsal victorious. "I got my step!" On opening night, the producers arranged for Fred Astaire to send Rock a telegram: "Congratulations. You got your step!"

The show opened in San Bernardino on June 13, 1973. Joy and Clarence drove out to see it, as did Mark and George, Rupert Allan and Jack Coates. Everyone was nervous. "I hope I'm not embarrassed for him," Jack said. "Oh shit, oh dear," Tom wrote in big letters across the top of his appointment calendar. "We were scared to death," Tom says. Backstage, he grabbed Rock and said, "You are going to kill them," went out in the audience, sat down and "fell apart."

The show began with Rock and Carol sitting on either side of the stage, getting ready for their wedding. Rock was sitting in a wing-back chair, and a draft in the theater had blown the curtain back against his legs. Suddenly the music started, Rock felt the curtain yanked up and away from him, "and there was this great black pit in front of me," he said. "I nearly died. My Adam's apple was beating in my mouth. Fortunately, the audience started to applaud when they saw us. They applauded so long that I had time to collect my wits and get my Adam's apple back to where it belonged." Rock had the first lyric in the show. He took a deep breath and began.

At intermission, Jack said, "I don't believe this. It felt like five seconds." When the show was over, Mark and George wept, "because he was so good," George says. "Rock was dynamite, not because he had mastered the craft of theater, but because his internal motor was running on high. It was partly sheer panic, he was scared out of his skull, and he was determined this would not be a failure but a success. You put that determination on top of the powerful motor, and Rock just bounced off the walls. He was like a freight train, and Carol rose to the occasion."

At the party after the show, Rock was euphoric. Mark went up to him and said, under his breath, "Loved your bows." Rock smiled and whispered, "All due to you." Rock had always joked that "inside this hulk is a frustrated song and dance man yelling to get out," and it was true. He fell in love with the theater on that first night. He liked the instant reaction from the audience; he liked knowing right away if the jokes made them laugh and the show made them happy. He did not have to wait ten months and check grosses to see how the film was doing. The personal exchange with the audience in the theater was electrifying.

Rock began talking privately about Broadway. That was his next imperative: to get ready to do Broadway. Tom says, "He was like a dope addict. He couldn't get enough of the theater." Carol Burnett said she had never had more fun on a stage than with Rock. "Usually, I like the rehearsals and opening night, and after two more nights I want to close. But with Rock, we had so much fun, we wanted to do it again. Of course, people would break down doors just to watch Rock stand up there and breathe, but he was truly wonderful."

The following spring, Rock and Tom planned a trip to Germany to buy a Porsche and drive through Italy and France, so Rock could show Tom "Yourpe," as he called it. "When you go to a country, you should speak the language," Rock said. "Let's take French lessons." They went to Berlitz, but Tom dropped out after a few lessons. "I'm no good at languages," he told Rock, who continued to the end, which was an all-day, total immersion program in which he was permitted to speak only French. When he came home, his head was spinning. "Don't talk to me," he said to Tom. "Fix me a drink. I can't think."

They flew to Munich, picked up the Porsche, drove through Switzerland and down through Italy to Portofino, where the orange roses were in bloom. Then they headed back along the Italian Riviera, listening to French tapes as they drove, and finally crossed into France, where they arrived at Èze in a rainstorm, out of gas, hungry and thirsty. They walked into a restaurant, Rock opened his mouth to speak the language, but could not call up a single word of French. After a bewildered pause, he said, in English, "Could we have a glass of water?" Rock and Tom both laughed so hard the waiter became offended and walked off.

This was the beginning of Rock and Tom's great expeditions. They took three or four trips a year, to every spot on the earth they had an impulse to visit. Rock had always loved traveling, and now he had a companion who was free to go when he was and who would not arouse suspicion. They took cruises on ocean liners and small private yachts, rented cars and planes, visited Acapulco, Sicily, Baja California, Portugal and Spain, Yugoslavia and Italy, Australia and Japan. At least twice a year, they went to the Mauna Kea on the island of Hawaii, which is one of the most beautiful and luxurious resorts in the world and was Tom's favorite place to "lump up." The only place they wanted to visit but never did was the Greek Islands. Shortly before Rock died, he said to Tom, "I owe you that."

In the summer of 1974, Rock and Carol Burnett did another tour of *I Do! I Do!* They had so enjoyed doing the play in Los Angeles that Joe Hamilton, Carol's husband and the producer, booked halls in Dallas, Washington, D.C., and St. Louis. The performances were sold out in advance. They opened in Dallas, where Rock and Tom rented a house and brought Joy to cook and Joy's friend Peggy to keep her company. Rock would not eat before the show, and afterward it took him hours to come down. He and Tom would sit up and drink, and eventually eat the dinner Joy had cooked and sleep until noon.

In Washington, they performed at the Kennedy Center. A cousin of Tom's arranged for a tour of the White House, and Joy still has a picture of her with Peggy, Rock and Carol Burnett in the Rose Garden. In St. Louis, they were booked into the Municipal Opera House, which was their first outdoor theater.

The first night, we get in bed on stage, just after we've been married. I'm in my nightshirt and Carol's in her nightgown, and after a bit of music, a tender embrace and a kiss, we slide under the covers and the lights black out for the next scene. Except, in St. Louis at

8:30 the sun is still up; the stage is still brightly lit. So under the covers, I look at Carol and say, "Carol . . . we're going to have to have at it, or . . . play tag." So while Carol was cracking up, I slid out of bed and tiptoed behind it to get ready for the next number.

A large contingent of the Scherer family lived in St. Louis, and they planned a family reunion to coincide with Rock's performance at the Muni. "Rock was not enthusiastic," Tom says, "because Scherer had deserted Rock and his mother." But Rock agreed to go, and his mother flew out from California with Mark Miller to see the show and attend the reunion.

Although it was summer, Kay wore her mink and every piece of jewelry Rock had given her. A woman relative, at one point, said to Kay, "I'm so happy that we relinquished Roy to you, because you've done such a wonderful job in raising him."

Kay said, "What do you mean, relinquish?"

"Well, you know we could have kept him, but we felt he should be with you."

Kay flushed and said nothing. On the ride back to the hotel, she fumed, "Relinquish. Relinquish!" Rock and Tom laughed and egged her on until she was in a rage. Tom had another conversation to report: He had been cornered by a Scherer cousin who had asked Tom, "Do you find me an honorable man?"

"Yes, sir, I certainly do," Tom said.

"I'm just a humble farmer. I've farmed all my life, tried to feed the hungry. Do you find me worthy?"

"Yes, I do. Farmers are the backbone of our nation."

The cousin moved closer to Tom. "Could you get me on *Let's Make a Deal?*"

Mark Miller flew back to California with Kay, and on the freeway driving home from the airport, Mark had a conversation with her that haunts him. "Kay drove like a man," Mark says. "She had a T-Bird called 'the juke box,' and her turn signal was constantly flickering. She used all four lanes of the freeway and she'd get angry if the cars didn't move over for her." As she was speeding and weaving, she said to Mark, in a tone pregnant with meaning: "Did you notice that Roy doesn't look like *any* of the Scherers?" She stared ahead.

191

"Katherine," Mark said, bracing himself for the next lane change, "do you mean what I think you do?"

"Mmmm," Kay said, and flicked on the signal.

"She didn't confirm or deny," Mark says, "and she was not the kind of woman you could question. You'd get silence. Like mother, like son. But it was odd that she brought it up. She didn't volunteer conversation."

Mark suspected that Rock had not been Scherer's son, that Kay may have been pregnant by another man and when Scherer found out, he deserted the family. But the birth certificate on file in Cook County, Illinois, shows Roy Harold Scherer as the father of Roy Harold Scherer, Jr., born on November 17, 1925. When Kay's relatives were told about Kay's conversation with Mark, they said they had no knowledge of what Mark suspected. "If it's true," one said, "that's something Kay took to her grave."

In 1974, Rock drew up a will that provided for all his assets to be placed in a trust fund upon his death. All income from the trust would go to Tom Clark, and if Tom died, to George Nader, and if George died, to Mark Miller. Rock knew that Mark and George pooled their funds, so it did not matter which was named ahead of the other. When all three had died, the residue of the trust would go to charities. What was strange was that Rock decided only one person should benefit from the trust. Why did he not divide up portions among the people he cared about? Mark says, "It was like Rock to make it all or nothing. He didn't want people to get lazy and live off the money he'd worked hard to earn."

The following year, Rock hired a new business manager, Wallace Sheft. After four years of large earnings on *McMillan and Wife,* Rock was in debt and didn't understand why. Sheft, who'd been introduced to Rock by Buddy Hackett, flew out from New York to meet with Rock and Tom. Sheft is a tall man with thinning dark hair, who does not waste words and sprinkles Yiddish phrases in his speech. Rock told him he was apprehensive because Doris Day and other stars had been swindled by people who managed their funds. Sheft said, "I have a small C.P.A. firm in New York, where I personally oversee and control everything. My wife and I are plain people. I don't need your money and don't want it."

He said his goal would be to make Rock financially independent, so he could decide to make a picture not because he needed the money but because he wanted to do the project.

Rock and Tom looked at each other and decided, right there, to place their finances in Wally Sheft's hands. They learned, later, that Sheft's nickname as a kid was "tight wallets." He has an obsession with saving money and getting the best deal. When Rock and Tom wanted to buy something, they had to clear it with Wally, who wasn't satisfied unless it was a bargain. He determined that Rock would need $250,000 a year to maintain his life-style, and eventually, Sheft would be able to generate that from investments.

As part of the housecleaning and refurbishing that followed Tom's arrival at Beverly Crest, it was inevitable that Joy, who had been with Rock for fourteen years, would have to go. Tom was irritated that at dinner parties, "Joy would be having drinks with the company." He was annoyed, also, that she was drinking on the job. "We'd come home and find unmade beds and cigarettes in the ashtrays, and Joy was in her room, drunk. She should have been fired, but Rock couldn't fire people."

Joy was unhappy from the moment Tom moved in. She felt he was imperious and condescending to her, and at night, "when he was drinking, he was downright nasty." The friction became intolerable. One night, when Rock and Tom came in to dinner, Joy was barely able to navigate from the stove to the table. She wobbled over, carrying a pot, braced herself against a chair and started serving tiny peas and mashed potatoes. She dipped into the pot for the peas, but she missed Rock's plate and spooned them onto the table. Tom could not help laughing, "watching Joy unable to hit the plate," but Rock picked her up, carried her down the hall to her room and threw her on the bed. "I don't want to see you again until you've been sober for two days," he shouted.

The next morning, Joy could not remember what had happened. "Did I do something wrong last night?" she asked Tom.

"Did you ever."

Rock was off Joy after that, and once he was off someone, it was final. He felt his own drinking had never interfered with his work, but Joy's drinking was.

Not long afterward, there was a confrontation between Tom and

Joy in which Tom yelled at her and she threw a box of cottage cheese across the room. Tom went to Rock and said, "You have got to deal with Joy. I can't handle it anymore."

Rock told Joy he wanted an all-male house. He was getting older and wanted to be free to do as he pleased in his home—to walk naked if he felt like it. "When I come in those doors, I want to be private." Joy asked the handyman to help her load her things into his pickup truck and drive her to her son's house.

After Joy left, there was a flux of people through the Castle, assorted housemen and butlers who were troublesome and did not last, until James Wright was hired in 1978.

Rock turned fifty in 1975, and Tom threw a costume birthday party that he later said was "the prettiest party we ever had." He removed all the furniture from the house and stored it in the playroom. He turned the red room into a nightclub, with a dance floor, a band, a bar and little tables. The big living room became a dining room, with eight tables covered with brown tablecloths, silver candelabra and chocolate-brown candles.

Dozens of ficus trees in pots were brought in and lit with tiny bulbs. There were so many flowers that the air was perfumed, and at Rock's table, an electric train was going round and round because Rock had never had one.

Rock and Tom had a screaming argument several hours before the party. Tom was growing more nervous as the arrival time approached, and Rock was trying to undermine his preparations.

"We can't use the playroom—why'd you put all the furniture in there?" Rock said.

"Where do you expect me to put it? Shut up."

"Fuck you."

"Fuck you."

Tom slammed the door, left the house and drove down to a T-shirt store and had them make up a shirt that said, in bold letters, ROCK IS A PRICK. He gave the shirt to Rock for his birthday present.

Rock stayed upstairs as the guests arrived. The most popular costume that year was Arab dress, and Buddy Hackett, Rupert Allan and Mark Miller came as Arabs. Tom wore kilts. Carol Burnett and Joe Hamilton came as flappers because Rock had been born in the twenties. Olive Behrendt, Roddy McDowall, Nancy Walker and David Craig came as fans, and stood by the door, screaming and asking for autographs. Juliet Mills and Michael Miklenda arrived on a motorcycle, which they drove right through the front door and onto the patio.

When everyone had arrived, Tom gathered them in the red room and signaled the band. They struck up "You Must Have Been a Beautiful Baby," and Rock made his entrance, strutting down the grand staircase wearing a diaper. Everyone whistled and howled. Rock greeted people, then went back upstairs and came down in the ROCK IS A PRICK T-shirt, which he wore the rest of the evening.

"It was one of those parties that worked," Tom says. The fires were blazing and the tiny lights winking and the music playing and drinks and food were flowing. Rock and Tom kept circulating. "We both worked our tails off," Tom says. "You gotta work the room." In the middle of the evening, they met at the bar and had a drink.

"Thanks, babe," Rock said. "It's a great party."

Rock was in his glory. He had survived a half century, and on this night, he was a star among stars. Heaven and earth were in the proper place.

CHAPTER 11

The most dangerous thing for an actor is to refuse to listen to anyone else, to feel you know more than anybody. You become your own worst enemy. I'm sure it's a manifestation of insecurity. It takes a great deal of security to say "I don't know" without feeling embarrassed, or "What does that word mean?" or "I don't understand." Most insecure people will say "Yes, I know all about that," thereby shutting off learning. They're losers.

In December of 1975, Rock went to London to perform in *I Do! I Do!* with Juliet Prowse. The producers had contacted Tom and asked if Rock would help them start a subscription theater. Tom said, "Okay. We want a riverfront suite at the Savoy, a car and driver and five hundred pounds a week." Then he thought, "Who the hell will we get as our leading lady?" Carol Burnett was unavailable, Lee Remick, who lived in London, said no, and then an agent for Juliet Prowse called and said she was interested. Rock and Tom were invited to fly to Las Vegas to see Juliet's show at the Desert Inn.

When Rock and Tom arrived and saw Juliet's name on the marquee, Rock said, "Do you realize, we've come to audition a headliner?" After the show, Rock and Tom went to her dressing room and Rock said, "I think you're wonderful. Would you please do *I Do! I Do!* with me?"

The three of them went to London and Toronto, and became inseparable for the three-month run. The reviews were bad, but they did good business. "The weight of Rock's name brought people in, if only from curiosity," Juliet says. Juliet was an accomplished dancer and singer, and she was feminine and romantic with her long, supple limbs and curly reddish-blond hair. She found Rock "easy to work with and such a hard worker. He gave one hundred percent all the time. As a dancer, he had two left feet. He was big and had big feet and they were clumsy. But as an acting partner, he was so sincere, you really *felt* love towards him in those tender moments." With many actors, she says, "nothing comes out of the eyes. One week Rock was sick and I had to do the play with an understudy. He was like a wall. I got nothing back, although he sang beautifully."

Every night after the show, Juliet had dinner with Rock and Tom in a restaurant that would stay open for them. Juliet says there was a lot of tension between Rock and Tom, "and it was fueled by all the drinking. Tom would say, 'Another tiny triple?' and out would come another round of triple gin martinis with the orange twist."

Juliet taught yoga, and lured the men into trying a session with her. "They got hysterical, and I was laughing, watching them try to do asanas. Rock was not that flexible. He did it once and said, 'Thank you.'" Juliet and Rock did needlepoint together, and they discovered that both had a "roving eye. Tom was a one-person person, but Rock and I liked variety."

When Rock and Tom came home from London, Mark and George noticed that something had turned between them. What had started as good-natured sparring—"You're wrong." "No, I'm not." "Yes, you are!"—was growing unpleasant. Rock and Tom were bickering constantly, each trying to prove the other wrong. "Rock loved a good fight, and Tom was a fighter," George says, but Rock had a nasty streak that was surfacing and Tom had two personalities. "He was a wonderful monster. When he was sober, he was kind, loyal, generous and incredibly charming. When he was drunk, he was cruel and insulting. He would cut your heart out and not look back." The split character made him unpredictable. "We learned through the years not to cross him," Mark says. "The minute you crossed him, you had problems, because Rock would turn around and side with the monster."

Rock and Tom never fought about important issues. "Something major would come along and they'd unite," Mark says. What they fought over was trivia. When James Wright was hired, Tom went out and bought uniforms, but Rock told James not to wear them.

"Get your ass in that uniform," Tom said.

"Take it off," Rock said. "Don't pay attention to Tom."

"Don't pay attention to Rock."

Mark Miller was often caught in the middle. Rock would come into his office and say, "We're not going on the *Q.E.II*. Cancel the reservation." Tom would come in later and say, "Book the reservation. Don't tell Rock. And don't tell Wally Sheft it will cost thirteen thousand to go to England. I've never been on a ship and I want to go."

Mark would call both of them into the office and tap on the table. "Committee meeting. Are you going on the *Q.E.II?*" They'd fight it out, and when Mark had his answer, he'd call the travel agent and Wally. "I learned not to be part of their deviousness. I'd make them face each other."

Jim Gagner, a young man who worked in the Castle for a year, says he found it difficult to have a meal with Rock and Tom. "I'd feel so much tension, I couldn't eat. Occasionally, the anger softened to gruff, like when they were playing Spite and Malice and would fight over whose card it was. But most of the time, they were like the characters in *Who's Afraid of Virginia Woolf?* Tom would say, 'I've ordered you this beautiful lunch. Isn't it marvelous?' And Rock would say, 'I'm not hungry.'"

The quarreling was exacerbated by alcohol. When Rock drank, he became "a viper," Mark says, and made Tom his whipping boy. Tom would walk into the room and Rock would taunt him. "Oh, it's Tommy Truth. What lies do you have to tell us today?"

"Fuck you," Tom would say, and walk out of the room. In front of friends, Tom would say, "I hope he dies a terrible death, bald. I hope he doesn't wake up. We'll all be better off and I will be rich, thank God. I can do what I want."

Most of their friends learned to ignore the bickering, and had no doubts that underneath it was a powerful bond. Jon Epstein, a close friend who produced *McMillan and Wife*, says, "People can spend their lives bickering and really love each other. I figured it would go on forever." Stockton Briggle, who directed Rock in *Camelot*, says, "Tom loved and protected Rock magnificently, but Rock didn't want so much protection. Tom had given up a successful career to be 'Mrs. Rock Hudson.' It's hard to respect somebody who gives up his own life and starts doing everything for you. They were never able to face this. They just drank more, socialized more and took more and more trips."

In the summer of 1976, America's bicentennial year, Rock toured in a production of *John Brown's Body* by Stephen Vincent Benét. It was a narrative poem that had been staged once before with Tyrone Power and Dame Judith Anderson. Rock had seen the performance with Bob Preble, and had become infatuated with Power. "All he could talk about was Tyrone Power," Preble says. Rock eventually met Power, and they flirted with getting together but never did.

When Tom committed Rock to do *John Brown's Body*, Rock was thrilled: "I've never had such beautiful words to say." They arranged for Claire Trevor and Leif Erickson to be the co-stars, and set off in high spirits. But the tour had to be canceled because of poor management. They were booked at college campuses, but most of the campuses were deserted in the summer, and they played to empty houses. Rock received the best reviews of his career, however. Flo Allen called Rock and read him the review in *Variety*: "Hudson proves himself a fine actor, revealing a strong side to his dramatic talent that has seldom been explored by films. . . . Hudson should now be able to take his place in the ranks of exceptional stage performers."

Rock wept when he heard it, and Jon Epstein had the review framed. Tom says, "After decades of bad reviews, I can't tell you what this meant."

The show had a chorus of young actors who traveled by bus, while Rock, Claire and Tom traveled by limousine and Leif flew his own plane. When they had their first night off, in Spokane, Washington, Tom gathered the company in the hotel lounge, where there was a piano bar. "I made it my job to be the social director," Tom says. "The star has to keep the company happy, and make everyone a family and keep things fun, or it shows in the production." Tom said to the young actors, "Okay, you kids, we don't know you. Get up and sing!" They took turns singing, and then they said to Rock and Claire, "We don't know you, get up and sing." Rock sang "Send in the Clowns," Claire sang "Moanin' Low" and Tom sang, "You Are My Sunshine." Tom says, "We all fell in love, it was one of the magic nights of all time. The hotel guests started leaning over the balcony and applauding. After this, we said, get rid of the limo, we're gonna travel on the bus with the kids."

When the show played in San Francisco, Rock and Tom had dinner with a group of men that included Armistead Maupin, who'd been introduced to Rock by Jack Coates. Armistead is a writer, a well-known gay figure in San Francisco, whose multivolume novel

Tales of the City appears in serial form in the *San Francisco Chronicle*. For Armistead, Rock Hudson had been an important model. "Rock was manly, he was successful, kind-hearted and funny and he was gay," Armistead says. "He'd been able to surmount the obstacles that face a gay person and had made it big."

The night that Armistead had dinner with Rock was, by coincidence, the night before his first column was to run in the *Chronicle*. After dinner, they walked back to Rock's suite at the Fairmont, and Rock secretly went to the desk and obtained a copy of the next day's paper. When everyone was seated and supplied with drinks, Rock stood up and gave a reading of the first installment of *Tales of the City*. Armistead was "blown away," hearing his words brought to life and amplified with meaning by Rock Hudson. There were sparks of affection and admiration between them, and it appeared to be the beginning of a friendship.

The following night, Armistead met Rock and Tom again for dinner at their favorite restaurant in the city, La Bourgogne. Armistead told Rock he had just come out publicly and with his family. "I've been enjoying my life more, and feeling in control of it for the first time." He suggested that if Rock told the truth about his life, perhaps in a book, "it could make a big difference to a lot of people. It would have an enormous impact in destroying some of the stereotypes about homosexuals. If you told the whole story, it would be amazing."

Tom Clark said, "Not until my mother dies."

They laughed, and moved on, and Armistead sensed that Rock was intrigued but "wasn't ready."

The following year, 1977, Rock toured in *Camelot*, and it was, in Tom's words, "the best summer that ever was." King Arthur was Rock's favorite role. It was a showy part, with challenging opportunities to act and wonderful songs, and Rock identified with Arthur. The piece was autumnal, about the glory that was, and it resonated with the autumnal mood in Rock's life.

Tom and Rock flew to New York to choose a director and members of the cast. The producer, Bill Ross, had a close relationship with Stockton Briggle, who had directed musicals for him before. Stockton is originally from Texas, an articulate man with sandy hair, fair skin and wire-frame glasses. He has a gift for seeing the humor in a situation and a zealous love of his work that is contagious. An admirer of Rock's, he was eager to direct *Camelot*, but Ross said, "I don't think you got much chance. They're seeing lots of big directors."

Ross set up an appointment for Stockton with Rock and Tom, and to prepare, Stockton locked himself in his apartment for two days with every book he could find on King Arthur. Immersed in the spirit of Camelot, he went to meet Rock and Tom at the Plaza, "my heart beating wildly." Rock was sitting with his feet up on the coffee table, and said, "Hi!" Stockton recalls, "He was a man of few words, and his 'Hi!' had a wonderful ring." Rock said, "Well, what's your point of view on *Camelot*?" Two hours later, Stockton was still talking. He said he saw the play as a "homoerotic three-person relationship" between Arthur, Guinevere and Lancelot. Arthur and Lancelot loved each other and both were in love with Guinevere, and she was torn by her love for the two of them and it ended by toppling the empire.

The next day, Stockton received a call that he would direct Rock in *Camelot*. "It was the greatest thrill of my life," Stockton says.

They had three months before rehearsals began, and Stockton flew to California to work with Rock. They sat in bathing suits by the pool and went over the book, analyzing why the story had never worked. Stockton says, "It was a big spectacle that had relied on the great voice of Richard Burton and the tricks he could do. But the story itself, the emotional curve of the piece, didn't work properly. It had been an empty hit."

Stockton remembers a night when he and Rock sat on the floor around the coffee table in the red room and went over the book page by page. They cut and rearranged scenes and rewrote lines to bring out the power of the emotions each character felt. "We put aside the king and queen nonsense," Stockton says. "We were building real, in-life characters, who had depths of feeling and moments of passion you could identify with." The hours flew, and when Stockton looked at his watch, it was 6 A.M. He and Rock felt intoxicated with the intimacy that comes from a creative collaboration. "It was almost a sexual thing," Stockton says. "Rock emanated such power when he was thinking and working. I've always believed a director has to seduce an actor into falling in love with him, into seeing his dream. The actor surrenders himself up to the director, and that's when you can work magic. But with Rock, it was the opposite. I fell in love with him, and at six in the morning, we closed our scripts, looked at each other and just burst into laughter. We knew we had done something we could be excited about."

The tour opened in Dallas, then went to Cohasset, Massachusetts, and Westbury, Long Island, zigzagging its way across the country. They played in tents and theaters-in-the-round, and, Tom says, "We were in love with the cast again and were a family."

The emotional peak of *Camelot* came each night when Rock, as the aging king who has lost everything—Guinevere, Lancelot, his kingdom—speaks to a little boy, Tom, about keeping the dream alive. He has a song where he asks the boy to tell everyone he knows the story of Camelot. Rising to his feet, Rock sings about that one magical moment in history that was Camelot.

Every night, when they came to that scene, Stockton would break down and cry in the wings, and Rock and the boy would weep onstage. "Rock had a problem with snot when he cried," Stockton says. "This was a ten-snot scene. It ran down his face, and I told him, don't try to wipe it, just let the snot go, people can't see it. When you get offstage, you can blow your nose." One night, Rock came off, grabbed a handkerchief and forgot to cut off his wireless mike. He blew his nose, and the audience heard "one of the great nose blows of history." The honking sound echoed through the theater, and then came the voice of Rock Hudson: "Damn, that felt good!"

Just before the tour ended, Rock called Mark in California—called him personally, instead of having Tom do it—and said, "I want a beauties party when we get home. Could you arrange it? Have a party with beauties waiting for me at the house."

Mark did as he was told. He invited about ten friends, and asked a gay optometrist in Hollywood to round up fifty beautiful young men and bring them to a swimming party and barbecue. Mark ordered a cake from Cake Art, decorated with characters from Camelot. When Rock and Tom got off the plane, they took a limousine to the Castle, walked through the door and saw fifty tanned young men in swimsuits splashing in the pool and lying on the patio. The dogs barked and ran to Rock and jumped on him, but none of the beauties stepped forward. They whispered and stared and smiled. "Rock loved it," Mark says. "Tom was less amused. He went upstairs to the bedroom, and his friends came up and had drinks with him."

Armistead Maupin was in Los Angeles for the party, and was dazzled. It was like being at Hugh Hefner's Playboy mansion, except all the perfect-looking creatures were male. "There were some of the best-looking men I'd seen in my life," Armistead says. Rock took him aside and said, "Look at that one. Look at those legs. He's an eleven on a scale of ten."

"Who are they all?" Armistead said.

"The blonds are named Scott and the brunets are named Grant," Rock said.

Armistead would write about Rock at this party, thinly disguised, in *Tales of the City*: "He was truly magnificent, a lumbering titan in this garden of younger, prettier men."

In the middle of the party, Rock came up to Armistead in the kitchen. "There's a man outside who says he knows you." Rock paused. "He's got a *woman* with him." Armistead went to the door and saw Warren Seabury, a public-relations man whom he knew and had told he was going to a party at Rock Hudson's. Warren had wanted to come, and had figured the best way to get into the party was to show up with an actress. There, on his arm, was Michelle Phillips, in a low-cut dress, looking ravishing. Rock had not known who she was.

"I don't know how to explain this," Armistead said. "Rock has just come back from a tour, and he left instructions that he wanted the fifty best-looking men in town waiting for him at his house."

Michelle laughed. "I understand. I've often left those instructions myself."

In the fall of 1977, Rock's mother died of a stroke. The year before, Rock had sent her on a bridge cruise around the world. She had caught the flu twice and never recovered her strength. She became bedridden, and Rock refused to go see her. "I can't handle it," he told Mark. "Will you go down there?" Rock did not see his mother the last six months of her life, and he said, later, he was glad he hadn't. "Because I remember her as she was—a real goin' Jessie, driving, speeding, a whirlwind."

Every two weeks, Mark would drive down to Newport Beach to make sure Kay was all right, shop for groceries, see that the house-keeper was there and had enough money. The housekeeper was a Central American woman named Bezelia, who was a cousin of the housekeeper who worked for Claire Trevor. Bezelia was loving and kind to Kay, but when Kay saw Mark, she said, "Why won't my son come?"

"Darling, he's busy. He's snowed under with work and can't get away," Mark said.

In October, Claire Trevor called Rock late at night and said, "Your mother's had a stroke." Rock and Tom were drunk, but they got in the car and raced down to Newport Beach. Kay was dead when they arrived. Rock went into the bedroom by himself for a time, and came out. He did not cry, but he was devastated. His mother was the only blood relative he had cared for or felt connected to. When he was growing up, it had been the two of them against the world, but he did not speak about it. "It was much too private," Tom says. "He would never expose those emotions to anyone." Occasionally, Mark would catch Rock staring into space, but that was the only outward sign that he was grieving.

Rock had just started shooting *Wheels*, a mini-series, and the producer offered to change the schedule so Rock could have a few days off, but Rock said no. He wanted to work, and went to the studio the next morning.

Mark and George made arrangements for the funeral, but Rock asked them not to go. They were stunned, but complied. When December came, Rock said he could not have Christmas at home, it would be too painful without his mother. "Let's get outa town," he said to Tom, and they took the train to New Mexico. Rock dropped all his rituals, he didn't get a tree or give presents.

Rock had begun what Mark was to call "the decline." He was drinking so much gin that the alcohol seeped out of his pores and "his breath was awful." He became bloated. Mark found it impossible to do any business with Rock or Tom until noon. "I'd make plans with them in the morning and at two P.M. I'd learn they hadn't absorbed a word I'd said. They'd stay up late every night and fall into bed dead-drunk. By two in the afternoon, Rock would wake up enough to start needlepointing in my office, and Tom would watch old movies." When Rock was shooting, he'd go right on drinking all night but would get up for a 7 A.M. call. His first words when he came home were "Get me a *drank*."

George grew annoyed and angry, watching Rock destroy himself.

"He was given so much; he had the ability to portray greatness. Only a few people on earth are given the gift to portray what is good and noble, and he was throwing it away."

In April of 1978, Mark and George were at the Mauna Kea in Hawaii for a week—a present from Rock—when Rock and Tom surprised them by stopping there on their way home from Japan. Rock and Tom got off the plane drunk, continued to drink in their room, went to the dining room with Mark and George and had more drinks, until the time change and the alcohol rendered them inoperative. Tom stood up to leave and went crashing over backward into the empty table behind him. Mark walked Tom to his room, leaving George with Rock, who couldn't articulate words and couldn't locate his mouth with his fork. George looked away, and when he turned his eyes back, Rock's head was in his plate. Mark had returned, and he and George got Rock on his feet, wiped the food off his face and walked him out through the crowded dining room, which had fallen dead silent.

While Rock and Tom snored it off in their room, Mark and George tried to settle their nerves by taking a walk on the beach. "We were mortified," George says. "We'd been brought up not to make a spectacle in public. Rock and Tom didn't care. It was the arrogance of being famous."

Rock's temperament, which had always been buoyant, was turning dark. His favorite expression was "Fuck him, I hope he dies." When a friend gave a dinner party for him, Rock said afterward, "Fuck him, I hope he dies." He was envious of anyone else's success or good fortune. If he read that another star had a sixty-five-foot yacht, he'd say, "Where does he get the money for a yacht? I hope it sinks." When he saw Richard Gere in *Bent* in New York, he came out irritable. "What's all the fuss about? I don't think Gere was that great."

Some of his friends thought Rock couldn't handle becoming an older man. In ten more years, he would be an old man. "This is a cruel business," Stockton Briggle says. "You're handed the world, and when it's taken away from you, what do you do?" For twenty years, Rock had had his pick of the most beautiful men in the country, and now, when young men spoke to him, there was a hint of patronization.

Rock's energy went into one-upmanship and fighting with Tom.

"He didn't put film projects together or do creative things," George says, "he drank and fought with Tom." When they had parties, Rock started drinking before the guests arrived. For the first hour, he was jovial and gracious. "Want a *drank*? What'll you have?" He would serve people and get things rolling, then he would settle into a chair and hold out his glass. He'd rattle the ice cubes, waving the glass in the air, until Tom would take it and fix him another. Tom would start watering the drinks, and Rock would take a sip and swear. "Jesus Christ!" He would stand, go to the bar and throw out the drink. "I see I gotta make my own *dranks*."

He wouldn't allow dinner to be served until ten. When everyone was seated at the table, Rock would tell anecdotes, and as he was getting to the punch line, Tom would interrupt: "No, no, you're telling it wrong."

"No, I'm not. I know the story . . ."

"You're telling it wrong!"

"All right, you tell the fucking story."

At some point in the evening, Tom would go upstairs and pass out, but Rock would stay to the end, no matter how drunk he was, afraid he might miss something.

Just before Christmas in 1978, Rock and Tom hired James Wright as their butler. James came to the interview with misgivings. "I didn't want to work for a movie star, because they're temperamental," James says. He had worked for William Goetz, the head of Universal, and for A. H. Meadows, the oilman in Dallas. In both positions, he says, "I had to be smartly dressed all the time in a black suit and tie, and I would say 'Madam' and 'Sir.'" James was born in England, raised in an orphanage and was trained to be the kind of butler you see in old movies, who walks into the elegant drawing room carrying a silver tray with glasses of sherry and says, "Madam, dinner will be served in fifteen minutes."

Tom began the interview with James, then Rock took over, gave James a tour of the house and said, "When can you move in?" James moved in with his little dog, Victoria, on Christmas Eve, thinking he would not last two weeks. "It wasn't me," he says. "I'm used to a house where it's debonair and sophisticated, and beautiful tables are laid. Mr. Hudson liked people to be casual, and he sometimes ate standing up at the refrigerator. I could wear anything I wanted, shorts and T-shirts. And I had two bosses, which was difficult. Mr. Hudson was the main guy to me, and he was easy. Mr. Clark was fluffy and fanatical. Everything had to be just so. He'd say, 'Dust dust dust! Why is there dust upstairs?' I'd say, 'We had a wind today, that's why. It was cleaned this morning.'"

James settled in, grew fond of "Mr. Hudson" and found that he liked the casual house. He discovered a restaurant, Café Theodore, where he would go every morning for breakfast. He made friends, whom he would have to the house if Rock and Tom were away. Rock told him, "I want you to use the house. Give parties. Show any movies you want."

James brought a note of cheerfulness and stability into the Castle. When asked "How are you?" James would say, enunciating crisply, "I'm *extremely* well, thank you!" He was not easily rattled. "I don't let things wear on me. I try and carry on." He likes propriety and form, yet there is an unconventional spirit underneath. He imitates people and makes wry, cutting remarks, and when he gets carried away, his voice rises to falsetto, his stomach shakes with laughter and he turns red in the face, red to the roots of his white hair.

Rock took James into "the family" almost at once. James soon knew everything that was happening in the house, because the heart of the house is the kitchen and James was always there, standing behind the counter, indomitable. He proved he could be trusted not to talk to the press, and that he was loyal, a man of his word.

As Rock's interest in theater grew, it was inevitable that he and Tom would spend more time in New York. In May of 1979, Rock bought an apartment that Tom had found in the Beresford on Central Park West and Eighty-first Street. Rock liked to wander through the city and ride the subways; he enjoyed the small-town feeling of the neighborhood, where he could walk to the market and the drugstore and know everyone by name. He and Tom went to plays, saw theater people and moved in a new circle of friends. "We'd gotten in a rut in L.A., and we loved the change of scenery," Tom says. "We were really social. We did not stay home a night."

In June, they left for a five-month tour of *On the Twentieth Century*, a play Rock had insisted on doing but which he did not enjoy as the run wore on. One of his co-stars was Dean Dittman, who would become a close friend for the rest of his life. Dean is a large man who once weighed three hundred pounds, a gifted character actor who played Daddy Warbucks in *Annie*. Gregarious and jovial, he loves to cook and entertain, and when the show closed, he invited Rock and Tom to many dinners at his apartment.

In Chicago, Rock learned that the show was in financial trouble, and took a pay cut so the production could stay afloat until they reached Los Angeles, where they had a subscription audience. One night in Los Angeles, Rock arranged to meet Tom for dinner at Joe Allen's after the show. Tom says, "Rock *was* able to drive from the theater to the restaurant, but only because I had dropped bread crumbs." They ate dinner, and went to Dean Dittman's for a cast party. They had a lot to drink at Dean's and then started home in two cars. Tom drove the Mercedes—thinking Rock was right behind him in the Seville—got home first and collapsed on the bed.

Rock fell asleep at the wheel and crashed into a palm tree on Doheny Road, demolishing the Cadillac. He crawled out the door and started walking up the street with shards of glass embedded in his forehead. A milkman spotted him and called the police.

"I'm okay," Rock told them.

"Who was driving?" the policeman said.

"Tom Clark."

The police took Rock home and went back to search the bushes for Tom Clark, who was asleep upstairs. James tried to wake Tom but couldn't, so he called Mark and George. "Get right over here, there's been an accident!" Mark and George took Rock to the hospital to have the glass removed, and George marveled that Rock had not been seriously hurt. "Another example of the angel on his shoulder."

In the early years, when Rock had been single-mindedly pursuing his career, sex had taken second place, but as his career waned, sex became predominant. Rock thrived on intrigue and conquest. "The minute the prey fell into the lair, the chase was over and a new one began," a friend says. Rock liked multiple partners, and had trysts with airline stewards in San Diego and with carpenters and maître d's in New York. He gave all-male parties, like the beauties party, where he would not know most of the guests.

Jim Gagner met Rock at one of the "boy parties." Jim had been a

roommate of Armistead Maupin's; he needed a job while he was trying to break into screenwriting, and Rock hired him to transfer his
35-mm film collection to videotape. Jim was Rock's type: a blue-eyed
blond, who eventually would become a yoga instructor. When he
met Rock, Jim was struck by "the power of his libido. His sexual
energy was so extreme, you could feel the heat. It made my ears
burn." Jim says that Rock's sexuality sucked people in like a black
hole. "If he could have you, he did. His sexual orientation was lots of
it. He could have sex once or twice a day with several different people."

Jim recalls how, at their first meeting, Rock had fixed his eyes on
Jim's and said, in a low, sensual voice, "Hiya, come on in." It was
clear from his look and tone what he was thinking, and Jim felt flattered and sexually aroused. "We had a great conversation and two
minutes later, someone else came by and I saw Rock turn on the
same heat."

After their talk, Mark Miller let Jim know Rock was interested in
him. "It was tempting—it made me think about being queen of the
Castle, having all the money I wanted, being able to travel. But all
kinds of warning signals went off. You could smell the poison coming
out of Rock's system." Jim was put off by Rock's drinking and what
he saw as Rock's "astronomical ego," and resisted a physical relationship. He worked at the Castle, but "it was a roller-coaster ride.
Rock was alternately nasty and charming." Jim would be in the playroom, working on the tape machines, and Rock would come in and
say, "Get that shit outa here! What are you taping that for?" The next
day, he would look in, all smiles, and say, "Why don't you take a
break? Let's go in the kitchen and make lemon crepes." And they
would cook together and laugh and Jim would be charmed again. "I
felt sorry for him. It was sad to see a fifty-three-year-old star so driven
to follow his dick around."

In July of 1978, Rock went to San Francisco for the weekend with
Tom, Mark and George. They had dinner with Jim Gagner and Ar-
mistead Maupin at a beautiful house on Telegraph Hill called the
"Duck House" because it had a frieze of geese flying around the top
of the building. After dinner, Armistead took everyone to the Club
Fugazi to see a revue he had co-written, *Beach Blanket Babylon*.
Then Mark and George went back to the Fairmont to sleep, and

Rock and Tom went on with Armistead for a sightseeing tour of gay clubs.

The next morning, at breakfast in the Fairmont, Rock gave a detailed report which startled and horrified George, who wrote in his journal, "My GOD." George felt Rock was getting a kick out of "shocking the hell out of me, like I was a fuddy-duddy, the straitlaced country cousin." George had always chosen to stay away from gay gatherings, and the description of clubs where mass sex was taking place between strangers seemed to him the beginning of the end of civilization. This was a time when gay sex had reached a height of tolerance and permissiveness, and the awful irony, of course, is that this was when the AIDS epidemic was taking root.

George was upset that Rock had gone to these clubs where he could be recognized, and had even signed his name. Rock said, "I wanted to see it, you should see everything in life." Rock admitted, though, that he was startled at how promiscuous things had become.

The tour had started out tame, at the I-Beam, a gay discotheque filled with sleek and muscular young men in tank tops. "A middle-aged man with a paunch and a red V-neck sweater didn't get noticed," Armistead says.

The next stop was a club called the Black and Blue. Tom Clark took one look inside and said, "This is too much for me. I'm going back to the hotel. You guys go on." The Black and Blue had a motorcycle hanging from the ceiling, and men in boots and black leather jackets standing around the bar. Every night at midnight, they played "Thus Spake Zarathustra," the theme song from *2001*. In the back of the club, pieces of corrugated metal were suspended from the ceiling, creating three spaces where orgies would take place. It was like a scene from Bosch: a pile of naked arms, legs, backs and wriggling behinds. Armistead and Rock stood against the wall, watching, and Rock thought it was funny. Armistead remembers thinking, "How ironic. I'm standing with the man who was *the* sex symbol of the world for two decades, and nobody's paying any attention to him. We could walk through this place like two women—completely invisible." Armistead leaned over and pinched Rock playfully.

"Is that you?" Rock said.

"Yes."

"Just checking."

The next stop was the South of Market Club, which was known, locally, as the Glory Holes. Rock signed up to join the club, using his real name. "You go through the motions of becoming a member, and then they let you into this sexual wonderland," Armistead says. The club re-creates the way, historically, homosexuals used to meet in public bathrooms. There would be a hole drilled in the wall between two stalls, and a man would stick his organ through the hole and see if it aroused any response from the other side. The technique had been dangerous, and at the Glory Holes, the proprietors devised a way to make it safe, or so they thought.

The club was a maze of plywood booths, connected by holes. There were three sides to a booth, with a hole in each side. "People would stick their weenies through the holes, and sometimes it would be stereophonic weenie," Armistead says. The club was softly lit with red lights, and there was a balcony where you could look down and watch the action in the booths. Armistead told Rock, "You're on your own. I'll meet you back on the balcony in forty-five minutes."

Armistead went off through the club, and when he came back, Rock was leaning against the railing, looking down into the booths.

"Have you been enjoying yourself?" Armistead said.

"Nothing happened," Rock said with a laugh.

After the Glory Holes, Rock took a taxi back to the Fairmont. "We'd had a man's night out, and it gave Rock a sense of freedom," Armistead says. "I think Rock felt he couldn't have done this in L.A. He valued that freedom, and I respected Tom for allowing it."

The Glory Holes, like other gay clubs and bathhouses, shut down a few years later, after men began dying of AIDS. Armistead says, "It may sound like it was the end of civilization, but there were good people there, people with intelligence and humor. There was a trust and a communal spirit that was very nourishing." He said the clubs were formed at a time when a great many men were coming out, and needed to feel accepted by a large number of other men. "The place was a real escape," he says. "No matter what your worries of the day had been, you could find complete abandonment there."

CHAPTER 12

I like to work with new actors; it's sort of a little game I have with myself. I love to watch them, to see what they do, what they come up with, if they're inventive. Their ideas may not work all the time, but it's important that they have something more than an ability to memorize lines.

In 1981, Rock agreed to do another series for NBC, *The Devlin Connection*, about a father and son detective team. Rock had sworn, after *McMillan and Wife*, that he would never do another TV series. He told a reporter, "As you get older, you learn to keep your mouth shut more, because you never know how badly you're going to embarrass yourself later."

NBC had wanted Rock on the air again and had done everything to persuade him. Rock's explanation to friends was "I like to work." For the co-star—his son—he chose a young and inexperienced actor, Jack Scalia, who had worked with him in a mini-series, *The Star Maker*. Rock had taken a liking to Jack and gotten to know him and his wife. Twenty minutes after Jack was told he had the part, Rock called him and said, "It's important for us to start a father-son relationship, so it will carry over onto the screen." Jack lived a few blocks from Rock on Central Park West, so they began taking walks through New York.

Jack is from Brooklyn, six one, with dark curly hair and the scrappy charm of the street kid who's grown wise, the jock with heart. When he was growing up, Jack and his friends used to taunt anyone who was acting cocky: "Who do you think you are, Rock Hudson?" Jack was a pitcher for the Montreal Astros, but he had to retire when his arm was injured. He became a model in New York, and took his first acting class in 1980.

When he started his walks with Rock, Jack found that Rock had "a privacy wall around him. It was like a curtain; he wouldn't let many people in and if he did, it was not for long. He'd let you in, let you in, let you in, then say, that's enough. I could sit and talk with him for hours, and not know any more than when we started."

From the first, Jack kissed Rock on the cheek and hugged him, "because that's the relationship I had with my own father. I could feel, sometimes, Rock was awkward with it, but he got used to it." Rock would ask Jack endless questions as they walked. Jack had been addicted to drugs and alcohol, and had "gone sober" in 1979, and Rock wanted to hear about the process. But when Jack asked Rock questions, he could never get an answer.

"There were a lot of parallels between Rock and me and the characters we were playing," Jack says. Rock played Brian Devlin and Jack played his son, Nick Corsello, whom Rock had walked away from and not seen since he was a baby. The characters did not know each other and were feeling one another out. "Nick had a lot of knowledge about his father, but didn't know him," Jack says. "I had a lot of knowledge about Rock, but didn't know him. And Nick had this great love for his father."

One afternoon, as they were walking past the Museum of Natural History, Jack said to Rock, "What does it feel like to have a son?"

"I don't know. Whenever I have one, I'll let you know."

"Cut that shit out," Jack said. "I'm Nick Corsello. Your son."

"Oh. That one." Rock laughed.

"How come you never talk to me directly?"

"Who, me?"

"How come you don't answer me directly?"

"What do you mean by that, Jack?"

"Don't start that, Rock."

"I'm not starting. I want to know what you mean by that."

"When I ask you a direct question, you don't give me a direct answer."

"There are lots of answers to a question," Rock said.

"Why don't you give me the one I want?"

"Maybe because you want it, Jack."

Jack would give up in frustration. "It was like a sword fight. Parry and thrust, parry and thrust. That was his way of keeping you from learning much about him."

Yet Rock showed Jack he cared for him a great deal. When Jack moved to California to do the show, he didn't know anyone except Rock and Tom. "I had two doting Dads. They told me where to live and helped me find a place." Jack needed work done on his teeth, and Rock sent him to his dentist, Dr. Phillip Tennis. The day of his appointment, Rock called and said he was coming to take Jack to the dentist for the first time. "You might feel more at ease." Rock introduced him to the dentist, Jack went into the examining room, sat down in the chair and there was a knock on the door. Dr. Tennis winked at Jack and said, "Who is it?"

"Me."

Rock opened the door and poked his head in. "Want me to come in?"

"No, but come sit down," Jack said. "I know you'll be happier." Jack says Rock proceeded to tell jokes and keep him laughing for an hour while the dentist worked on him. That evening, Jack told a friend: "Rock Hudson came to my house today, drove me to my dentist and told me jokes for an hour while I sat in the chair, then drove me home. You're telling me this is not a make-believe world in Hollywood?"

Jack came to feel he and Rock were similar in temperament. They both were Scorpios, born in November, both were secretive and private. Rock said, "We're a lot alike, but we're also different. You're not as stubborn as I am."

"You think so?" Jack said.

"Yes, and I'm gonna prove it to you."

They began playing a game: Whenever they went out together, Rock would stop at the door and insist that Jack go first. They once stood outside Jimmy's restaurant in Beverly Hills for fifteen minutes.

"I went in first the last time," Jack said. "You go first this time."

Rock shook his head and folded his arms.

"I'm not going first again," Jack said.

"Okay, we'll spend lunchtime out here. We'll have 'em bring out food. Waiter!"

"Okay, I'll go in!" Jack said.

"I told you I was more stubborn than you."

*   *   ‘ *

They began shooting *The Devlin Connection* in October, and from the beginning, Jack says, "We knew the show was in trouble. Rock was unhappy that they weren't playing on the chemistry between us—the relationship we'd been working to build." Tom Clark says that Rock was unhappy with the producer, who was going through an emotionally trying divorce, and with the scripts. There had been a writers' strike all summer, so they had raced to get scripts done at the last minute and they were substandard. "There was chaos on the set."

The first day, Rock and Jack were walking out of their trailers and saw buzzards circling in the sky. They were told a man had asphyxiated himself in a car nearby. Rock looked at the car, at the buzzards, and then at Jack. "And it's only our first day of work," he said.

Rock did not give Jack explicit help, but he made himself available to rehearse and make suggestions. If Jack seemed to be having trouble with a scene, Rock would take him aside and say, "You feel okay? Want to run the lines? Let's take a few minutes and talk about it." Jack recalls, "This is my first big job, I'm working with Rock Hudson, and I was frenetic. I would want to run the lines four hundred times in five minutes, and he'd sit there with me." Jack asked Rock, "Why are you doing all this?"

Rock told him how, when he was new to acting and making *Magnificent Obsession*, Jane Wyman had gone out of her way to help him. When he had asked Jane why, she had told him, "If we have anything to give another person, it's the experience we've been through. So I'm giving it to you, and I know one day you'll pass it on." Rock said to Jack, "It's my turn to pass it on now." Jack walked back to his trailer and cried.

Jack started calling Rock "the big guy," and the writers used it in the scripts. Jack says he's sure Rock was not six feet four, as he has always stated, but six six. "I'm six one, and Rock dwarfed me. I've played a lot of basketball, I've stood next to a lot of tall guys, and Rock was not six four. He had enormous hands—his hand could engulf my whole face." They had one scene where Rock was supposed to slap Jack, after Jack had insulted him. "Coming from the

215

New York school of acting, I said, 'Rock, you better hit me, so I can get the full effect.'"

Rock said, "You sure?"

"I think it would work for this scene. Give me a whack."

Jack says he never saw Rock's hand, he felt it. "It's called 'ringing your bell'—like the sixty-second warning you get before a nuclear attack." After he'd been whacked, Jack flubbed a line and the scene had to be reshot. He was standing, rubbing his jaw, and Rock said, "Well?"

"Rock, you better hit me again."

Rock gave him another bell-ringing whack, and Jack got every word right. Rock walked up and said, "That was very good."

"The reason it was good is, I didn't wanna get hit a third time."

"I was wondering when you'd wise up," Rock said.

They finished shooting three episodes and were in the middle of the fourth when Rock woke up in the middle of the night with shooting pains in his chest. He went down to the kitchen, and when Tom came downstairs at 6 A.M., Rock was white and his arm was numb clear to the fingers. "I'm glad you're up," he said. "I can hardly breathe." Tom rushed him to the emergency room at Cedars-Sinai Hospital, where they did a cardiogram and found no evidence that Rock had had a heart attack. He went back to work, but his doctor, Rex Kennamer, ordered extensive tests.

In New York, Rock had occasionally had shortness of breath and chest pains while walking home from a restaurant, but he had written it off as indigestion. He was proud of his health and stamina. If he got a cold on Monday, he would be well by Tuesday, while everyone else in the house would sneeze and suffer all week. Rock often said, "I'm gonna live to be a hundred and the rest of you will be dead."

When the test results came back, Dr. Kennamer found evidence of blockages in three coronary arteries, and advised Rock to enter the hospital for emergency bypass surgery. Production was shut down on *The Devlin Connection*, and Rock was concerned about Jack. He called the studio executive in charge and said, "No matter what happens, I want you to take care of the kid."

The night before his surgery, Rock looked out the window of his hospital room at the word HOLLYWOOD carved in the hillside. "I wonder if I'll ever see that sign again," he said.

"Oh, come on," Tom said. "You've got the greatest doctors in the world, and you're strong."

"I can't help thinking, if I go now, I've really had a wonderful time."

He spoke on the phone to Mark Miller and Dean Dittman. "I'm waving good-bye to Hollywood and all my friends in the hills," he said. Rock told Mark later that he thought they had spoken for the last time.

Rock survived the surgery—which became a quintuple bypass—and recovered with surprising rapidity. Tom donated blood to replace the blood Rock had received, and in 1985, it occurred to Tom that Rock might have contracted AIDS from blood transfusions. Cedars-Sinai was in West Hollywood, where there was a large gay population. In 1981, at the time of Rock's bypass, no one in his circle of friends had heard of AIDS. They were beginning to hear rumors in the gay community of a rare cancer that was killing homosexuals—"There's something out there, be careful"—but it did not have a name.

In 1981, Dr. Michael Gottlieb at UCLA and Dr. Alvin Friedman-Kien of NYU alerted the Centers for Disease Control in Atlanta that they had identified several cases, in gay men, of two rare diseases—*Pneumocystis carinii* pneumonia and Kaposi's sarcoma—both of which are usually seen in people with a depressed immune system. Reports from other doctors in large cities led to the identification of AIDS as a new and distinct disease. The first articles about it appeared in popular magazines in 1982. It was believed that AIDS was transmitted sexually, but there was no link yet to blood transfusions.

Dr. Gottlieb, who was called in when Rock was diagnosed as having AIDS in 1984, said it was "virtually impossible to determine with certainty" where Rock got AIDS. He said this was true of all sexually transmitted diseases "because the true number of lovers is known only to the person who has the disease."

Jack Scalia went to visit Rock three days after the bypass surgery. He was still in pain, and Jack helped prop him up in bed. Rock said he couldn't wait to get home and smoke a cigarette.

"Are you out of your mind?" Jack said.

"It's a test. I'm gonna smoke one, that's all."

"That's a lot of shit."

"I can do anything I want," Rock said.

"I know you can, but if you smoke one, you're gonna start smoking again."

Jack's hand was not far from Rock's on the bed. Rock reached over and put his hand on Jack's—it was the first time he had initiated any physical contact. His eyes welled up and a tear ran down his cheek.

"What's going on?" Jack said.

"I'm scared. Really scared."

More tears fell.

"It's all right," Jack said softly, "it's all right to do this."

Rock put his head down a minute, and when he lifted it, his eyes were dry. "No. I'm okay. I'll be fine."

"Rock, you're a son of a bitch for stopping. It was very special, what you were doing. I wish you would have continued."

"I don't want to. I'm fine."

Jack found it startling and "a little scary" that Rock could shut it off so fast. "I got a feeling of great loneliness in him. He had learned to protect himself too well; he never shared his life with anybody."

Tom brought Rock home from the hospital the next week, and a few days later, found him in the kitchen smoking. "I got up in the middle of the night, came down and lit a cigarette and I don't care," Rock said. Tom recalls, "I knew there was no point in arguing. He smoked up to the very end, and cigarettes didn't get him, did they?"

Rock and Tom tried many techniques to stop smoking. They heard about the "hip hypnotist," Pat Collins, who had a nightclub act. Tom called her and said, "We need to stop smoking. Would you like to come here and have cocktails?" Pat arrived in evening clothes, wearing elaborate makeup and jewels. She and her secretary sat in the living room, chatting and drinking, and finally Rock said, "Well, we want to stop smoking." She took first Rock, then Tom, up to the bedroom, had them lie down on the sofa and close their eyes, talked to them and planted the suggestion. When she left, neither Rock nor

Tom was sure if they had gone under. "We lit up so fast your head would spin," Tom says.

Rock did not change his diet after the surgery. He still ate gizzards, which are high in cholesterol, and used lots of salt and butter. He did not go for cardiac-rehabilitation exercises, but he did start walking. Jack Scalia would call and say, "Let's walk around the Hollywood reservoir. I'll pick you up."

Rock succeeded in cutting back his drinking, from fifteen drinks a day to two. According to Mark Miller, Rock would occasionally get drunk one night, but not again for three weeks. "He woke up from the drunkenness of the seventies," George says. "The meanness and sniping fell away, and he was returning to the Rock we had known in 1952—a warm human being, who laughed and played games." Rock felt as if he'd been given a reprieve; he took stock of his life and wanted to change all the things that had made him unhappy.

His doctors said that if he made it through the first year, he had a good chance of enjoying a normal life-span. He was told he might have periods of forgetfulness, irritability or paranoia, particularly a fear of traveling, and that, on the positive side, he could expect renewed vigor sexually.

In December, he went on a two-week cruise to recuperate, with Tom, Ross Hunter and Jacque Mapes, Claire Trevor and Pat Tolson, a friend from New York who was a stage manager. They met in Houston, took a limousine to Galveston and boarded a Greek ship, the *Stella Solaris*, which sailed around the Caribbean and through the Panama Canal. Rock read, took the sun, ate and played bridge. They had six bridge players so there was a constant game going. When Rock returned home in early January, he had gained back weight and seemed in prime health. "I've never felt better in my life," he said.

They resumed shooting *The Devlin Connection*, but because they'd had to start again with a new crew and producer, they lost momentum and any sense of what the series was about. It went on the air in October of 1982, and for the first time in Rock's television career, he had poor ratings. After thirteen shows, the series was canceled.

Although it had not been unexpected, the failure of the show was a blow to Jack Scalia, who did not see Rock as frequently after they stopped working together. At Christmas, Rock stopped by Jack's house for a tree-trimming party, and while talking with Jack and the actress Stepfanie Kramer, who appeared in *Hunter*, Rock described a Christmas he had had in Winnetka as a child. Rock said that when he was eight, his stepfather, Wally Fitzgerald, had bought him a Flexible Flyer for Christmas. Rock had been wanting the sled all year, and went right out to ride it with his friend Billy. He had an accident and broke the sled the first day, and hid it at Billy's. Wally kept asking where the sled was, and finally went over to Billy's where he found it in the garage, split in two. Rock said his stepfather hit him and swore he'd never let him have another sled.

In the summer of 1985, when Rock was flown home from his ill-fated trip to Paris and was at UCLA Medical Center, Jack asked Stepfanie to help him think of a gift to bring Rock in the hospital. "It's a big deal, his coming home, and I want to get him something."

"I know what he'd like," Stepfanie said. She asked a prop man to help her, and they found an antique Flexible Flyer made in 1929. They wrapped it like a Christmas present in green paper with red ribbon, Jack strapped it on his motorcycle and took it to the hospital. He had been warned Rock might not recognize him, but when he walked in the room, Rock smiled and instantly reverted to their old swordplay.

"What've you got there?" Rock said.

"Where?"

"Right there."

"Oh, that's a present."

"I wonder who it's for," Rock said.

"Who do you think it's for?"

"I don't know. You brought it in."

"It's for you, Rock."

"Are you gonna open it?"

Jack unwrapped it and put it on Rock's lap.

"Flexible Flyer," Rock said.

"You and Billy, right?"

"I remember it." He rubbed the shiny surface of the wood. "Put it up against the wall, so I can see it when I wake up."

Rock took Jack's hand, for the second time since they'd known each other.

"Rock, I want you to get better, there's a lot of things we haven't talked about," Jack said.

"Oh? Like what?"

"I just want to talk with you."

"What do you want to talk about?"

Jack smiled. It was the old conversation, and he knew where it was going. So he said, "Heard any good jokes lately?"

In the summer of 1982, Rock called Mark and George in the desert and told them Edith Scherer, the third wife of his father, Roy Scherer, had died. Scherer was eighty-three and senile, and hadn't realized his wife was dead. A neighbor saw her lying on the sofa and knew immediately she wasn't sleeping. She called the police, who called Rock, who called Mark and said, "What do I do?"

Rock had been sending his father fifty dollars a week for thirty years, but he had avoided seeing him. "I cannot handle this," he told Mark, who said what he always said to Rock: *I understand.*

Mark arranged for Edith to be buried, and decided Scherer should be placed in a home because he could not care for himself. Rock and Tom wanted him to go to the Motion Picture Country House, which was for retired actors and had a long waiting list. There were hundreds of homes where Rock could have placed his father, and Rock himself owned an interest in a rest home in Westwood. But Rock insisted on the Motion Picture Country House, so Mark and others had to pull strings to get Scherer admitted. Mark drove Scherer there, but Scherer kept walking away, and the administrators said they couldn't look after him. Mark called the daughter Scherer and his second wife had adopted, Alice Marie, who lived in Oregon. Mark put Scherer on a plane for Oregon, and a few months later, Alice Marie called and said Scherer had died. When Rock was told, he asked to be left alone for ten minutes, and never mentioned it again.

In the fall of 1982, Stockton Briggle received a call from Rock at ten in the evening. "Can I come over?"

"Of course," Stockton said, although he had been preparing to go to sleep. Rock said Tom was in bed, drunk, and he wanted to talk. Stockton had never known Rock to call like this, and wondered what was on his mind. Rock drove over, they sat up talking and Rock

221

drank Scotch until finally, at three in the morning, Stockton put Rock in his car.

It was a night in which Rock poured out his sorrows, unburdened himself of all the fears and torments and demons he'd been holding inside and concealing. It is one of the few instances I have been able to find in all of Rock's life where he confided in someone about his anguish. "For some reason, he unburdened himself to me," Stockton says. "I think it goes back to the awesome relationship we developed during *Camelot*—the incredible night we spent together reshaping the show." Rock trusted Stockton and felt that the director understood him.

Rock told Stockton that after his bypass surgery, he felt like a man who'd been given a second chance. "It's time to make my own decisions, my own choices. It's time to do what I want to do without other people running my life." He said he hated working in television because everyone settled for too little and schedules were more important than quality. "I'm tired of doing crap. I'm sick to death of getting mediocre roles with mediocre writing." He felt bitter that his long years of work in films had gone unrecognized and unappreciated.

Stockton said his favorite film of Rock's was *Seconds*, and for a moment, Rock's eyes lit with pleasure. Rock said he couldn't understand why the film had not drawn more attention to his acting abilities. He had a range and complexity that had barely been tapped.

His thoughts kept turning to illness and death. He spoke about his father, Roy Scherer, and how much he had hated him, and how he had loved his mother and been devastated when she died. He explained to Stockton that he couldn't bear illness, and hadn't been able to face the fact that his mother wouldn't recover, so he had cut himself off from her.

Rock seemed so miserable and lonely, Stockton tried to reassure him. "Your work is greatly respected by lots of serious people, and you're loved by millions all over the world."

"But no one loves *me*," Rock said.

"You have Tom."

Rock made a scoffing sound.

"I know Tom loves you."

Rock said, with a grunt of disgust, "There's nothing there anymore. It's purely social."

222

When Rock left his house, Stockton was shaken. "It was an astonishing night. Rock was in enormous pain, and his whole life had been spent in efforts to camouflage the pain. This was like a Walpurgisnacht, and yet, when I saw him next, he never acknowledged that it had taken place. I never saw him like that again."

Not long after his visit to Stockton, Rock moved into Tijuana to sleep, while Tom continued to sleep in the blue bedroom. Rock had asked Mark Miller to move his office out of Tijuana and down to what had been the projection room, next to the playroom. Mark was glad to be closer to the front door, and to be out of the firing line between Rock and Tom.

Rock told Tom he was sleeping in Tijuana because he was sweating at night and could sleep better there. (It's hard to imagine anyone having a restful night in Tijuana, with its red walls, red carpet, red plaid furniture and raised red platform with a bed behind red drapes.) Tom didn't buy the excuse, but he didn't force the issue. He thought it was part of the "peculiar behavior" the doctors had warned him to expect after Rock's heart surgery. Tom says, "I thought, this too shall pass."

Another piece of peculiar behavior was that Rock started going out for walks every afternoon. He would leave around two, take the car somewhere "to walk" and come back around six, cheerful and whistling, looking freshly showered and with his hair still damp. James Wright said to Mark Miller, "I bet you he ain't going out to walk. He's meeting somebody." James said later, "Somehow it always shows. When you live with somebody, you get to know his ways. Mr. Hudson wasn't the sort of person to go for long walks. He was always jolly when he came back. His eyes were sparkling. He'd go straight to the freezer and have a bowl of vanilla ice cream with chocolate sauce and walnuts. Then he'd go up to his bedroom and start tatting (needlepointing), and Tom would come down to the kitchen and turn on the television. Mr. Hudson didn't care for television, and wouldn't have it on in the bedroom. I got the impression from Mr. Hudson that he'd had enough of Tom."

Rock was, in fact, going out in the afternoons to see Marc Christian, whom he met in the fall of 1982. Christian's full name is Marc Christian MacGinnis, and he was the type for whom Rock had a weakness: tall, blond, bisexual, with blue eyes and, when Rock met him, a mustache and beard. He was a "health freak" and worked out at a gym. He did not have a regular job, but told Rock he was putting together a history of popular music from the time the phonograph was invented.

Christian was twenty-nine and Rock was fifty-seven, but Christian had been involved with a woman who was even older than Rock— Liberty Martin (pronounced Martine), who is now sixty-five. Marc and Liberty have been together, on and off, for eleven years, sharing her one-bedroom apartment in Hollywood. They have a relationship, which, Liberty says, "We don't understand ourselves. How could anyone else?" Liberty is exotic looking, with long black hair that she wears swept up and skin "like a baby's. I've never had a knife on my face." She describes herself as "very Greek—we're fighters for justice." When Rock was buried at sea, Liberty was on the boat and wore a large blue hat and dangling earrings in the shape of silver stars.

At first meeting, Marc Christian seems shy, sincere, gentle and articulate. But it is difficult to get a fix on him. His eyes have a flat, opaque quality, and when asked a question, he may give one answer one day and a different answer the next. If pressed, he may slip into yet a third explanation, and it's hard to grasp hold of anything solid. For example, he said on *The Larry King Show* that he was a musicologist, and had a job with "the Institute of the American Musical, here in Los Angeles"; in an interview with the *New York Native*, he said he worked at "the Record Institute." There is no listing in Los Angeles for either organization. On the question of where he met Rock, Christian told Mark Miller in 1983 that they had met at Brooks Baths, a straight bathhouse where Rock used to go for a sauna and massage. In 1985, when Christian filed suit against Hudson's estate, he said he met Rock at a fund-raising party for Gore Vidal's Senate campaign. He even made a little joke about it on television: "Gore used to say he was walking for the Senate. It was a low-key campaign." Marc and Liberty did work as volunteers on Vidal's campaign, but it ended in June of 1982, and Christian said he met Rock in October of '82. In 1986, Christian changed the story; he told me he met Rock at "a political campaign, somewhere in the Valley. I believe it was the Bottle Initiative." Proposition 11, known as the Bottle Initiative, was a bill to require deposits on bottles, and was on the ballot in California in November of 1982. What's disturbing is that people don't usually forget the way they met their lovers, particularly important ones. They are asked how they met and tell the story again and again; it becomes a piece of shared history.

However they met, Rock and Marc started spending afternoons together at Liberty's apartment. "Rock would come here, have coffee with me and Liberty and then we'd go out," Marc says. "Rock always had to live his life in secrets. He kept things from Mark Miller, he kept things from everyone. This was like Rock's secret world, a haven. We'd play music and talk, or we'd drive up to Mount Baldy." Marc says Rock asked him to go away for the weekend, but they did not go far—they stayed in a motel in North Hollywood. Their secret meetings went on for a year before Rock invited Marc to live with him at the Castle.

Rock had a lifelong problem of not being able to confront people, to fire help or ask lovers to leave. Perhaps because his father had deserted him, he did not want to be in the position of rejecting another person. Instead, he would use indirect measures. As Phyllis Gates said, "He froze people out." Rock would grow silent, hostile, and make things so uncomfortable that the person would decide on his own to leave. But this method did not always work. Rock had been cold to Tom for some time and had moved out of the bedroom, but Tom stuck it out, believing "this too shall pass."

On September 7, 1983, Mark Miller drove Rock and Tom to the airport to leave for New York, where they were planning to spend the fall. As Tom walked off to take care of the baggage, Rock came around the side of the van and whispered to Mark, "I'll be back next Tuesday."

"But . . ."

"I'm not going for three months. *He* is. I'll call from New York and let you know my flight."

"You're on," Mark said.

When Rock and Tom arrived in New York, Claire Trevor threw a big party welcoming them back. They went to see *La Cage aux Folles*, and talked with the producers about Rock's doing the show. Two days later, Rock announced, "I'm going back to California tomorrow."

"We just got here!" Tom said. "Claire's given us this big party. I'm not going home now."

Rock said he was going anyway. Tom did not know it was the end of the relationship. He told himself that Rock was probably reluctant to be away from his doctors and Cedars-Sinai Hospital, because of the heart surgery. "Several times, he had canceled trips at the last minute with weak excuses. I figured he didn't want to leave the womb."

Mark picked Rock up at the L.A. airport on September 13, and was distressed to see him in baggy pants, a shirt that didn't match and old, scuffed loafers. "He looked bedraggled, and it embarrassed me. I don't like to see a movie star get off a plane looking like shit. It's bad for his image," Mark says. When he asked about Tom, Rock said, "I hope he stays in New York the rest of his life. I never want to see him again."

On October 7, Tom flew back to L.A. with Claire Trevor, who was staying at the Castle. Tom knew, by now, there was a rift, but he wanted a reconciliation. He believed that Rock and he could work things out if they had a chance to talk. When they did, Rock told him he had fallen in love with someone else, Marc Christian. Rock said, "Nothing will change. You go live in New York and let me spin this out." Tom said, "I have too much pride. I'm out."

A few nights later, James heard a fight between Rock and Tom in the kitchen. It was about nine-thirty, Claire had gone out to dinner and Rock and Tom had been drinking. James says, "I was in my room, which is next to the kitchen, and I heard this terrible row. They were shouting at the top of their voices. I heard Mr. Hudson say, 'I want you out of this house and out of my life. I should have kicked you out eight years ago. It was finished eight fucking years ago. It's finished!'

"Tom said, 'Oh yeah? I've done everything for you. I got you all the work you've done. . . .' And then I heard Mr. Hudson hit Tom. I heard Tom fall down on the bloody ground and say, 'You see what you've done? You punched me in the eye.' And Mr. Hudson said, 'It serves you fucking right. If you keep on, I'll belt you in the other eye.' Tom said, 'Go ahead, I dare you.'" James heard someone walk out the swinging door and there was quiet. James was stunned; it was the first time he had heard Rock, drunk or sober, tell Tom to leave.

On October 27, Tom flew to New York with Claire Trevor, and stayed in the apartment at the Beresford. Four days later, Rock left for Israel to shoot *The Ambassador*. Wally Sheft was nervous that Tom would sue for palimony—he had been with Rock ten years—but Tom said, "I'm not the suing type." Tom was certain there would be a reconciliation. "If Rock would just come here and talk to me, we could straighten out our lives in ten minutes," he said. Rock called Tom from Jerusalem, and said he would stop in New York on his way home and they could settle things. Tom waited, but Rock never came. He flew directly back to Los Angeles, and Tom did not see him again until Rock was at UCLA Medical Center. Tom started rebuilding his life on his own, but he did not give up. "There was never any question in my mind that we'd get back together."

CHAPTER 13

Love? It's overexaggerated. There are many forms of love, of course, like love for a child or a parent, love for dogs or plants or fried chicken. I love loving, but being in love with someone has been too romanticized. People have come to expect much more of it than there really is.

Rock was euphoric, at first, to be away from Tom. He told Dean Dittman he had had "five wonderful years and five years of servitude." When a relationship that has deteriorated into fighting and recrimination is suddenly stopped, there is instantaneous relief. "No one's beating me up anymore. I'm free!" It is only later, gradually, that one comes to realize what else is missing: the positive qualities that kept the relationship in place.

Rock was enchanted with his new lover, and had romantic expectations of the future. With Marc Christian, he told friends, he could recapture the passion and sexual ecstasy he had known in younger years. Stockton Briggle says, "Rock was totally smitten with Marc, he couldn't keep his hands off him." When Rock was in Israel, he called Dean and said, "I wonder what Marc's doing. Why don't you call him? I can't wait to get back home and see him." He wrote passionate letters to Marc, who responded in kind.

Just before he left for Israel, Rock brought Marc Christian to the Castle and introduced him to the staff. Rock said to James, "Would it be all right if I let Marc move into the house while I'm away?"

"All right with me," James said.

"Thank you," Rock said. He gave Marc the keys to the Cadillac Seville, and told Mark Miller, "Marc will be house-sitting, he'll guard the house on James's days off, and he'll prevent Tom from moving back."

John Dobbs, an aspiring actor who was Rock's houseman and came in days to clean the house, says, "At first, everyone was joyous he was replacing Tom Clark. I liked Marc. He was intelligent and he treated me as an equal. He was farther to the left, politically, than the rest of the house, so I felt I had an ally."

Mark Miller sensed, instantly, that Marc Christian was more than a house-sitter, which Rock confirmed privately. Rock told Mark to put Christian on salary, so he could have health insurance. Christian was paid $400 a month from Rock's company, Mammoth Films, to look after the film library. He was given use of a car, membership in a gym and a private workout instructor. Rock said, "Send him to Dr. Tennis, we're gonna fix his teeth, and we're going to restore his father's Chevy Nomad station wagon." Rock explained that Christian's father was dying of lung cancer, and to restore his 1959 car would lift his spirits. "Give Marc the money to get started on the car, and don't tell Wally." Rock also wanted to send Marc to acting school with Nina Foch. Mark Miller says, "It was a crusade, like *Pygmalion*. Rock wanted to change the young man's life. He said he'd been living with a woman who had some kind of hold on him, and Rock was determined to break it." Mark Miller thought Christian was pleasant and would cause no problems for anyone. "Tom Clark had been so difficult at the end, we were relieved to have somebody new."

George Nader says, "Where Tom had been flamboyant, difficult and wonderful, Marc Christian took it slow and treaded on no toes. Like a snake enters the garden, that young man entered this house."

Marc Christian said he had never lived with a man before, and was reluctant to move in so soon after Tom Clark's departure. "I told Rock I didn't want to be his satellite or appendage," Marc says. "I'm very opinionated. I have a pretty good ego and can hold my own in a conversation, and Rock liked that. I was not some little blond twerp who couldn't talk."

The only person who was not happy with Christian's arrival was James. A short time after Christian moved in, James went to a party and several strangers came up to him and said they had heard Marc Christian was Rock's new lover and had moved into the house. "They described him perfectly, and said he was very well known around town." James was shocked that word had gotten out so fast. "Mr. Hudson was extremely discreet about these things." James told Mark Miller the next morning, "I hear he's bloody well known, and the word is out all over town." Mark said nothing to Rock, because "when someone is in love, you don't want to make waves."

James says that with Christian in the house, "things were easier for me, but I hated it. I could see what sort of person he was. I'm a good judge of character, I've had to be, and I thought he had no interest in Mr. Hudson. He was using Mr. Hudson. He was a user." On the surface, though, James was cordial to Marc.

Marc did not give James orders, as Tom Clark had done, but he would create chaos and walk away, leaving it for James to clean up. "He'd come down to the kitchen, make his stupid bloody energy drink and leave his garbage all over the place. He kept having all his friends up to the house, and they'd leave the place a mess. Mr. Hudson's bedroom was a shambles—Marc would drop his clothes on the settees and they'd stay there for days on end. Mr. Hudson always hung his things up. He was a considerate person. I told Mr. Hudson, 'I'm not picking up after him,' and he said, 'Don't, let him pick it up himself.'"

George Nader came to the Castle to celebrate his birthday shortly before Rock left for Israel. George had not seen Rock in some time, because he had moved to Palm Desert and was living there year round. Mark was commuting every week, spending four days in town, working for Rock, and three days in the desert. Rock had conceived the idea, the year before, of getting hold of episodes of the *Loretta Young Show* George had done in the early fifties. George had appeared in the pilot with Loretta and on sixteen programs. They had been some of the best roles George had ever had, but he had never been able to see the shows again. Loretta Young had prevented NBC from showing them in reruns, and they were made before the time of the video recorder. "I thought it was a golden age that had vanished forever," George says.

Rock set out to find the shows and have them transferred to videotape. He had no idea how difficult the task would be. It took him and Mark Miller eight months, and required volumes of paperwork. Rock had to call in favors from heads of studios and sign a sworn statement that he would not use the tapes for commercial purposes. At first the shows could not be traced; then they were found in a warehouse in New Jersey, and five shows were copied and sent to Rock, along with a bill for $2,000.

Rock wrapped the tapes himself in an elaborate package and presented it to the unsuspecting George. As George undid the wrapping and realized what was inside, he broke down and sobbed. "It was priceless. I'd stopped acting ten years before, and I thought I'd never see this work of mine again," George says. Rock was embarrassed by the emotion, and laughed, but later he told Mark, "God, I'm glad we did that."

Rock left for Israel on November 1, 1983, and Marc Christian moved into the Castle on November 5. When Rock came back on January 4, 1984, Marc met him at the airport. That night, James saw them in the living room, hugging and kissing. They had set up a Christmas tree in the room, and Marc and his friends had put little notes on it. "Mr. Hudson was so happy and pleased," James says. "He was just thrilled to be with Marc again."

Rock and Marc went out for lunches and dinners and on shopping trips to buy Marc clothes. "It was wedded bliss," Mark Miller says. Marc showed a videotape he'd made as a joke for Rock, a tape of himself impersonating Doris Day, in a blond wig and makeup, miming to one of her records. Christian told Mark Miller he and Rock were going to Europe. Rock had always loved taking his new mates to Europe, showing them the Ritz, the Savoy, and all his favorite restaurants, but at the end of January, Rock said, "We're not going," and gave no explanation.

With Marc, Rock started going to gay restaurants and bars he had never set foot in before. When Mark Miller learned about it, he asked Rock why.

Rock shrugged. "Marc likes it."

"Oh. So you don't care anymore, about . . ."

"What people think?" Rock said.

"I was going to say, your image."

"Marc says that kind of thinking is fifties shit. No one cares anymore. Hell, I'm not even recognized most of the time. Last week, we went to the Hayloft, and no one even looked twice."

"Rock, that's bullshit and you know it," Mark said.

"I'm going on sixty. It's time to do as I please."

"You can go on acting until you're eighty. Look at Henry Fonda and Jimmy Stewart—the parts get older, but they're still there. But you can't if you go around throwing it in people's faces; you've always said that yourself."

Rock brushed him off with his customary wave of the hand. The next day, though, Rock was sitting in the kitchen, doing a crossword puzzle, when Marc came in and proposed they have dinner at a gay restaurant he liked, Café d'Étoile. Rock said no.

"Why not?" Marc said.

"Boring. Been there too much lately."

"But they're expecting us . . ."

Rock looked up from the puzzle and stared at Marc. "No," he said, and waited. When Marc did not respond, Rock deliberately took a sip of his coffee and went back to work on the puzzle.

On January 17, just two weeks after Rock's homecoming, Mark Miller came to work and found Rock sitting in the kitchen in a rage.

"Marc didn't come home last night," Rock said.

"Oh? Cute."

"Mmmm." Rock said Marc hadn't called, he simply stayed out all night and appeared the next morning, as if nothing had happened. Rock refused to question him; it was beneath his dignity.

Marc soon established a pattern: He would get up at midmorning (Rock started calling him "the sleeping prince"), set the video recorder to tape *Days of Our Lives*, leave for the gym, and when he came back, immediately turn on the TV and watch his soap opera. Once a week, he would drop into Mark Miller's office, turn in his receipts for meals in restaurants and purchases in stores, get his money and go on his way.

James would ask Rock, "Will Mr. Christian be in for dinner?"

"I don't know," Rock would say. "He never tells me where the fuck he's going." Rock would walk into Mark Miller's office and start needlepointing. "Where does he go all day?" Rock asked Mark. "He says he's going to the gym. How long does that take? He calls at five and says he'll be home in thirty minutes. I wait three hours and he doesn't show up. Fuck him."

A wall went up between Rock and Marc that was evident to everyone in the house. James says, "I felt sorry for Mr. Hudson. Marc Christian was treating him like a piece of dirt. There was no warmth or caring. Mr. Hudson would come down to the kitchen first, then Marc would come down and there'd be no words exchanged. They didn't have big fights, it just wasn't lovey-dovey ever again."

Rock and Marc led separate lives. At night, Rock would go have dinner with Dean Dittman or Ross Hunter and Jacque Mapes. Most of Rock's friends did not care for Marc. Stockton Briggle says, "As a friend of Rock's, I tried hard to like him, but I found him cold and calculating. Nobody knew his real past." Occasionally, Liberty would invite Rock and Marc to dinner, and they'd take separate cars. John Dobbs says Marc complained to him that Rock would never go out with him. He wouldn't go to movies, he wouldn't do anything Marc proposed. Marc said Rock had introduced him to his gay friends but not his straight ones. "He hadn't met Elizabeth Taylor. He told me he was lonely, and started trying to fill his days."

On February 24, Rock and Marc went to visit Mark and George in the desert. George met Marc for the first time, and was surprised to see "no affection between them, no jokes, no sweetness, no connection on either side. No sense of, this is mine, isn't it great? You'd have thought they were two strangers stranded together for the weekend." The four went to dinner Saturday night at the Beach House, and Rock grew sullen when it was clear that no one in the place recognized him. He began barking rude orders to the waiter. George looked up and suddenly felt sick at what he saw: "It was like a caricature of the aging star. Thirty-five years and this is what's left: a man whose cheeks are starting to fall in, who doesn't look good, sitting with a guy half his age that he doesn't like and who's using him."

Rock had lost weight in Israel, but George didn't think the weight loss was flattering. Rock, however, was pleased and proud. He'd go into Mark's office and say, "I've lost another two pounds!" Mark was envious. "We were eating the same food. Rock had a chocolate sundae every day. We'd discuss what we ate and why he was losing and I wasn't." Mark weighed 225, and Rock was down to 210. Mark noticed, about this time, that Rock had a peculiar smell, which was familiar but which he couldn't place. Then he remembered, and told George: "It's the smell my brother Philip had when he was dying." They were silent. Rock is dying? Impossible, George thought. Rock is invincible. Rock is never going to die. Rock has an angel on his shoulder. Mark rationalized: Rock had started drinking gin again; it was probably the smell of gin seeping out of his skin.

Sometime in 1984, Marc Christian stopped sleeping with Rock in his bedroom and moved into Tijuana. Mark Miller says it was the spring of 1984. James thinks it was later. Christian told me, "I never officially moved out of the room. Rock snored and had sweats at night—I thought it was from the alcohol. It was intolerable to sleep with him when he was sweating, it was like being in the ocean, so I'd get up at night, a few times a week, and go sleep in the red room." Christian said in his deposition, taken under oath, in his lawsuit against Hudson's estate, that he and Rock had a constant sexual relationship until February of 1985. Christian said he was faithful to Rock, and to his knowledge, Rock was faithful to him.

James says Marc started staying out all night once or twice a week. "I'd go upstairs early in the morning, and be surprised to see only Mr. Hudson in bed. I'd check the red room and Marc wasn't there. I'd check the garage and the Seville was gone, so I knew he hadn't come home." Other nights, James says, Marc would have friends stay overnight with him in Tijuana, "while Mr. Hudson was sleeping in the blue bedroom. I knew it galled Mr. Hudson, but he wouldn't let on. I'd say to Mr. Hudson, 'Why have him around? You're not happy with him, he's upsetting you and you never know where he is. Why don't you get rid of him?' Mr. Hudson said, 'I'm going to,' and I'd always say, 'The sooner the better.'"

The cool disinterest Rock had adopted toward Marc turned into outright hostility. John Dobbs says, "Within three months of Rock's return from Israel, he exuded a cold loathing of Marc. He called him 'that asshole' or 'that ditz.' If Marc said 'Good morning,' Rock wouldn't answer. I couldn't have taken it. I would have packed up and left. But it didn't seem to bother Marc, he just went on about his business. I think he felt, I'm not going to be abused by this movie star."

To Christian's face, everyone in the house was pleasant. He received all the money he wanted, the charge accounts and cars. But there were always rumors whispered in the halls: "Any day now, Rock will get rid of him."

On February 29, Mark Miller, sensing that relations were strained, took Rock aside. "It's time to have a talk about something. What do you know about Marc's background? People say he's well known around town." According to Mark Miller, Rock told him the following: "When I came back from Israel, Marc told me, 'There's something I want you to know. Some of your friends might know, and I want you to hear it from me first. I've only done it a few times, when I was hard up and desperate for money. I was sent to people's houses, and I took money for sex.'" Rock said he felt disgusted, duped. He had taken Marc in, thinking he was innocent and trustworthy. Rock said Marc had then told him how he'd "hooked him." Marc had learned that Rock went to Brooks Baths every afternoon for a sauna while he was shooting *The Devlin Connection*. Marc had gone to Brooks Baths and hung around the dressing room until he succeeded in meeting the star. Rock said, "I promised him I'd fix his teeth and car. Give him the money for that, and I'll get rid of him."

Marc Christian says he has never taken money for sex, and never had such a conversation with Rock. But it is evident that in the spring of 1984, some event or sequence of events led Rock to turn against Marc.

When Rock went to dinner at Dean Dittman's, he mourned that the romance he had set such hopes on had turned to ashes. He said Marc was getting "all the advantages and wasn't putting out—not just sex, but companionship." He ranted about Marc with such violence that Dean said, "You've got to get rid of him because you're suffering and you're making me suffer with these conversations."

Rock said, "I'm working on it, in my own way." Dean says, "Rock could never face things directly. He wouldn't tell Marc to leave. He was sure that Marc would pick up the message and would be 'too embarrassed to stay.'" Dean tried to tell him it wouldn't work. "You spent five years giving Tom Clark the message. Are you gonna wait another five years? You don't have five more productive sexual years. You're fifty-eight years old. You better get out there in the field while you can still get a hard-on."

Rock laughed, and nodded, and the next time he saw Dean, nothing had changed. Dean asked, "Does he have something on you? Is that why he's still in the house?" Dean says Rock waved his arm and didn't answer, "but the subtext was, Rock felt he did have something on him. He was afraid of Marc. Rock had begun seeing other people and didn't want Marc to know. He said, 'I never want him to have that on me.'"

Rock was starting to be drawn to a new person, Ron Channell. Rock had hired Ron to come to the house and work out with him in October of 1983, just as Tom Clark was leaving. Rock told Mark

Miller that Ron was "John Foreman's workout man," which Mark learned, later, was not true. Rock had met Ron on his own, at a gym. At first, Ron was businesslike; he and Rock did exercises together in the playroom to music Ron would bring. Ron's voice could be heard over the music: "Come on, guy. Harder!" Ross Hunter, who overheard them one morning, said, "How can you work this man out? He's so skinny, there's no meat on his bones. What are you trying to do?"

In February of 1984, when Rock was becoming disenchanted with Christian, he encouraged Ron to spend more time at the house. Ron would come at 10:30, stay for lunch, then Rock would say, "Let's go shopping," and ask, "What are you doing tonight for dinner?" Rock showed films to Ron, paid for him to go to acting school and even did a screen test with him, because, he said, "The boy's talented and I want to help him." Rock showed him *Iron Man* one day, and Ron started calling him "Speed." Rock was tickled by this, and would call Ron's number in the morning and say into his answering machine, "Hi, it's Speed. You up yet? How soon you coming over?"

John Dobbs says, "There was something electric between the two of them. Rock delighted in every moment he spent with Ron, and Ron genuinely cared for Rock. They laughed together, which was something Rock and Marc Christian rarely did." Rock and Ron once walked into Mark Miller's office, laughing hysterically, and said, "Guess who we are?" Rock sat down on Ron's lap and moved his face in exaggerated gestures. When Mark couldn't guess, Rock said, "Edgar Bergen and Charlie McCarthy."

Mark says, "James and I watched Rock fall in love with Ron. They had secrets and would giggle like crazy. Those were some of the happiest times I saw Rock have in all his life." James says, "Mr. Hudson was a different man when Ron was around. Ron gave him that feeling of happiness and freedom."

Ron was a new physical type for Rock: He had dark skin, brown eyes and very dark hair. Ron knew that Rock was infatuated with him and that he hoped the relationship would grow to something more than friendship, but Ron kept things on the buddy level, like guys in the locker room. He indicated that he was straight and didn't feel as Rock did, and yet there was an element of flirtation and pursuit. They fell in love as two new friends do, excited about discovering each other.

Marc Christian saw what was happening and barely spoke to Ron. Rock had given Ron permission to borrow any videotapes he wanted from the vault, and when Marc discovered this, he went into the kitchen where Mark Miller was talking with James. According to Mark Miller, Christian was furious, and said, "I don't want him coming in the house and taking tapes without my permission! If they're not careful, they'll find themselves in the *Enquirer* as lovers. I'm not afraid to go to the *Enquirer* and say I'm Rock Hudson's lover. You think I am? Test me." James said afterward, he thought Christian was serious and that the threat was real. "I said, that guy is out to ruin Mr. Hudson."

Christian says he never threatened to expose Rock. "It would have ruined my acting career." He says Mark Miller told him not to be concerned about Ron. "Relax, kid. You've got nothing to worry about. These things happen in every affair."

While Rock's days were increasingly occupied by Ron Channell, his evenings were the province of Dean Dittman. Dean says Rock would get depressed at night if he had to be in his house alone. "I became his social director, after Tom Clark left. Tom had been a marvelous instigator, but Rock didn't instigate things." Dean says he and Rock would speak on the phone every morning and every night. "His favorite time to call was five-thirty. He'd wait until then to see if he got a better invitation, and if he didn't, he'd call me. Rock knew that for me, every night is New Year's Eve. It's a disease—I love to entertain. Around dinnertime, I'll think, there's no one to cook for. God! And I'll round up a group."

Dean lived in a high-rise apartment building in Hollywood, and his apartment was furnished all in green: green carpet, green velour walls, green couches and chairs, in one of which Rock would hold court. Dean was a "flowerholic," and Rock would bring him roses from his garden. Rock would usually come early and watch Dean cook, and before the guests arrived, Rock would methodically light the crystal "space candles" around the room. Dean had a doorbell that could be programmed to play music; when it was someone's birthday, the doorbell would chime "Happy Birthday," but most of the time it played "Home Sweet Home." Dean's apartment was destroyed by a fire, which police believe was the result of arson, on the night Marc Christian gave his second deposition in his lawsuit. There is nothing left of the green apartment, but when Rock was alive, it hummed with festivity.

Dean says, "Rock was very much like a child of mine." In 1984, when Rock was asked to be one of the presenters at the Academy Awards, he stopped at Dean's on his way to the ceremony. "He wanted approval," Dean says. Rock had lost weight and hadn't bothered to have his tuxedo refitted. It was baggy, and Dean took it in with safety pins. "Even after we pinned it, it was loose, but it wasn't so tentlike." Rock went on television with safety pins in his tuxedo, for what would be his last Academy Awards. Ten minutes after presenting the Oscar for best actress to Shirley MacLaine, Rock walked back into Dean's apartment, where a dinner party was in progress. Everyone cheered.

One of the guests at Dean's that night was a young man named Pierre, whom Rock had met with Dean at a gay bar in Long Beach. Rock had been fascinated with Pierre: He was a boat builder, in his twenties, and, of course, blond and blue-eyed. Rock was reluctant to give out his phone number, so Dean got Pierre's number, called and invited him to dinner at his apartment, along with Rock. Pierre played piano and wrote songs, one of which was about saving the bald eagle, and Rock sat at his feet, enthralled. In April, Rock went to Mexico with Pierre for a week, and stayed at the home of Pierre's father. But the romance was not consummated. Pierre later told Dean, "In Mexico, I looked at Rock and looked at my dad, and they were the same age. I couldn't do it."

Rock had not told anyone in the Castle, even Mark Miller, about Pierre. He told Mark he was going to Mexico and would make his own travel arrangements. Between the time Rock returned from Israel and his death in 1985, he went to Hawaii twice, Europe twice, New York, Florida, Louisville and Washington, and never once took Marc Christian with him. Most of the time, he took Ron Channell.

When Rock was out of town in the spring of 1984, Clarence Morimoto, the gardener, discovered Marc Christian in Rock's bed with another man. It was Clarence's habit to go up to Rock's bedroom in the afternoon to water the roses on the balcony. "If he's home, I always knock on the door and say, 'Rock, are you there?'" Clarence says. "If he's out of town, I go right in." On this afternoon in the spring, Rock was off traveling and the bedroom door was closed.

Clarence opened it and walked through the dressing and bathing area to the main part of the room, where the carved wooden bed was. "When I passed the bathroom area, I could see, at the bottom corner of the bed, Marc Christian with a blond boy. I don't know his name. I could only see them from the waist up. They were on the bed, no clothes on, and both were caressing each other. I could see Marc's face, I'm sure it was him, but they didn't see me and I didn't say anything. It was such an embarrassing place to jump in." Clarence turned, walked out and softly closed the door.

On May 15, 1984, Rock was invited to have dinner at the White House. He had met the Reagans at Hollywood functions, but they had never been close; he had voted for Reagan because he was a conservative Republican. The dinner was a black-tie affair, and Rock was seated at Nancy Reagan's table. He told Mark Miller later he had been "bowled over" by her. "She's funny, charming, and does she know how to keep a table moving." Nancy had told Rock he was too thin, he should fatten up, and Rock had answered, "You're thin, also." Rock was down to 195.

A week later, Rock was in Mark's office, sitting in the lion's-head chair, when a photograph taken of him with the Reagans at the White House arrived, autographed by both of them. He hadn't asked for the picture, and thought it was a "classy touch" for them to send it.

Rock and Mark studied the picture: It was taken from the side, and showed a large red sore on Rock's neck, just below the hairline. Rock thought it was a pimple, but it had been there almost a year.

"Rock, you've gotta do something about that pimple on your neck," Mark said. "Why didn't you wear Erase? You knew you'd be photographed."

"I don't wear makeup, except on film. Never have."

"It looks terrible, it's bigger, and it should have been gone by now. You should go see the skin doctor."

On May 24, Rock went to see a dermatologist in Beverly Hills, Dr. Letantia Bussell, whom he'd been referred to by his internist, Dr. Rex Kennamer. She told him the growth was too large for her to remove. She took a biopsy, and suggested Rock go to Dr. Frank Kamer, a plastic surgeon, to have it removed. Dr. Kamer had done eyelid surgery on Rock in 1981, and Rock made an appointment for June 5.

A few days after Rock had seen Dr. Bussell, and before his appointment with the plastic surgeon, Dr. Bussell called with the biopsy results. "Are you sitting down?" she said.

"No," Rock said.

"I think you'd better sit down. It's Kaposi's sarcoma. You have acquired immune deficiency syndrome. AIDS."

Rock immediately went to Dr. Kennamer's office for blood tests, and told no one. On June 5, he asked Mark Miller to drive him to the office of the plastic surgeon, Dr. Kamer, to have the "pimple" removed. Mark had no hint of the gravity of the occasion. He took Rock in at 7 A.M., and was told the procedure would take about three hours. He chatted with the receptionist, then went down to his car and listened to classical music on KUSC. Dr. Kamer did an excisional biopsy of the sarcoma and the lymph node underneath. "I made the definitive diagnosis, and it broke my heart," Dr. Kamer says. "Mr. Hudson was one of my favorite patients. I knew, when I looked at his neck, it was Kaposi's sarcoma. He didn't look well, but his mood was up. He said he was gonna lick it, he'd licked other things, and if he didn't, it had been a good life."

Mark drove Rock home with a large bandage covering his neck. They ate franks and beans that James had fixed—it was one of Rock's favorite lunches. Then Rock went to his bedroom to take a nap, and Mark went into his office. "He didn't seem upset," Mark says. "He was a perfect poker player, as Kay had been."

At 2:25, Rock came into Mark's office and sat down in the lion's-head chair. "I have to tell you something. I have AIDS." He stared at Mark a long time.

"Oh, shit," Mark said.

"I don't know why I haven't told you before. Dr. Bussell called last week and said they found it in the biopsy. They're concerned it'll be in the lymph node. They've arranged for me to see a specialist from UCLA, and you have to go with me. You have to come to all the doctors with me. I sit and listen and I don't hear a word."

"Oh, shit."

Mark recalls, "My first thought was, run, get out and never come back, so you don't get it and die too. I got up and walked out of the

*With Milton Bren, Claire Trevor and Marilyn
Maxwell, Newport Beach, 1959*

Dorothy Malone, Rock and Kirk Douglas in
The Last Sunset

Rock Hudson

The Undefeated, *1969: the Giant and*
the Duke

Tom Clark and Rock on MGM lot during
filming of **Pretty Maids All in a Row,** *1971*

With Claire Trevor and Leif Erickson on tour in 1976 with John Brown's Body

With Carol Burnett in I Do! I Do! *on stage in Washington, D.C.*

With Juliet Prowse in I Do! I Do!
on London stage

MAX ECKERT ESTATE

Rock Hudson's living room at the Castle

Dear Rock —
So good to have you here with us —
With warmest regards
Nancy + Ron

**With Ronald and Nancy Reagan at the
White House**

room, but my body stayed. An inner voice said, 'Do not desert. Don't get out of the chair, don't even offend him by starting to get out of the chair.' Somehow, I held myself in that chair, but I was in utter panic."

Mark knew nothing about AIDS, and Rock knew nothing, except that you don't survive it. *Newsweek* had done a cover story in 1983, calling AIDS "the health threat of the century." But Rock was the first man they knew personally to contract it. "I thought it was a disease that fairies on Santa Monica Boulevard got," Mark says. "My mind was whirling—could you get it by kissing, touching, was it in urine? Rock used my bathroom, he coughed in my face, he touched my hand, we shared food. When he was cooking, he'd take a taste, then put the spoon back in the pot."

Rock talked about who should know and who shouldn't. "Under no circumstances is Marc Christian to know. He can't keep anything to himself. He'll tell Liberty, and they'll tell the world."

"May I tell George?" Mark said.

"Always. I trust George with my life."

Rock went back to his bedroom, and Mark immediately called George in the desert. He told him to write the date and time in his diary, then he told him the news. George recalls, "He could have said, Rock is going to be executed. It was just like the knife going down with a terrible sound." George asked if he could speak to Rock, and Mark told him to call that night.

"Hiya," Rock said.

"I know the news," George said. "I'll do anything I can. What can I do?"

"Silence," Rock said.

"Fine. Are you sure there's nothing else?"

"No. Just absolute silence."

"Fine. We love you."

George was worried about Mark, and that night he went to the supermarket and bought a paperback titled *AIDS*. He read it at one sitting, and was relieved to learn the disease was not transmitted through casual contact but by the exchange of semen or blood. Mark was probably not at risk, but this left Rock, sentenced to die. Rock had told Mark that the first week, he had sobbed every night and couldn't sleep. The nights were the hardest for him. How could they help?

On June 7, Dr. Kennamer cleared his office of patients and Dr. Michael Gottlieb came in from UCLA for a two-hour consultation with Rock. Dr. Gottlieb was one of the premier researchers in the country working on AIDS. Dr. Kennamer is a "celebrity doctor," tall, thin and gray-haired, fashionably dressed; his practice is geared toward people accustomed to receiving special attention.

Dr. Kennamer and his associates, Dr. Gary Sugarman and Dr. Jeffrey Helfenstein, have refused to discuss Rock's case. Dr. Bussell also refused; only Dr. Kamer was willing to answer questions, as was Dr. Dominique Dormont in Paris. Dr. Gottlieb spoke briefly in August of 1985, and later refused to comment further. As a result, the information that follows comes largely from Mark Miller, who accompanied Rock to all his medical appointments, and from Dr. Dormont, who spoke candidly and at length.

Rock had been a patient of Dr. Kennamer's for twenty years. The doctor shook Rock's hand sadly and said, "I'm sorry this had to happen to you." He left Rock and Mark alone with Dr. Gottlieb, who examined Rock and confirmed that he had AIDS. In a kind and gentle voice, he told him about the symptoms and course of the disease. Rock said, "Is it terminal?"

Dr. Gottlieb paused, too long. "If I were you, I would get my affairs in order."

Rock was in a rage afterward. "He wouldn't tell me if it was terminal. He wouldn't answer me directly. Everyone in the office was saying good-bye. 'Oh, Rock, why you, of all people?' It's like they just gave up, instead of saying, hey, let's fight this." Rock told Mark, "I'm going to fight this. And besides, I think they're wrong. I don't have it. I won't have it. I won't. I will not have this!"

Dr. Gottlieb said there were four stages patients usually go through: fear, denial, rage and acceptance.

Rock said, "What about sex?"

The doctor said it was not advisable to have sex because there was the possibility of transmission. If Rock did have sex, he should use a condom.

The doctor asked if Rock had a sexual partner.

"Yes, well, that is, there has been . . ." Rock waved his arm. "It's over with."

Dr. Gottlieb asked if the partner lived with Rock.

"He's still in the house, but it's finished."

According to Mark's recollection, Dr. Gottlieb said that in his experience, sometimes it was best to tell the partner and sometimes it was best not to. Some partners would flee in panic. Some would start developing symptoms of AIDS, even though they did not have the disease. Some would stay and be supportive to the end. Dr. Gottlieb acknowledged that because Rock was famous, he would have to weigh his decision even more carefully.

He asked if Rock's friend had any symptoms of AIDS: weight loss, dry cough, night sweats. Rock shook his head no, and Mark said, "He's very healthy. He doesn't drink or smoke, doesn't use drugs to my knowledge."

Rock said, "I'll take care of it."

Rock then asked, "How long do I have?"

Dr. Gottlieb said there was no way of knowing.

Driving home, Rock and Mark were silent. Mark remembers feeling as if they were floating in space—quiet, motionless. He watched Rock behind the wheel and thought, "I'm looking at a dying man, he's dying right there."

Rock broke the silence. "It's like the plague. I've got the fucking plague. Nobody will come near me. If this gets out, I'm ruined. My career will be over. I'll never get another acting job. No actor will work with me." Rock said he felt ashamed and unclean, like he'd let everyone down. "I can never have sex anymore. I don't even dare touch people."

"What about Christian?" Mark said. "What are you going to do about him?"

"He goes immediately. Now—today."

"Rock, you can't do that. He's been exposed," Mark said.

"Bullshit, I could have gotten it from him!"

"That's not the point. What if he comes down with it, without health insurance? He'll be back living with Liberty on her sofa. He has no money, his parents have no money, Liberty has no money. Morally, you can't turn him out in the street."

"You're right," Rock said. "We'll leave him in the house, keep him covered. He's already sleeping in the other room. But I'm the one who has this, so, please, let me handle it my way, okay? He is *not* to know. Understand?"

251

Mark started to argue, but he knew the hard, flat tone of Rock's—when he used it, his decision was final.

"What about Ron Channell?"

Rock shook his head. "I struck out with Ron. No worry there."

Dr. Gottlieb had said that one member of the staff should be told, so he could make sure proper hygiene was maintained and would know what to do if Mark Miller wasn't there. But Rock insisted the staff not be told. "Not James, not John Dobbs or Clarence. I'll take care of the cleanliness; I'll make sure no one gets AIDS."

Rock said he wanted to send an anonymous letter to three people he'd had sex with in the months prior to learning he had AIDS. Mark drove to Palm Desert with a draft of the letter, and George wrote out the notes in longhand and mailed them from his post office, so they couldn't be traced to Rock.

Hi

This note shall remain anonymous for obvious reasons.

Since we have had intimate sexual contact where sperm has passed between us, I feel it only fair to tell you that I have just found out I have AIDS.

I am most sorry to tell you this.

I suggest you have tests made to make sure you're ok.

Most sincerely

One of the letters was sent to a twenty-two-year-old man in New York, who had had a fling with Rock after his dinner at the White House and guessed immediately that it was he. Obviously, Rock was concerned about the people he might have infected. But Marc Christian contends that Rock never told him he had AIDS, and that Rock continued to have sex with him until February of 1985. Rock told his friends and staff that they hadn't had sex since the spring of 1984. Rock's coldness to Christian and the fact that they led separate lives would seem to support this. There were no witnesses to sexual acts between them. Rock is no longer here to defend himself, so we have Christian's word against the evidence of Rock's behavior and statements to friends.

Since Rock informed three other lovers that he had AIDS, why did

252

he not tell Christian? This is difficult to understand: Christian may have been exposed to AIDS and may have exposed other people. We can only try to imagine what Rock thought and felt in the extraordinary circumstances in which he found himself in 1984. We can attempt to piece together Rock's reasoning, his point of view, from those who were closest to him at the time and shared his secret: Mark Miller, George Nader and Dean Dittman.

As they see it, Rock's intimate relationship with Christian ended shortly after Rock's return from Israel. Christian told Rock he had taken money for sex, and had set out to "hook" Rock at Brooks Baths. Rock believed it was possible that Christian had brought the AIDS virus into the house. Most important, Christian had threatened to blackmail Rock by going to the *Enquirer* or other publications, and revealing that he was Rock's lover. What would he do with an even more damaging, and valuable, piece of information—that Rock was dying of AIDS?

Rock felt he was fighting for his life and his career, which, through the years, had become indistinguishable. He kept saying, "As long as I can work, I'm okay." George Nader says, "I feel very certain about what Rock felt. He had spent almost his entire life creating his persona and career, so that his career and his life had long ago become commingled. If anything threatened his career—it was tantamount to an assault on his life." Rock had faced threats before, but the threat from Christian was so great, Rock felt, he had to defend himself by the only means he had: silence.

Rock made his decision and never wavered. But Mark Miller suggested that Christian should be examined, somehow, by a doctor. Mark went to his own doctor, Barry Unger, and said, "I have a problem. My employer has AIDS, and he has a friend whom he's chosen not to tell. Would you give the friend a complete physical and check his white count?" Mark then said to Christian, "When's the last time you had a physical?" Christian said he couldn't remember, it was long ago. "You should have one every year, why don't you go to my doctor and Mammoth Films will pay?" Dr. Unger saw Christian on September 27, 1984, and reported to Miller that Christian was in outstanding health and there was no impairment evident in his immune system. His blood was not cultured for AIDS because at that time, the test could be done at only a few laboratories in the world.

It was Rock's intention to tell no one else he had AIDS, but shortly after receiving the diagnosis, he had broken down and told Dean Dittman. He had gone to Dean's for a dinner party and arrived an hour early. He walked over to the bar, took out his wallet and said, "Look what I got." He threw a package of rubbers onto the counter.

"Why, Rock, have you gone back to women?" Dean said.

"No. I have AIDS."

As Dean stared at him, Rock said his doctors had told him if he had sex, he should wear a condom. The trouble was, he couldn't figure out how to put it on gracefully. "I've never worn a condom in my life. Won't I give the show away if I suddenly have to put one on?"

Guests began to arrive, and Dean and Rock could not talk further. It was a warm night, and the guests drifted out to the balcony. Dean was in the kitchen, cooking, when Rock came in, leaned back against the sink and started to sob. "Why me, Dean? Why me?"

Dean closed the door and took hold of Rock's shoulders. "Rock, I will not accept this for you, and you must not." Dean said later, "I committed myself to be his strength. I'd never seen Rock cry, I'd never seen weakness in him. He *is* Rock." Dean knew Rock was not religious and not receptive to talk of an afterlife. But he was an actor, he understood the power of acting. "You're a brilliant actor," Dean said. "You have to rehearse the right part. If you rehearse fatality, you will get it. Let's rehearse life. We won't speak about death. We'll speak only about life."

Dean says Rock was overcome with shame. "He felt he'd committed a crime against his public. That was his main concern— that the public would find out. He said one night, 'I hope I die of a heart attack before they find out I have AIDS. If only that would happen.'"

Dean felt honored that Rock had chosen him to confide in, and took up the task of being Rock's support. "I had to fill Rock's life. He stopped calling people, and in Hollywood, if you don't invite people, you stop getting invitations. Also, he was becoming so dour and withdrawn, he wouldn't participate in conversations. He had no social life anywhere but here." Dean consulted his doctor to see if there was any danger of exposing his other guests to AIDS. "I needed to know, if someone accidentally picked up Rock's glass and drank from it, could they get AIDS? Because if they could, I was taking people's lives in my hands." Dean was told that the AIDS virus does not survive in air, and could not be transmitted on glasses and plates.

As the months went on, Dean says, the guests he invited for Rock became "less interesting, but safer. I didn't want people in the business to see him looking poor, because they would gossip." Dean never went to sleep at night without calling Rock. "He'd take a pill, I'd talk to him and he'd drift off to sleep, so he didn't have to lie awake all night, alone and terrified." Occasionally, Dean tried to introduce God and metaphysics into their talks. "Life is life, life is always life and can never be unlife," Dean said.

"I don't want to hear that," Rock said.

Rock told Mark Miller he was sorry that in a weak moment, he had told Dean. He swore it wouldn't happen again, and it didn't.

Rock entered a period where he refused to believe he had the disease. He began staying out late, drinking and smoking more, even though he had been told that alcohol and cigarettes lower the white-cell count. He went to the opening of *Evita*, ignoring a warning to avoid crowds because he was susceptible to any sickness present. When Mark reminded him of the doctors' counsel, Rock silenced him with a wave. "I told you, I don't have it!"

Rock was losing weight rapidly, and friends began to ask Mark and Dean if he had cancer. Mark and Dean would say, no, but maybe he has anorexia—is that possible? Mark said it often struck men at his age who tried to recapture the weight of their youth and went too far. No one really bought the story of anorexia, but no one was willing to believe, either, the vague rumors that Rock had AIDS. People discounted it as gossip; it was too horrible to believe. Elizabeth Taylor said she thought Rock had cancer, but she didn't feel she could ask him about it.

In July, Dean received a letter from a woman in New York whose son had AIDS and had learned of a new drug, HPA 23, that supposedly could suppress the AIDS virus. The drug was being tested in Paris, and the woman's son had gone there for treatment and was improving. Dean showed the letter to Rock, who gave it to Mark, who called Dr. Gottlieb and asked about HPA 23. Dr. Gottlieb said he could arrange for Rock to be given the drug by Dr. Dominique Dormont at the Percy Hospital outside Paris. He warned that it was experimental and might lead nowhere, but on the other hand, it might prolong Rock's life.

Mark and Dean started to work on Rock. "It was a ray of hope," Mark says. "In Paris, they were doing something. Here, they could do nothing." He told Rock, "You gotta do this, kid, you've got nothing to lose."

Rock agreed, and Dr. Gottlieb said he would have to go for seven or eight weeks. Who could go with him? Mark didn't want to leave George for eight weeks. Rock said he wouldn't go with Marc Christian. "Why should I take him to Paris and sit in my hotel room alone every day?"

"What about Ron Channell?" Mark said.

"Great idea," Rock said. He had thought of taking Dean, but Dean knew he had AIDS, and it would be a heavy-hearted journey to the court of last hope. With Ron, he could pretend they were on holiday. Rock had received an invitation to the Deauville Film Festival for a George Stevens Retrospective, and that would be his cover. He invited Ron to go to the festival with him and take a vacation in Europe. They could continue their workouts, and Rock would keep him on salary.

On August 20, Rock flew to New York ahead of Ron to revise his will with Wally Sheft and his attorney, but did not tell them he had AIDS. He removed Tom Clark and put George Nader in first place as the beneficiary of his trust, with Mark Miller second.

On August 27, Rock met Ron in New York and they took the Concorde to Paris. The next day, Rock left Ron at the Ritz Hotel and took a cab to Percy Hospital. Rock told Ron he was working on a film project, and had to go to "story meetings" every morning. On the second or third day, he accidentally took off his shirt in front of Ron, revealing a bruise on his arm from the IV needle. "What the hell is that?" Ron said. "Oh, I banged into a chair on my way to the bathroom in my sleep," Rock said.

Percy Hospital was an old installation, built by the Americans in World War I as a temporary hospital for American soldiers. Dr. Dormont, a lively man of thirty-six, established an immediate rapport with Rock. He found that Rock's condition was good, "the disease was not very advanced, but his immune system was badly impaired." Dr. Dormont recommended that Rock stay in Paris at least three months and get daily shots of HPA 23. It was the course of treatment they had found most effective. He explained that the drug doesn't stay in the body so it's necessary to have injections every day to inhibit the virus.

Rock said he could not stay that long, he had work to do in films. Dr. Dormont said there was a shorter course of treatment, but it was more intense: Rock would come to the hospital every day for a week and have three-hour infusions of the drug. He would then take a week off, have another week of infusions and continue for four cycles. Rock agreed, and they started that morning. When I interviewed Dr. Dormont in December of 1985, he said, "If Rock had agreed to stay in Paris for a long-term course, probably the disease would have stabilized. But he felt the work in films was more important. My impression was, he was thinking Rock Hudson couldn't be killed by this virus."

Mark Miller called Rock to see how the first day of treatment had gone. "Awful," Rock said. "I feel terrible, the drug made me nauseated." Mark was standing in the kitchen of the Castle, and when he hung up, he started to cry. James thought he was laughing. "What's so funny?" he said, but when he turned, he saw Mark in tears.

"I wish it was funny. It isn't. Rock has AIDS. The boss is gonna die."

"You're joking!" James did not show much emotion, he consoled Mark and tried to be positive, but he could not sleep that night. George Nader suggested that James leave the house immediately or he might be branded as having worked in an AIDS household and have difficulty finding another job. James refused. "I love Mr. Hudson. You don't leave a person at a time like this."

In Paris, Rock felt fine after the first day of treatment and was full of energy. He met Dale Olson, his publicist, and he and Ron and Dale took long walks through the city. Rock called Dean Dittman in California and said he was having the best time he'd ever had, rediscovering Paris through Ron's eyes. He had taken Ron straight from the airport to the Eiffel Tower, as he had taken Jack Coates in 1968.

He said Ron was childlike in his excitement. "I can't believe it, I'm in Paris!"

After the first week, they drove to Deauville, where Rock received worldwide press coverage. Dale was pleased because he'd been trying to get Rock publicity to stir up film interest. After the second week in Paris, Dale arranged for Rock and Ron to stay at the château in Bordeaux where Dom Pérignon champagne is made. "It's one of the great experiences of life," Dale says. "You stay in a beautiful old château, champagne flows like water and you have meals prepared by one of the finest chefs in France."

Rock and Ron went on to Rome, London, Barcelona, Nice and St. Tropez. While they were traveling, Rock's agent called Mark Miller and said that Esther Shapiro, the creator and producer of *Dynasty*, wanted to see Rock about doing a part on the show.

Esther Shapiro is a warm, soft-spoken and canny woman of Sephardic Jewish ancestry. She had been a fan of Rock's since seeing him in *Giant*, and had always wanted to do a project with him. She and her husband, Richard Shapiro, had created the character of Daniel Reece, a wealthy rancher, with the idea that if the character worked, it could be the basis for a spinoff series. She decided to go after Rock. His agent at that time, Marty Baum at C.A.A., said, "I don't think he'll do it, and he's in Europe." Esther said, "I can usually persuade people. If you will get me a meeting, I will go anywhere."

Esther flew to Paris for one day, and Rock asked her to come to the Ritz and have tea. "I felt like a fan, not a producer. Here I was, flying fourteen thousand miles to have tea with Rock Hudson. I'd heard rumors he was sick, but he looked wonderful to me. He was wearing khaki pants and a bush jacket." Esther's view of Rock was similar to that of Susan Saint James and Dick Ebersol in Atlantic City. Rock's presence was still so dazzling that it overpowered the eye, and people did not notice the physical signs of illness and deterioration that showed up in still photographs.

Rock started telling her all the reasons he hated doing television. She told him that on *Dynasty*, they operated more like a repertory group and the actors had time to work on material. "It was like an Indian war council," she says. "One side speaks, there's silence, then the other side gives their position." This went on for about two hours. "I didn't push head on, because I sensed he wouldn't respond to that. I said, please don't feel pressured, just because I've flown all this way. I've heard no before, and if I hear it from you, I'll go on."

Rock asked, finally, if she wanted him to read a script.

"Yes, I'd love that."

"When are you going back?"

"Tomorrow," she said, and Rock asked if she would have dinner that night with him and Ron. "I was flabbergasted. The whole trip was worth it." Rock took her to a nouvelle Italian restaurant, Béato, near the Eiffel Tower, ordered a bottle of vodka and they stayed until the restaurant closed. "I read the script," Rock said. She nodded, and did not ask what he thought. Rock began telling her again how he hated doing television. "What would be the downside if you did the show?" she said. "Do you think it would hurt you in any way? I don't think it could help, you've already arrived."

Rock said he didn't think a soap opera was his milieu, but he admitted he liked to work. He looked at Esther and smiled. "What the hell. Maybe I'll just do it."

After Rock's fourth week of treatment with HPA 23, Dr. Dormont cultured his blood and found no AIDS virus present. He told Rock the treatment had been successful, the virus had been inhibited, but he cautioned him that he still had the disease. "The culture can be negative and the person still has AIDS," Dr. Dormont said. "The virus creates disorders in the immune system, after which the disease progresses independent of the virus." He said the AIDS virus would grow back, so it was important for Rock to return to Paris for treatment as soon as possible.

Rock said he wouldn't be able to come back before February because he was going to do a TV show, *Dynasty*.

Dr. Dormont said later, "I'm sure he heard what I said, but he didn't want to understand all my sentences. He understood what he wanted to understand." Dr. Dormont waited for Rock to return in February, March and April, but to his disappointment, Rock never came. The doctor received a case of champagne and flowers, sent by Mark Miller, but he did not hear from or see Rock until July of 1985, when Rock collapsed and was taken to the American Hospital.

In October of 1984, just before Rock was due to fly home to Los

Angeles, Marc Christian learned that Ron Channell was with him. Ron's father had called the house and asked Christian, "When are the boys gonna get back from Paris?" Christian called Mark Miller in the desert and said, "Why didn't you tell me? Why was this done behind my back?"

"Marc, you're not having an affair with me, you're having an affair with Rock. It's up to Rock to tell you. Don't look to me for your information."

"But you and I are friends. You should tell me things like this."

"I work for Rock," Mark said. "When Rock says don't tell, I don't tell."

On October 7, Mark Miller picked up Rock and Ron from the airport and brought them back to the Castle. Marc Christian had gone away for the weekend. When Rock was alone with Mark in the kitchen, he told him he had great news: The serum had worked. There was no more AIDS virus in his blood. Mark nearly fainted with joy and relief. Rock did not tell him the rest of Dr. Dormont's message, that he still had the disease, and that he would have to stay on HPA 23 or the virus would grow back. What Mark Miller heard was that Rock was saved. The virus had been killed. Rock looked wonderful, he hadn't lost any weight in seven weeks, and he was elated. "I can work, I can do *Dynasty*," Rock said. "I don't have AIDS. I've licked it! I told you, I never had it in the first place."

CHAPTER 14

Fright is one of the worst things in the world. I've been plenty frightened at times, like when I was in an automobile accident, a head-on collision. I remember I was so frightened my hands wouldn't work. A terrible feeling, like a disease you can't control. I don't like things I can't control.

Within a few weeks of Rock's return from Paris in October of 1984, the bubble had burst. "I've lost another ten pounds. What the hell is happening?" Rock said. The skin of his face had the creased and saggy look of elephant skin. He was sleeping twelve hours a night, and collapsing after lunch to sleep for another two hours. Mark Miller says Dr. Sugarman was upset that Rock had agreed to do *Dynasty*. He asked why Rock was jeopardizing his health, he might not get through the show, he might not see Christmas.

Rock would listen, at this time, to no one but Ron Channell. Ron persuaded Rock to start eating breakfast, which he had never done, and Rock would pick at eggs and toast and maybe eat half a portion. Rock started wearing only his jockey shorts around the house, and the staff was shocked at the way his bones protruded. John Dobbs blurted, "Mr. Hudson, you've got to eat more."

When Mark told Rock he had informed James of his illness, Rock did not speak to James for three days. "He acted as if I wasn't there. He was so embarrassed and ashamed, he couldn't face me. But then he came round," James says.

Rock was depressed and silent much of the time. "The famous laughter we all love is going," Mark said. He would tell Rock stories he knew would make him laugh, "and he'd barely react. Before, no matter how low he was, I could always get him to giggle. I could make him fall on the floor, but now I couldn't. I was losing him."

At the end of October, Rock started work on *Dynasty*. He had made a commitment to do six episodes, with an option for four more and a spinoff series the following year. The cast felt honored to be working with him, and were charmed by his kindness to other actors, his unpretentious manner and humor. Rock told riddles and kept people fascinated with anecdotes about such legendary figures as David O. Selznick and George Stevens. John Forsythe told Rock he should write a book. "You've got all these wonderful stories, you should find a writer to help you put it together."

Rock and Mark Miller had often discussed writing a book, and had always decided the time was not right. When Forsythe kept bringing it up, Rock said to Mark, "Maybe it's time."

"Okay, let's write the book," Mark said. They sat down in Mark's office, on opposite sides of the two desks that were pushed together, facing each other. They took out yellow legal pads and held their pens poised. Minutes went by; they stared at the pads, looked at each other and burst out laughing. "That's as far as we got with the book," Mark says. Rock told Forsythe, "I wrote a few paragraphs and made a big decision: no."

When he was shooting, Rock joked and chatted with the cast, but when he was not required on the set, he went to his trailer and slept. He did not eat with the cast, because he had no appetite and was beginning to throw up meals. The assistant director would come to his trailer to call him for scenes, and once she had trouble waking him. She spoke to him, touched his arm, then had to rock and shake him. "It took me a long time. He was really out—completely unconscious."

Rock's memory was failing, and he had to have cue cards, which was humiliating. It meant he could not perform the most basic part of his craft—memorizing lines. The makeup man, Jack Freeman, who had worked with Rock before, said, "His coloring was pale. I did what I could to make him look better, but it was evident he wasn't well or strong. And yet, his face would light up at times and he'd look wonderful."

During his second episode, in January of 1985, Rock agreed to do the additional four episodes. He ended up doing a total of nine because the story written for his character came to an ending point at nine. Esther Shapiro says, "I would have kept him forever. I thought he was magical on screen. He looked tired at the end, but it was the end of the season. None of us thought he was seriously ill." Esther says that if she had known he had AIDS, she is not sure they would have hired him. "I would have had to take it up with the production company and the network. The ill have rights, and other actors have rights too."

Rock was pleased with his appearance on *Dynasty*. He would ask friends, "See *Dynasty* last night? I think I look good. I look the way I did when I started acting." Rock was disconcerted, though, when he received a script for an episode in which he would have to kiss Linda Evans. He walked into the kitchen where Mark Miller was sitting and threw the script on the table. "Jesus Christ. I've got to kiss Linda. What the hell am I gonna do?" He had been given the script a week before it was to be shot, and all that week, he agonized. It had been reported in the press that the AIDS virus had been cultured in saliva, although there was no evidence that the disease could be passed through kissing. Rock did not consult his own doctors. Dr. Gottlieb says, "I would not have advised a passionate kissing scene with anyone."

Rock discussed and fretted about the kiss with Mark. "Do I run to Gottlieb and Sugarman and say, there's a kiss, what do I do? Do I reveal it to Linda Evans, to Esther Shapiro and Aaron Spelling?" Rock kept coming to the conclusion that he could do nothing. Mark says, "He was trapped. He felt, either you announce you have AIDS, or kiss the lady."

I asked Mark why Rock did not tell the producers he had an infection in his mouth and could not kiss anyone. Mark said, "You couldn't suggest things like that to Rock. He would wave you away and say, 'It's my kiss, not yours.' He felt he could not ask them to change a script; it would have aroused suspicion."

Rock made what Mark calls a "career decision." Rock's career had always been the ruling priority; all other considerations came afterward. It was the ruthless, tunnel vision he had applied to all decisions in his life, and it did not change. Rock knew, though, that "way down the line, I'm gonna pay for that kiss." His mood changed toward the show, and he started making a pun of the title, Die Nasty.

Mark says that he, Rock and George still believed they could keep Rock's affliction quiet. "We didn't know there would be an announcement." They talked about bringing Rock to the desert and installing him in a condo with discreet male nurses round the clock. "We thought Rock would have a slow demise, and it would be hushed up forever. All of a sudden, there would be an announcement that Rock Hudson had died of cirrhosis of the liver. He would die quietly; we should have known better with Rock."

On the day the kiss with Linda Evans was shot, Rock used every gargle, mouthwash and spray he could lay his hands on. He came home and told Mark, "The fucking kiss is over with. Thank God." He said it was one of the worst days of his life.

The episode went on the air February 6, and George Nader watched it alone in the desert, frozen with dread. He taped the show, played it back and stopped the action. To his relief, he says, "I could see where Rock kept his lips closed and hit Linda on the side of the cheek for a brief, chaste kiss. He did not open his mouth, no saliva was exchanged."

Esther Shapiro, in retrospect, agreed. "It was not much of a kiss. It couldn't be passionate because Linda loved her husband and was pulling away from Rock." Esther was not angry when she learned Rock had AIDS and hadn't told the company. "I was horrified Rock had AIDS and was going to die." She said she didn't think about the disclosure issue. "The man was ill and wanted to work, he had a history of denial all his life. It was understandable to me."

No one on the *Dynasty* set seemed upset about Rock's lack of truthfulness. A spokesperson for Linda Evans said, "She's not concerned about getting AIDS. She's said, medical evidence tells her you cannot contract it through kissing. She is not a worrier; she's a fatalist, and believes things happen for a purpose." In September of 1985, Linda Evans appeared at an AIDS benefit in Los Angeles and said, "Like everyone here, and all his friends around the world, I would like to express my love and support to Rock Hudson."

The cast and crew had developed a fondness for Rock, and their reaction when the news broke was grief. One director said, "It was a damn shame this had to happen to such a wonderful man." Ironically, no one on the set voiced what people were saying outside: "How could he have kissed Linda without telling her he had AIDS?" Fans of Linda were furious. One man, who owns a small business in Los Angeles, said, "He flat-out exposed her, and I can't forgive him for that. I don't trust these doctors who say it can't be passed through kissing. They don't know everything yet. Linda should have been told, so she could make the decision herself if she wanted to take the risk."

Mark Miller woke up in the middle of the night, worrying that Linda Evans would get AIDS from the kiss. "Even though I knew Rock couldn't give it to me by touching, I still shrank from his touch.

When he asked me to rub salve on his back, I'd go in the bathroom afterward and scrub down like a surgeon. On *Dynasty*, there he was, rolling around the ground with Linda, kissing her, even though his mouth was closed." Rock, however, did not give the matter a second thought, once it was over. It was a lifelong pattern: He did not seem vulnerable to guilt.

When Rock's birthday had approached in November of 1984, Mark Miller asked Marc Christian if he wanted to throw a party. Rock had been saying that he regretted falling out of touch with the friends he'd had in the fifties and sixties. After Tom Clark had moved in, Rock had stopped seeing people like Lynn Bowers and Pat Fitzgerald, Bob Garren, Chuck Tilley, Dr. Joe Carberry, Jimmy Dobson and Wolfgang Bruch. Tom had moved Rock into a more elegant, social crowd, and Rock said, "I should never have allowed that."

Mark Miller said to Christian, "Why don't you invite the old-timers, along with his current friends, to a birthday party?" They made up a list, and Christian went to the phone. He first called Ross Hunter and Jacque Mapes, who said they were busy Saturday, which was Rock's birthday. Christian called Dean Dittman, who said he was busy, and Jon Epstein, who was also busy. He came back to Mark's office and said, "Everyone's busy Saturday." Mark said, "Okay, let's change it to Friday."

What Mark Miller did not know was that Dean was throwing a birthday party for Rock on Saturday, and at Rock's request, had invited Ron Channell and not Marc Christian. Dean did not know Mark Miller was behind Christian's party. Christian called everyone back, and many said they were busy Friday also. Some of the old-timers declined because they had been snubbed for ten years and saw an opportunity to get even.

Ross Hunter finally called Mark Miller and told him about Dean's party. Mark realized he'd blundered. "I couldn't tell Christian about Dean's party because Ron Channell was going. I had to let him go ahead with the other party." Mark asked Rock what to do and Rock said, "Let him go ahead, I don't care."

Mark Miller did not attend either party because he was in the desert on the weekend. On Monday, November 19, he asked Rock,

"How'd the parties go?" Rock made a thumbs-down gesture. "No sixtieth. I'm leaving town next year."

Rock was beginning to accept what was happening to him, and to resign himself not to fight it. He said, in November, that he was through with doctors. He complained that when his blood was taken, the doctors never called him with results. "No one calls and says, hey, there's improvement, or, uh-oh, there's a setback. Sugarman takes blood, then nothing. Silence. There *can't* be any good news, so why the hell go on pulling the fucking blood? I've had it—no more blood tests and that's that!"

Rock had no further interest in sex. Where in the past, he had loved to hear details of sexual adventures, and was pleased if someone sent him a "care package" of pornography, in the fall of 1984, he did not want to hear or see anything relating to sex. Dean Dittman says, "If a sexy scene came on television, Rock would shut it off. You couldn't discuss sex around him; he was dying because he'd had sex."

Mark Miller felt Rock was giving up. "Sex and career had been the most important things to him. Now, he couldn't have sex, and his career had waned to the point where he was doing a soap opera on television. He was dreading the future, he saw a way out and decided to take it."

Rock still worried that his illness would "get out in the press." Mark said, trying to be light, "If that happens, you're to leave town immediately, understand?"

Rock fell in with him, pretending innocent confusion, "But where will I go, sir?"

"To the Yucatan, or western Australia. You can live out your days in remote parts of the world."

"You've gotta go too, then, sir." Rock dropped the game and stopped smiling. "You're right. I sure as hell won't stick around here, watching the rejections pile up."

Rock had stayed home alone three nights in a row, for the first time since he had arrived in Hollywood in 1948. "I had no place to go," he told Mark. "Ron Channell was busy and so was Dean." The phone hardly rang anymore, where, in prior years, all four lines would ring night and day. "Rock loved the phone; he could be talking on one line, have someone on hold, and if the third line rang, Rock would yell, 'I'll get it!'"

Rock spent long periods in Mark's office, sitting in the lion's head chair, staring into space. Mark would be answering letters or balancing accounts, and Rock would say, "I'm gonna die." He said it like a child taunting his mother, "I'm gonna eat worms."

"I'm gonna die."

"No, you're not," Mark said, taking the part of another child.

"I am too," Rock said.

"No you're not."

"Yes I am. Na na na na."

"Stop it," Mark would say, and they'd laugh.

In December, Rock and Dean started learning a duet to sing at Christmas parties, "Perhaps Love," recorded by Plácido Domingo and John Denver. Rock took the John Denver part, and Dean took Plácido Domingo's. Rock enjoyed working on the song, but they were not invited to any parties where they could perform, and Rock ended up staying home by himself on Christmas day. "For Rock, invitations had almost ceased," Dean says.

They went to a tree-decorating party at Stockton Briggle's, and Stockton remembers Rock sitting by himself, looking thin and unhappy, staring wistfully at the tree. Stockton went over and sat beside him, put his arm around Rock's shoulders and kept it there. "He seemed so vulnerable, like he needed support." When Rock left, he told Dean he felt bad he couldn't share what he had with Stockton. When Stockton learned this, after Rock's death, he was saddened. Stockton himself had been told, ten years before, that he had cancer and might die. "I shared it with *everyone*. I was determined to beat it and I did." Stockton says Rock could have spent his last year surrounded by loving friends. "But he had to tell the world or nobody. He chose to isolate himself and die alone."

On Christmas Eve, Rock and Dean went to a party at the home of Martha Raye, who had been Rock's co-star on *McMillan*, but Rock left early because Tom Clark was expected. Dean had toured with Martha that year in *Annie*, and one night on the road, when both were drinking, Dean had slipped and told her Rock had "the big A." Dean had sworn her to secrecy, and was furious with himself for the breach.

When Tom Clark arrived at the Christmas party, he went straight up to Dean and said, "What's wrong with our boy? You've *got* to tell me, does he have AIDS?"

"Tom, if he has it, I have it. No, he couldn't possibly have AIDS," Dean said.

"If he does, I'll be right there, even if he throws me out," Tom said.

Dean saw Tom go off in a corner with Martha Raye, and feared what might happen. Later that night, when Dean returned to his apartment, Tom called and said, "Martha Raye just told me you told her Rock has AIDS!" Dean denied it, and called Martha and demanded that she call Tom and deny it; they had angry words and have been estranged ever since. Tom Clark says, though, that he never really believed it. He didn't learn Rock had AIDS until the news was announced in July of 1985.

By January of 1985, the rumors that Rock had AIDS were more persistent. Wally Sheft called from New York and grilled Mark, "Does he have AIDS?" Mark said, "Why don't you ask Rock?" Wally put the question, tactfully, to Rock, and he said no. Later, Rock said, "Maybe I should have told Wally. But why? It changes nothing."

As Rock spoke, his hands moved ceaselessly over his body, scratching, trying desperately to relieve the itch. He was covered with rashes, in his genital area, on his face, and he couldn't have cortisone to alleviate it because it would affect his immune system adversely. He had Vincent's disease in his mouth, and two front teeth were loose. He developed contact impetigo, which was highly infectious and covered his chest, back and legs with itching sores. Rock said he could not sleep at night because of the maddening itch. He walked around in jockey shorts because clothing was intolerable—it aggravated the itch.

After Rock's workout one morning, James walked into the bedroom and found Rock lying on the bed with a thermometer in his mouth. He pointed at James and said, "You didn't see this."

Mark and James started a campaign to persuade Rock to go back to Paris, to be treated again by Dr. Dormont. Mark showed him a letter from a friend they had sent to Dr. Dormont after Rock had gone, Bob Darcy. (This is a pseudonym; he asked that his name be withheld.) Bob had been in Paris six months, and wrote that he was gaining weight and swimming two miles a day. Doctors in San Francisco had told him he wouldn't see his next birthday, but he was celebrating his birthday in Paris!

"It's cold in Paris," Rock said.

Mark said he would go over first, rent an apartment, furnish it and Rock could fly in.

"I don't want to hear about fucking Paris! There's no work in Paris."

"Forget your career, you want to live," Mark said.

"I'm not gonna live in Paris alone, and how can I explain to Ron, we're gonna go live in Paris, in the cold. For what? Ron's in acting school—I can't take him away."

Mark said, after Rock died, "I did everything to get that man back to Paris. If he'd stayed in Paris, he would be alive today. Bob Darcy is alive today."

In February, Rock took Ron Channell to Hawaii for a week's vacation at the Mauna Kea. He lay in the sun, which seemed to alleviate his rashes, but when he returned to the Castle, his weight was down to 182. He sat at lunch with the staff and did not eat. If he did, he would excuse himself afterward, go upstairs and throw up. The only thing he could keep down was Nutriment. "I get nauseated just walking through the kitchen," he said.

He was slower in his speech and walk, and often had trouble understanding simple questions. Mark began to crack under the strain of watching Rock fade, and being forced to lie and cover up. Mark would drive to the desert every Thursday, sit down at the bar and fall into a catatonic stupor. It would take him until Sunday to regain his spirits, and then it was time to drive back to the house where Rock was dying, "to Plague Palace, to hell," Mark says. "Yet you could not desert. At least I couldn't desert. That's the Iowa farm boy."

In March, Rock asked Mark if he could come to the desert some weekend and visit. Mark was surprised, as Rock had never liked Palm Desert. "Sure," he said, "let's ask George." They called George, and Rock said, "Is it okay if I come down?"

"Of course, it would be great. Come, and bring whomever you'd like."

"Can't I just come by myself?" Rock said.

"My God, Rock, sure, just get your ass down here."

They made a plan for Easter weekend, and on Thursday, April 4,

Rock and Mark drove out in Mark's Jeep Wagoneer. George had not seen Rock in more than a year, since the weekend he had come to visit with Marc Christian in February of 1984. George had been warned that Rock looked poor, but the sight of Rock's face was still a jolt. It was hard to believe it was the same face George had known for three decades, the face that the camera had loved.

Rock put out his hand, George grabbed it, then threw his arms around Rock and slapped him on the back. That was another shock—that he could feel the bones beneath Rock's sweatshirt. Rock looked directly in George's eyes, said "Hiya," and it was clear that they were going to be together without pretense. George says, "There were many levels of intimacy Rock and I could use. We could be very superficial, stay on the surface and not probe. Rock could turn on the grandeur and play the movie star, or we could get down to a man-to-man, no-shit basis right away. When Rock said 'Hiya,' I knew we were on that no-shit basis."

The house in Palm Desert was low and modern, with windows on all sides looking out on the palm trees and brilliant greens of the Bermuda Dunes Country Club, and beyond that, the mountains of Palm Springs, which change color through the day from tan to salmon to deep purple. George had moved out of the master bedroom for Rock's visit, because he thought Rock would be more comfortable with a private bathroom close at hand.

They went to dinner that night at the French Quarters, which Mark and George called "the fort," because it had once been the desert training headquarters of General Patton. Rock pushed food around his plate and ate a little, but toward the end of the meal, he asked Mark, "Where's the men's room?"

George looked at Mark with raised eyebrows. Was Rock going to be sick? Mark nodded.

Rock returned ten minutes later, smiling, as if he'd been gone just a minute. He gave no sign of feeling ill.

The next morning, Rock came out to the pool in a pair of sloppy old blue shorts. He asked if it would be okay if he took his shorts off, because he had a rash in the groin area, which the sun would help. Mark and George said that was fine, there was a fence around the property. Rock spread a beach towel on the grass and lay down on his back, while George sat in a chaise longue, under a shade tree.

George had had several bouts with skin cancer, so he wore jeans, a long-sleeved shirt and a hat. While Mark was puttering in the kitchen, Rock and George sat in the yard and talked about the pets they had had through the years. They argued about which had been the most intelligent, which the most charming. Rock's favorite was his first Irish setter, Tucker, and George's was Matty, a Doberman-Airedale given to him by Rory Calhoun.

They sat in silence a while, and then Rock sighed. "Well, I guess you're right . . ."

"I'm always right," George said.

"Like hell! You've never been right." Through the years, Rock and George had had a fierce rivalry about who was wisest, and Rock had insisted he was always right and George was always wrong.

"For once in your life, you're right," Rock said. "People are no damn good."

George let out a hurrah. "What converted you?"

"The phone's died. At the house."

"You sure the bill's been paid?"

Rock lifted his head and looked sternly at George. "No one calls . . . ever . . . about anything. Ross and Jacque have stopped calling. My agents don't call. Even the fucking doctors don't call."

"Rock, it's no consolation, but that happened to Mark and me a long time ago. When I stopped acting. 'Taint much fun, I know."

Rock said he was sick of spending all his evenings with Dean Dittman, and having to listen to his lectures about God and positive thoughts.

"What's with the sleeping prince?" George said, using Rock's nickname for Marc Christian. According to George, Rock replied as follows.

"More of the same." Rock turned over and lay on his stomach, so he was facing George directly. He gave a grim smile. "He trapped me, you know? And then he laughed about it."

"How do you mean, trapped you?"

Rock looked toward the house and bellowed, "Mark, how long till lunch?"

"About ten minutes," Mark yelled.

Rock turned back to George, and told him how, shortly after his return from Israel, Christian had confessed to him that he'd taken

271

money for sex. "With that shit-eating grin of his, he said he *only* did it when he was really so hungry he just *had* to," Rock said, imitating Christian's voice. "I told him to get the hell out. He just laughed and said to listen because there was more. It seems I'd been set up—the 'accidental' meeting was planned." Rock related how Christian had waited for him to come into Brooks Baths. "And when I did, he kept waving his dick at me until I finally noticed him. The rest is history. Jesus Christ, I still can't believe it. Yours truly, set up and seduced."

"For God's sake, why didn't you throw him out?" George said.

"He said he'd go straight to the *Enquirer*, he had a friend who was a reporter, and they were all ready and waiting."

There was an uncomfortable pause. "That ended it for me, for good," Rock said.

George wrestled with a question he'd been wanting to ask Rock for some time: Why he hadn't told Christian he had AIDS. George tried to gauge whether this was the moment. "Uh, Rock, when you found out about . . ."

"The Plague? I just told you, for God's sake, I was finished with Christian, we hadn't had sex for months. And if I said anything to him, he'd run straight to Liberty and she'd have it all over town."

"But . . ." George tried to voice his concern that Christian had been exposed.

"Listen to me." Rock's voice was steely. "You know Christian's story. So fuck him. Because it goes with the territory."

They stared at each other, and then Mark appeared at the back door. "Lunch, you guys."

On Saturday, Mark and George had planned an excursion to Joshua Tree National Monument. "Yeah! Let's go, let's do it," Rock said. They climbed in the Jeep, turned on the radio and drove to the national park, planning to make a two-hour loop and have dinner at the Valley of the Moon restaurant. Rock had never been to Joshua Tree, a desert preserve filled with exotic cactuses, wildflowers and fantastic rock formations. "Goddamn, that's beautiful, look over there!" Rock said. They had come upon "the cholla gardens," a stretch of desert that was packed with thousands of cholla cactuses, whose yellow spines were iridescent in the afternoon sun. They walked along a path through the cholla, then returned to the Jeep and drove on.

They soon began to see Joshua trees: large yucca plants, brown and bent, which seemed to have been stuck in the sand like sentries with extended, thorny arms. On the local radio station in their car, Patti Page came on, singing "Mockin' Bird Hill." They all started screaming with laughter, and Mark nearly drove off the road. "Mockin' Bird Hill," after all these years! It was the song Rock had played again and again in 1951, the song he had loved when they were young and struggling, when they were first getting to know one another. It was the record Mark and George had threatened to fling out the window if Rock played it one more time. Mark pulled over and stopped, and they laughed until tears were streaming down their faces.

Then a quiet fell upon them. Mark started the car, and they drove the rest of the way without speaking. The sun was setting, and the landscape became barren as the moon, except for the Joshua trees with their spiky arms and eerie shapes. George felt "some other level of communication was taking place. It was as if the noisy vocal system had to be shut down, so the wordless could occur." And George knew: Rock has come to say good-bye.

When they reached the end of the park, they switched to four-wheel drive and followed a gravel road that appeared to lead nowhere. Far in the distance, they could see faint lights; then, closer and closer, they saw clusters of cactus and ocotillo, and finally, an old stone building with a sign: VALLEY OF THE MOON.

The spell was broken when they walked into the restaurant. The owner recognized Rock and made him welcome. Out came platters of farm-style, home-cooked dishes: fried chicken, mashed potatoes, country biscuits with honey, and Jell-O for dessert. It was the kind of food Rock loved most in the world, and he ate as much as Mark had seen him eat in months. After the Jell-O, though, he said quietly, "Where's the rest room?"

George says, "It was heartbreaking." They drove home by the quickest route, sensing that Rock was exhausted.

On Easter Sunday, Rock slept until ten. He and Mark did needlepoint in the front room, while George read the paper. Rock carped about Mark's "sloppy work," and showed him where he had made a mistake turning a corner. "Jeez, it's the easiest thing, any ass could do it."

"Bullshit," Mark said. "Show me."

Rock undid Mark's work, showed him the correct stitch and did a few rows himself. Then he went back to his own piece.

Rock inquired about Mark and George's finances. "If something happens to me, will you two be all right?" Mark went over what they had, and explained that they could get by very well by living simply. They did not need Rock's money; he should feel free to dispose of it as he wished.

Mark and George had planned to take Rock to Borrego Springs that day, but George felt Rock was not up to it. "Why don't we just laze around here?" George said.

"Yeah, I think that's a good idea," Rock said.

George realized that no special efforts were necessary. "Rock didn't want or need entertaining. He was happy just being with us quietly." George was touched that Rock had made a point of coming for this visit, and that obviously it was important to him. George felt Rock's revelations about Marc Christian had been like a last confession. "If Rock hadn't known this might be our last time together, he never would have told me those things. He was too proud, he would have kept it to himself."

The knowledge that this was a parting visit was never verbalized. At one point, George said, "You know, Rock, now that you've been able to lose all that weight, you should get a complete facelift. Have the whole thing done."

"Come on!" Rock had had his eyelids done, under pressure from a cameraman, and had thought it was the height of vanity.

"You've got hollows and lines . . ."

"Me? Lines? Nah."

"Yes, in certain lights. A few lines. Why not do it, what the hell, have the whole thing pulled up and tightened. It'll look great on screen."

Rock gave a hearty laugh, and shook his head. "Thanks, George. I think I look like a million bucks."

In May, there were rumors, repeated to Mark Miller, that Marc Christian had AIDS and had given it to Rock. When Christian came into his office on May 28, Mark said, "Have you heard the latest rumor about yourself?"

"What is it?" Christian said.

"That you have AIDS, and you gave it to Rock."

"What! That's ridiculous." Christian said, "Does Rock have AIDS?" It was the first time Christian had raised the question with Mark.

"Why don't you go ask him?" Mark said.

That night, Rock was alone in the kitchen when Christian came in and told him the rumor. "Do you have AIDS?" Christian said.

Rock gave him a withering look. "No. Do you?"

"No," Christian said. "But there's something wrong with you. Why don't you get help? Why don't you go to a good physician, instead of the quacks you're going to?"

"I'm fine."

"Have you been checked for cancer?"

"Yes."

"Have you been checked for AIDS?"

"Yes, I've been checked for everything and I don't have it!" The familiar veil dropped over Rock's face, so no expression could be detected. He said to Christian, in a cold, intimidating voice, "What would you do if you had it?"

"I don't know. I'd probably commit suicide," Christian said.

In June, there was a crisis over Christian's 1959 Chevy Nomad station wagon. The car had been at Image Makers for more than eighteen months, being restored, and Mark Miller had been paying invoices each week. In May, he had totaled up what Rock had invested to date—$20,000—and when Rock was advised, he said, "That's it. I won't pay any more." Mark had relayed this to Christian, who nevertheless ordered more work done on the car. When a new bill arrived from Image Makers in June, for $10,000, Mark told Christian he would have to pay it himself.

"Wait a minute," Christian said. "The car is not finished. You can't leave me in the lurch." Christian said he had discovered that the manager of Image Makers, Mike Frawley, had been jacking up the prices because he thought it was Rock Hudson's car. "This man has charged you three or four times for the same part. He's been stealing from Rock, by writing up orders of the same parts time and again. I'm trying to protect you, I have all this evidence. You can't just pull out on me."

Mark said, "There have been too many problems. We're going to wash our hands of it."

"If you want me to, I'll just take the car off the lot," Christian said.

"If you can do that without breaking the law," Mark said.

Christian consulted George Nader's attorney, Margaret Saal, and concocted a plan to get the car off the lot without paying the bill. He told Frawley that Rock wanted the car registered as a vintage car, and asked Frawley to accompany him to the Department of Motor Vehicles. When they drove off the lot, they stopped at a light and Liberty Martin got in. Christian says he then "ordered Frawley out of my car. This was legal, I had found, because he knew I was taking the car off the lot." A policeman was called, and when Frawley was unable to produce a lien against the car, Christian was allowed to drive it away. "And so I took the car, in order not to incur any more expenses," Christian says.

Mike Frawley says he was conned by Christian, who kept asking for work to be done over again. "The car was painted twice and upholstered twice, at his request. Many of the chrome parts were replaced several times, at his request. The car is so old, you can't get new parts, you can only get good second parts. Christian had me combing the papers for parts, and if we found one in better condition than a part we'd already installed, he'd have me replace it." Frawley says Christian brought in Liberty Martin's Ford Torino, "told me to fix it and charge the parts to Rock Hudson's company, Mammoth Films. So some of the duplicate parts were for Liberty's car."

When Frawley stopped receiving payments from Mammoth Films, he asked Christian what was wrong. Christian told him Rock was upset the job was taking so long and would not pay any more until the car was completed. Christian said Frawley should stop sending bills to the house, Christian would take them up personally. Christian assured him he would be paid upon completion. Frawley asked his staff to work round the clock to finish the car in three weeks, and sent a final bill to Mammoth Films for $10,000. "I felt confident I was going to be paid when Christian tricked me into driving off the lot with him."

Christian told Mark Miller how he had "liberated" the car, and laughed about it. Christian went to Rock and said, "My car is ready, can I bring it up here?" Rock was in the kitchen with Ron Channell; they were about to start their workout.

"Definitely not," Rock said.

"Why?"

"You know how you got it. I don't want those people bothering me and coming up here after it."

"I live here too, this is my house, and it's my car."

Rock yelled, "I don't want that fucking car on my property and that's that!"

"How can you speak to me like that in front of a servant," Christian said, pointing at James.

Rock walked out; Christian picked up a chair and hurled it across the kitchen.

Ron Channell, who was at the kitchen door when Rock came out, said, "If I were you, I'd go right back in there and tell that guy to move out."

Marc Christian stormed into Mark Miller's office and swore he would bring his car there whether Rock liked it or not. Mark buzzed Rock in the playroom, and asked him to come into the office. "Talk it out, guys, come on," Mark said. Christian and Rock went back and forth, and resolved that the car could be parked at the Castle, but it would have to have a car cover on it at all times.

Meanwhile, James was in a rage and told Mark Miller he wanted to quit. "How dare Marc Christian call me a servant! He doesn't own this house. I'm an Englishman, I have an honorable profession."

Mark Miller went to Christian and said, "Listen, straighten out your relationship with Rock. Go talk to him. Either you straighten it out, or leave. The house is in an uproar, James is in an uproar. Nobody speaks. Rock won't even speak to you."

That night, while Rock was at the table poking at his dinner, Christian came in and sat down quietly across from him. "Can't we return to what we had two years ago?"

"No," Rock said. "I don't give a good shit about you anymore. As a matter of fact, don't even bother to speak to me. We have nothing to say. You've put me through the wringer for two years. It's too late."

Christian's mouth dropped open. Rock turned his attention to his plate, making it clear the interview was over. Christian waited a moment, then stood and walked out.

The following week, Ron Channell called a meeting with Rock and Mark Miller to discuss Rock's health. They sat down in Mark's office, and Ron made an earnest pitch for action. He wanted Rock to consult a new doctor, to see a dietitian and psychologists. It was time to mobilize all the powers of science, psychology, religion, anything that might help restore his health. Rock sliced open mail with a letter opener as Ron was talking. Ron plowed on, like a coach trying to fire up a team that was hopelessly behind. "What say, men, shall we do it?"

Dead silence. Rock said, "Let me think about it."

Ron slumped in his chair.

Rock was failing by the day now because he was getting no nourishment. He was down to 170—fifty pounds less than when the disease had started—and he seemed to have shrunk. No longer did he tower above other men; he seemed a normal size, about six one. For the first time in his life, Rock had nightmares and would wake up screaming. He was sweating so profusely in his sleep that James had to put plastic sheets on the bed. Rock told Mark Miller, "I stink at night. What is that terrible smell?"

On July 5, Dean called and said Ross Hunter had told him, "I hear Rock's being drugged by the staff." Mark repeated this to Rock, who said, "Yes, and I wish you'd stop it."

Rock had agreed to go to Carmel on July 15, to tape a show with Doris Day for her new cable program, *Doris Day's Best Friends*. A press conference had been set up, and *Life* magazine was planning to shoot what might be a cover picture: the reunion between Rock Hudson and Doris Day. Mark tried to persuade Rock not to go, the doctors tried, Dale Olson tried, but it was useless. Mark told them, "I don't think Rock realizes the change that's taken place in his looks."

Rock left for Carmel on Monday, "hanging by a thread," and the following day, Mark made an executive decision: Rock was going back to Paris. He made reservations for Rock and Dean to leave on Saturday, and asked Dr. Gottlieb to call Dr. Dormont in Paris to alert him. Mark called Wally Sheft and told him Rock was going to Geneva to be treated for anorexia. Mark would not inform Wally that Rock had AIDS until after Rock had collapsed in Paris.

In Carmel, Rock arrived late for the press conference, dressed in ill-matched, loose-fitting clothes. When it was over, the reporters were visibly shaken and swarmed around Dale Olson. "What's wrong with Rock? He was barely coherent."

"He's had the flu," Dale said. "I was afraid we'd have to cancel."

"It looks worse than that," one reporter said.

"No, I don't think so," Dale said.

U.S.A. Today ran a picture of Rock and Doris, and Dale started getting calls from around the world. "Is Rock dying?" Tom Clark called Dean and said he was alarmed by the picture. "The whole town is buzzing." Liz Smith printed an item that Rock was in the hospital, and friends called the house, asking where to send flowers.

Doris Day and her son, Terry Melcher, were so concerned they tried to cancel the shoot, but Rock was adamant that they go forward. They started filming on Tuesday, July 16, and that evening, after dinner, Rock invited Dale to his room. "I've ordered some drinks, come and talk to me," Rock said. Dale found Rock lying on the bed of the suite, with a fire going, music playing, and on the table, four Scotches and four vodkas.

"When you order drinks, you order drinks," Dale said.

"Well, it takes 'em a long time to get here, so I thought I'd order several."

Dale realized it was going to be a long night. "I spent a lot of time around Judy Garland," Dale says. "She was so terrified of being left alone, you couldn't leave until she passed out. That was the feeling I got from Rock that night." Dale kept saying, "I'd better go, you've got to sleep," and Rock said, "No, no, don't leave."

Rock wanted to talk about personal matters, things he had never come near discussing with Dale. He talked about people: who had been his real friends and who hadn't. Dale remembers being surprised, some of the people Dale had thought were Rock's friends were not.

"You know, the most important person who was ever in my life was Tom Clark," Rock said. "You could laugh with Tom, and he was great to travel with. He was loyal, and he made the house sing. He was terrific."

"Really," Dale said.

Rock acknowledged that his life had fallen apart after Tom had gone. The music had died. He had truly loved Tom and hadn't known how much.

"Maybe you should see him again."

"No, I don't think so. I'd like to, but I don't think so."

Rock did not mention Marc Christian. Two years before, Rock had asked Dale if he could do anything to help Marc with his music project. Rock had showed him, with pride, the tapes Marc was compiling on the history of pop music. A few months later, Dale had told Rock he had some ideas about getting an institution to sponsor Marc's research, but Rock had waved him off. "Don't bother with that. It won't come to anything."

Rock knew Dale was a longtime friend of Shirley MacLaine, and asked about her. Dale said she was doing a television show involving reincarnation. Rock was intrigued; he said he didn't believe in God, at least not the way God was generally pictured, but as to reincarnation, "I think there's truth to that."

At three in the morning, Dale announced he was leaving. "You've got to get some sleep, Rock, or I'm gonna cancel the shoot. You can't go in front of the camera with no sleep. You can't do that to Doris." Dale went to bed, and when his wake-up call came, Rock was up already, shaving, ready to work.

Doris Day's Best Friends was shown on the Christian Broadcast Network shortly after Rock died, and it is a touching little piece. It opens with Doris and Rock on a split screen, as they were in *Pillow Talk*. Doris is in her living room, putting flowers in a vase. She dials a number on the phone, and Rock, on his side of the screen, picks up.

"I love my roses," Doris sings the words, more than says them.

"Well . . . good. Pretty roses for a pretty blonde." Rock is folksy, relaxed, and you can feel the warmth through the screen. Doris says she's thrilled he's going to be the first guest on her show. He says he'll take the first flight up. She says there's a problem. "We're on kind of a tight budget, could you take the bus?"

Music starts, and we see Doris waiting on a country lane for a rickety old white bus. "Here he comes!" she cries. Doris and Rock are nearly the same age, but the contrast between them takes the breath away. She jumps up and down with spring and vitality, while he moves slowly, stiffly, off the bus.

"Give me a hug," Rock says.

"Ohhhh, I haven't seen you," Doris says, as they clutch each other.

They drive, in an antique yellow convertible, to her home. She sings, "My Buddy," as they walk around the grounds and gardens, stopping to admire a tree or throw a stick for a dog. They look so comfortable, so right together, Doris with her bouncing step and Rock shambling beside her, his hands in his pockets. When they sit down on the patio, one of her dogs flops at Rock's feet.

"Did he get tired?" Doris says.

"No, I did," Rock says.

"I walked you around pretty good," Doris says. "I miss those laughs we used to have."

"I do too. I haven't had a good laugh like that . . . since."

"We really had fun making movies."

"I wish we'd made more," Rock says.

"We should do it again."

Doris invites him to stay for dinner, but Rock says he has to catch his bus. There's a final hug at the bus stop, and Rock kisses her on the lips, keeping his mouth closed. She sings, "My Buddy . . ." as the white bus rattles away.

Doris said later, "When we were walking around out there together, it crossed my mind, it might be the last time. But I didn't really know. I hoped and prayed that it wouldn't be. I didn't know what was wrong with him, but I knew he was determined to do that show if it took his last breath. It was his final thing, and it was with me, and I really cherish that."

Doris made Rock promise that he would eat more. Rock collapsed on the plane and slept all the way to Los Angeles, but in the middle of the flight, he opened his eyes and looked at Dale. "I think I'm going to Paris."

"Oh, why?"

"Doris is mad at me. There's a doctor in Paris I've got to see, because I guess there's something wrong with me. I don't like it that Doris is mad at me." He closed his eyes and slept.

After Mark and George had put Rock on the plane to Paris, in the brief interlude before the sky fell in, Mark's mind kept returning to a talk he'd had with Rock the month before. Mark had learned more from Rock in that ten-minute talk than he'd learned in thirty-four years, and he was still running it through his mind, plumbing it.

Rock and Mark had been sitting in the office, alone in the house on a quiet afternoon. "Let's take a walk," Rock said. He stood and extended his arm to Mark, which was the signal to "practice our bows." Mark slipped his arm through Rock's, and they walked out to the deck where they could talk privately and be sure no one could eavesdrop.

As they strolled, they pretended to be noblemen, wearing velvet costumes.

"Do you think the queen is in the palace?" Rock said.

"The countess is here, I saw her carriage."

With heads held high, they made their way across the patio, past the pool and fountains and onto the deck. They leaned against the railing, looking down on the terraces of citrus trees and roses, and below, the hazy city. It was peaceful, no sound but the twittering of birds.

Rock said he wanted to get started on the book. "It's time."

"I agree with you there."

"What the hell do we put in a book?" Rock said.

"Well, for one thing, who have you loved? I mean really loved, we're talking about love, not infatuations or fucks."

"Only two people," Rock said. "Phyllis Gates and Lee Garlington."

Mark was fascinated, it was not the answer he would have guessed.

"Lee just drove me crazy," Rock said.

"I knew that at the time, even though . . ."

"You didn't like him, did you?"

"No, I found him supercilious."

"He led me a merry chase," Rock said. "Goddamn I loved him."

Months later, when told what Rock had said, Lee Garlington was astonished. "I had no idea Rock had cared to that extent." Phyllis Gates, when told, said quickly, "He was lying. Rock never loved me. To me, he wasn't a very nice man."

Mark Miller hesitated to question Rock. "He opened up so little that when he did, you took what he gave you and didn't press." Mark said, simply, "No one else?"

Rock shook his head no. "Those are the only people I've really ever loved in my life. The rest, I thought I did but I didn't. Soon after I got into the situation, I realized I didn't love them. It was sex, or infatuation, but it wasn't love. Then I had to figure out how to get rid of them."

"Why is it that you cannot say those two words: get out?" Mark said.

Rock laughed. "I don't know, but I can't."

Rock turned from the railing and put out his arm. "Shall we?" The two gentlemen resumed their regal posture, and walked back across the expanse of red tile, pausing, here and there, to bow.

CHAPTER 15

I have no philosophy about acting or anything else. You just do it. And I mean that. You just do it. However, I can say that with ease after thirty-five years. You go to a newcomer and say "Just do it," and it doesn't mean dits, does it? You've got to do the big circle to come back and be able to say "You just do it."

Someone asked me once what my philosophy of life was, and I said some crazy thing. I should have said, how the hell do I know?

Rock was flown home from Paris on a chartered 747 on July 30, 1985, and taken by helicopter to UCLA Medical Center. When Mark Miller arrived the following day, he asked Dr. Gottlieb, "Should he see friends?" Dr. Gottlieb said yes, Rock should see as many people as possible so he would want to return to life.

Mark drew up a list of visitors, and Rock approved everyone except Marc Christian and Tom Clark. Mark hired a guard and private nurses to watch Rock, and the hospital set up a lounge next to his room for visitors. Mark would schedule one guest in the morning and one in the afternoon. He brought them up and gave them a speech: Rock doesn't look as we remember, try not to register shock; he may not recognize you or talk, you'll have to do the talking; and don't stay too long. After the visit, the guests would go into the lounge and "fall apart," Mark says. When stars like Elizabeth Taylor and Carol Burnett came, Dr. Gottlieb made himself available to answer questions.

On August 8, Juliet Prowse came to see Rock and when she learned he hadn't seen Tom Clark, she said, "Would you like to see Tom?"

"Sure," Rock said.

She told Mark Miller, who went himself to ask Rock and when Rock said yes, Mark called Tom. "Get over here right now."

Tom drove to the hospital with Jon Epstein, who'd been scheduled to visit at 1 P.M. "I was shaking like a leaf," Tom says. Jon went in first with Mark, and after a few minutes, Tom walked in. Rock's face lit up.

"How you doin', pal?" Tom said.

"Pretty good," Rock said. Then he smiled. "It's the pits, isn't it? The fucking pits."

Little was stated, but from Rock's eyes and voice, Tom knew, "It was all right between us. I got in that room and, bingo. It was as if I'd never been away. And you know what? He looked beautiful to me. I was expecting him to look worse, because of the Doris Day pictures, but he looked radiant."

Jon Epstein left to give them privacy, as did Mark, who says, "It was terribly touching. I hadn't seen Rock greet anyone with such joy since he'd collapsed. The look in his eye seemed to say, Thank God you're here, buddy, I need you.

Tom took over Mark's duties at the hospital and practically moved in. He would arrive at eight in the morning and leave at nine at night. He read to Rock, watched television with him and cajoled and bullied him into eating. "Now eat your mashed potatoes," Tom would say. "How the hell are you gonna get well if you weigh two pounds?"

"All right, I'll eat!" Rock said.

Tom scheduled visitors and gave them the speech, adding, "He has no idea about the hoopla over AIDS. Don't mention it." Someone did slip, though, and told Rock he was on the cover of *Newsweek*. "Why am I on the cover?" Rock asked Mark.

"Because everyone loves you," Mark said.

Within two weeks, twenty-eight thousand letters for Rock had arrived at the hospital or the house, some addressed simply: "Rock Hudson, Hollywood." Fans sent Bibles, handcrafted gifts and cookies; members of churchs made scrolls and wrote little messages expressing their love and applauding Rock's courage. Among the gifts was a button that said, in red letters, I LOVE ROCK, with a heart in place of *love*. Tom put it on his shirt and never took it off.

Rock was calling Tom "Babe," as he had in prior years, and seemed to be assuming that Tom was coming home with him. Mark said, "I have to hear Rock say he wants you in the house. I want to be sure I'm following Rock's wishes and nobody else's." So in Mark's presence, Tom asked Rock, "Is it okay if I come home?"

"Well, of course," Rock said.

Later, when they were alone, Mark told Tom that he was not in Rock's will and that Rock was too sick for any alterations to be made. "So if you're doing this with the idea that you can be reinstated, that's not possible. You have to decide if you want to continue nursing an AIDS patient."

Tom said he didn't care about AIDS or the will, he was grateful to have this time with Rock. "If he'd died in Paris and I hadn't been able to be with him again, I would have been desolate."

Marc Christian had flown to Paris the day after Rock returned to California. At Mark Miller's request, Bob Darcy met Christian at the airport, helped him find a place to stay and took him to Percy Hospital where he was examined by Dr. Dormont. While waiting for the results of his blood culture, Christian went to the South of France with Darcy. Christian was impressed that Darcy looked so well and did not seem sick. They stayed together in Mougins, a little town outside Cannes, went to the beach during the day and at night to a gay bar called the Zanzi. "All the Europeans were scared of Americans," Darcy says. "When they heard the accent, they'd say, 'You all have AIDS,' and walk away." Darcy was surprised that Christian "did not seem all that freaked out. I would have been panicked. He seemed more concerned about Rock than himself." Darcy had known Rock for years and said, "Rock was one of the nicest, most generous people I ever knew, but I was angry he hadn't told Marc he had AIDS. Marc did *not* seem angry, which I found strange. My anger was stronger than Marc's."

On August 7, Dr. Dormont reported that Christian's culture was negative; there was no AIDS virus in his blood, and no antibodies to the virus. The staff at the Castle jumped up and down and hugged each other when they heard the news. A few days later, Christian returned from France.

On August 12, Wally Sheft called Mark Miller from New York and said he, Rock and Dr. Gottlieb had conferred and decided that Christian should leave the house before Rock was brought home, because his presence would disturb Rock. Mark called Christian and asked if he could meet him at the Castle at six. Mark asked James to be present, because he wanted a witness besides George. The four sat down in the large living room.

"Rock wants you to move out of the house," Mark Miller said.

"Why, is he afraid of publicity?" Christian said.

"No, he just wants you out. These are his last days, and that's what he wants."

"Why doesn't he tell me himself?"

"He doesn't want to speak to you."

"I don't believe it." Christian's voice began to rise. "How do I know you're telling me the truth? You lied to me for a year! If I wasn't told about AIDS, why should I believe what you're saying now? I don't have to leave this house. This is my house. It's not your house *yet*!"

George said to Mark, "That's it. You delivered the message. Let's go." He and Mark started walking out, but as they reached the bar, according to Mark and George, Christian shouted, "You're trying to kill Rock, Dr. Gottlieb is trying to kill Rock. I could have gotten Rock to go back to Paris for more of the drug and you couldn't." George kept Mark walking in front of him, sensing that Christian was trying to incite him. Mark turned. "I tried to help you, I did everything I could to help you . . ."

"You tried to murder me!" Christian yelled.

George kept pushing Mark toward the door and they left.

Christian says he did not acuse anyone of trying to kill Rock or himself. He says he was enraged because "I was told a different story every day about why I had not been informed about AIDS." He kept hearing from Mark Miller: "Let me tell you something that's been kept from you. I was not allowed to tell you before. This was Rock's decision, not mine. I've been following Rock's orders for a year and a half." Christian was frustrated to the breaking point, and decided to consult an attorney, Marvin Mitchelson, who was well known for palimony cases.

Mark Miller told Rock that Christian was refusing to move out unless Rock asked him personally. "Fuck him!" Rock said, waving his hand in dismissal. But Mark kept after him, and Rock finally agreed to see Christian. Mark drove Christian to UCLA, brought him into Rock's room and then stepped out in the hall, where he waited with Tom Clark and the private nurse, Tammy Neu. The door was open and Mark could see Christian standing at the foot of Rock's bed, but could not hear the conversation. It was a short visit, and after five minutes, Christian walked out. "Did he ask you to leave?" Mark said.

"No, I had to ask him—do you want me to leave? He said yes. So I said, okay, I'll leave. I just need some time to find an apartment."

Mark said, "Isn't that typical of Rock? He couldn't say the words, even on his deathbed."

Tom Clark and Tammy Neu confirmed that Christian said, on leaving Rock's room, that Rock had asked him to leave. John Dobbs, who was Christian's closest ally in the house, says Christian told him the next day that Rock had asked him to leave.

When Christian filed suit against Hudson's estate, however, he said, "Rock never asked me to move out." His version of the talk in the hospital room is as follows: Hudson asked how the house was, how the dogs were. Christian said, "Why didn't you tell me you were sick?"

"When you've got a disease like this, you're all alone."

"I wouldn't have run from you. I didn't run from my father's cancer. I would have been there to help you." Christian then asked Rock, "Do you want me to move out?"

"No, why would you do that?" Rock said. "Carry on as usual."

On August 24, Mark Miller learned that Christian had gone to see Marvin Mitchelson. Christian assured Mark he was not planning to sue, but he felt he deserved some compensation for being exposed to AIDS and had gone to "find out my rights." Mark said, "Trust me, you'll be taken care of in some way. Don't take this to court. It will hurt Rock and hurt you."

"No way," Christian said.

Mark told him they were bringing Rock home that night, and that Tom and a nurse were coming with him and would need to use Tijuana. Christian said he was moving out that day, and would be gone before Rock arrived. He packed his things in boxes and piled them in the playroom.

Rock had been longing with every breath in his body to see the Castle again. "Right out that window and up the hill is home," he kept saying. Mark and Tom had rehearsed a plan to take Rock out of the hospital at three in the morning so they would not be harassed by the press. On Saturday night, Mark and Tom had dinner at Matteo's in Westwood, then called James to see if Christian was gone. James said he had left, all was clear. Mark and Tom returned to the hospital at nine, and asked the chief of security if there were reporters downstairs. He said no. "Let's go right now," Tom said. They put Rock in a wheelchair in his pajamas and robe, and Tom pushed the wheelchair, surrounded by guards, down the halls and out a back exit. They got in Rock's new Mercedes; Rock sat in the back with Toni Phillips, the nurse, and Mark sat in front with Tom, who started to drive down Sunset. Tom was sweating and his hands were shaking. "Relax, nobody's following us," Mark said.

"Why're you driving so fucking fast?" Rock said.

"I'm not driving fast, I'm going twenty-five miles an hour. Shut up," Tom said.

Mark smiled to himself. "We were right back to ten years before."

They arrived at the Castle and helped Rock through the first front door. The dogs ran up and jumped on him, and Rock sat down on the wooden bench. "Hello Bozer, Sister, Casey!" Then he made his way slowly across the red-tile patio. James came out of the kitchen and stood at the door, trying to contain his emotion.

"There's James," Tom said.

"Hi, James!"

They went through the second front door, Tom took Rock's arm and said, "We go to the right . . ."

"I know, I know! Can't I look at my house?" Rock wanted to stand and stare in every direction, to re-fix the details in his mind. He walked up the stairs and stopped on the landing to look down at the red room: the oversized couches from *Pillow Talk*, the giant candles flickering in parchment shades, the ceiling made of tree limbs. At length, Rock went into his bedroom and climbed into the bed with the winged and crowned male figure on the headboard. Mark says, "It was wonderful to see him in his bed. He'd gone full circle, halfway round the world and back, at a cost of a quarter of a million." Mark said a silent prayer of thanks, and, thinking everything was settled, drove home to the desert.

The next morning, James was up in Rock's room with the nurse when he saw the light come on on the desk phone. James went down to the kitchen and saw Tom watching a football game on television. "Who's on the phone?" James said. "Mr. Hudson isn't, the nurse is not, you're not."

"I don't know."

"It's the line Marc Christian used to use. Let me go look in the playroom."

Two minutes later James returned. "He's come back."

"You're joking," Tom said.

"No, he's in the playroom. He sneaked right back in the house last night without telling anybody. He's sleeping on the sofa bed, and his things are all over the room. He's even put posters on the wall."

Christian said, later, that he hadn't been able to find an apartment. Tom called Mark Miller in the desert, who called Wally Sheft in New York, who consulted his attorneys and found that because of residency laws in California, Christian would have to leave voluntarily, or Rock would have to sign an affidavit and have the marshal evict him. Rock's attorneys suggested that they leave Christian in the house and ignore him. Wally asked Mark and George if they would move to Los Angeles to oversee the Castle during Rocks' final weeks.

"It was a mess," James says. "Both Tom and Christian were in the house at the same time, and I was caught in the middle." James says that Christian had a friend stay with him almost every night in the playroom, "sleeping with him in the same bloody bed while Mr. Hudson was lying up there dying." Christian says he had friends stay with him because "I was afraid I might be poisoned."

Tom did not want Rock to know Christian was still in the house, so he was careful not to bring Rock downstairs if Christian was around. Tom was civil to Christian when they met in the kitchen. "I decided, I can't deal with anything other than what's going on upstairs," Tom said. "All my energy is going up there and I'm not going to waste it."

On Monday, August 26, Mark Miller called a meeting of the staff. He explained that Wally had put him in charge of the house, and he and George would be staying in their condo in Hollywood four nights a week and going to the desert on weekends. "Tom, you're in charge of the patient," Mark said. "James will run the house, and I will disburse the money." Tom was not to order the staff about; James had made it clear that one order from Tom and he would quit. Marc Christian was to do as he wished. "I will ask Rock daily if he will see you." Ron Channell was to have access to Rock whenever he wanted.

Ron Channell would breeze in every day, wearing shorts and a tank top, and Rock would always brighten when he saw him. Mark recalls, "Ron was now in the position Jack Coates had formerly held—the knight who could jump to the throne at will." Ron Channell asked Mark if Rock would pay for him to take dancing lessons, so he could perform in Las Vegas. "Rock has always said he'd help me with my career," Ron said. "Let's go ask him," Mark said, and Rock said, "Sure, why not."

Tom was on duty at the Castle twenty-four hours a day, fearing that something might happen to Rock if he left, but once a week, he went to his condo to pick up mail. One day when he was out, Mark and George went up to Rock's room and sat down on the blue ottomans facing the bed. "You should know what's going on in your house," Mark said. "We want to tell you, because for years, it's been kept from you."

"I wish you would," Rock said.

Mark told him Christian was still in the Castle, sleeping on the sofa bed in the playroom. The news did not seem to upset Rock; on the contrary, George says, "a secret twinkle came to his eyes—they darted about the room as he thought about the situation. Rock loved intrigue, and I think he got a kick out of imagining Tom in Tijuana and Christian in the playroom."

"Has Christian got a job yet?" Rock said.

"I don't think so. Do you want to see him?"

"No, fuck him," Rock said. "When's Ron Channell coming by?"

"He'll be here at five-thirty."

Mark and George also wanted to convey to Rock what had happened as a result of his announcement that he had AIDS. "We wanted him to know what he'd done for the world, before he slipped too far to be able to understand it."

George began, "Rock you're a hero around the world and the world loves you."

"You are the biggest thing since the pay toilet," Mark said. "You're ten times more popular than you ever were as a movie star."

"Why? I haven't done anything."

"The announcement that you have AIDS stunned the world," Mark said. "You've made AIDS the number-one story in every newspaper; you've put it on the cover of every magazine. You've made the disease real—the world is tuned in to AIDS because of you."

"You're joking."

Mark said thousands of people were donating money for AIDS research, and governments were allocating major funds. The dinner that Elizabeth Taylor was helping sponsor in Los Angeles to benefit AIDS had had to be moved to a larger ballroom after Rock's announcement. "Before your announcement, they'd sold two hundred tickets. Now they've sold twenty-five hundred, and they've raised a million dollars."

"All that because I said I have AIDS?"

George explained that Rock was the first well-known person to contract the disease; if it could happen to Rock Hudson, it could happen to anyone. "We've got thirty thousand letters downstairs. You're getting more mail and publicity now than in all your years as an actor—through sixty-two films."

Rock turned on his side and propped his head on his elbow. "Isn't that neat."

Mark said to George, "Wouldn't you know Rock was gonna be immortal?"

George joked: "We've made you a Goddess." It was a line from *I, Claudius* that had long been a private joke.

"Please, a *God*," Rock said.

The three started to choke up; Mark and George felt they had to leave or they would weep, and Rock was starting to cry despite himself. It was almost beyond his comprehension: The very thing he'd been resisting with all the strength of his being had happened and it had brought only good. Mark and George shook his hand and slapped his back, went downstairs and broke.

In September, when the Santa Ana wind started to blow and the weather turned hot and dry, Tom said to Rock, "Let's go sit on the deck, there's a full moon tonight—it's your favorite kind of night." Tom walked Rock outside and settled him in a chair. The wind had blown all the impurities from the air and the view was spectacular. They could see as far as the Palm Springs mountains, where the airplanes turned on their landing lights and began the gradual descent over the city to Los Angeles International Airport.

Rock and Tom talked about some of the places they'd been, and Tom had the feeling Rock wanted to talk about dying. "I would not let him, because I had decided he was not going to die. I probably let him down, but I did not want to hear any negative thoughts."

As they sat in the warm, windy air, Tom said, gently, "You're not fighting this, Rock. You and I have fought some big battles and won. Will you fight with me?"

"No, I don't think so," Rock said.

"Why?"

"I'm ready."

"Well, I'm not ready for you to leave."

"See that plane?" Rock said. "We're on it coming back from Rio de Janeiro." They talked about their trip to Rio and how they had danced in samba lines in the street, and then they picked out other planes and talked of other journeys, to Japan, Australia, Sicily, Hawaii. After they'd sat there for an hour, Rock said he was tired and wanted to sleep.

"We had some fun in the house those last weeks," Tom says. One night, Rock said, "If you weren't such a chicken, you'd get out a deck of cards and play Spite and Malice." Rock played cards with Tom and beat him, "and we swore at each other—'You dirty prick!'—just like we'd always done."

Every morning, Tom would come into Rock's room at six to see how he'd slept, have coffee with him and read the paper while Rock did the crossword puzzle. At nine, Tom turned on *The $25,000 Pyramid*. When Tom had left in 1983, Rock had said, "Thank God, we don't have to see the fucking *Pyramid*, anymore," but when Tom moved back, the *Pyramid* came back on. They watched movies on cassette and cable, but Tom was reluctant to turn on network television because the *Enquirer* was running ads, promoting stories about Rock and Linda Evans.

September 6 was Tom's birthday, and when he went to Rock's room that morning, Rock was on his feet between two nurses, holding a cake and singing "Happy Birthday." Tom was moved that Rock, sick as he was, had remembered the day and planned a celebration.

Friends came to the Castle in a steady stream, bearing pies and cakes, soufflés and soups. It was tiring to Rock to see visitors, but when Tom put his hand on Rock's as he lay with his eyes closed and said, "Elizabeth is here," Rock smiled. "Oh, good."

Joy came one day with a pot of gizzards, but Rock was not able to eat them. "Your name is sure on everyone's lips," Joy said. "Talk about coming out of the closet. . . . You came out of the house!" Rock laughed. "And you're doin' a lot of good, too." Joy and Rock talked about how they had fought over the crossword puzzle and who had been better. "You sure loved the dogs," Rock said.

"I did, and in between those seven dogs, you're in there someplace."

The third week he was home, Rock started having days when his mind would cloud, and just walking to the bathroom would exhaust him. He weighed 140 pounds, and when George went to massage his shoulders, he felt nothing but bones. Rock would not be able to leave his bed for days, but then he'd get up, walk down to the kitchen on his own and entertain visitors.

On September 11, George and I went into the bedroom to try to interview Rock. The massive bed was cranked up and Rock was sitting in his blue pajamas under a navy quilt. The dark wooden shutters were closed, and the room was filled with the intensely sweet scent of ginger, which Clarence had cut and placed in a vase.

Rock had been watching a movie, *Blood and Sand* with Tyrone Power. Tom said, "Now here comes one of your all-time favorites, *The Postman Always Rings Twice*, with Lana Turner." Rock looked at the screen and sighed: "Lana Lana Lana."

George asked Rock about Lester Luther, the voice coach who had taught him to lower his voice. "I went out in the hills and yelled," Rock said. He fell silent. "I didn't have any . . . shoot." He looked confused. "I don't remember. I truly don't remember."

George tried again. He asked about an acting coach Rock had had, a woman.

"She was just terrible!" Rock said.

Partly because of the way he said it—like a child calling the teacher stupid—and partly because I was uncomfortable, I laughed. Rock perked up.

"She was so dumb!"

George and I both were laughing now, and Rock stirred in the bed, enjoying the sound he was eliciting. His eyes came into focus and he repeated it—"She's so dumb!"—while we laughed harder. His face was full of color and he looked happy.

In the evenings, when the house was quiet and everyone had gone, Tom would get in bed with Rock and hold his hand. "Sometimes he'd clutch my hand and sometimes he wouldn't," Tom says. "I'm sure he understood me. I'd talk and talk, saying positive things, letting him know he was not alone."

Everyone admired Tom for the way he cared for Rock. Stockton Briggle says, "Tom was selfless; he had nothing to gain, he'd been cut out of the will and he might have been risking his health by being so close to an AIDS patient." Tom carried Rock to the toilet and into the shower and stood with him there, so he could bathe himself instead of having the nurses do it. Clarence said to Tom, "I'm so glad to see you back to help him in his last days. A man can ask no more and do no more."

On Saturday, September 21, Tom was alone in the house with Rock and one of the nurses. Rock had been given a blood transfusion but had not responded well, and was being fed intravenously. The doorbell rang. Tom opened the door and saw a tall, well-dressed woman holding a Bible. "I've come to bring a message to Mr. Hudson from God," she said.

"That's just not possible," Tom said.

"It must be possible, because God told me I was going to see Mr. Hudson. Would you mind if I waited out here, because I know I'm going to see him."

Tom closed the door, went to fix his lunch, ate it, went back to the door and saw the woman was still there. "I'm sorry, lady, you're gonna have to wait off the premises."

"All right. I'll wait outside the gate because I know I'm going to see him."

Tom walked upstairs and, he recalls, "There was Rock and he looked so sick, I came down and got the lady and brought her up. That is so unlike me I cannot tell you! I throw nuts off the property all the time." The woman stood at the foot of the bed and said, "Mr. Hudson, I have come with a message from God."

Rock opened his eyes and smiled at her.

"God has asked me to tell you you're not going to leave us yet. He has a ministry for you here on earth that will be a far greater reward than your film career has been. The cancer will leave your body and you're going to be just fine."

Tom escorted her downstairs and learned her name was Eleanor. "Now I can tell you about my day," she said. Eleanor said she prays to the Lord and sometimes he answers. "This morning, I was praying and the Lord said, 'I want you to go see Rock Hudson and take him a message.' I said, 'I can't do that, I'm shy.' The Lord said, 'Yes, you can and you will.'" Eleanor had read that Rock was at UCLA, so she drove there, only to learn he'd been discharged. She got back in her car and was driving down Sunset when she saw a man selling maps to the movie stars' homes. She bought one, but Rock's home wasn't on it. "I told the Lord, 'I tried, you see I tried, and I can't.' The Lord said, 'Yes, you can. Do it.'" Eleanor saw Pat Boone's house on the map and, knowing Boone was religious, drove there. Shirley Boone came to the door, and when Eleanor told her why she'd come, Shirley "nearly fainted. They were holding a prayer vigil for Rock Hudson right there in the house." Shirley said she would find out where Rock lived, and a few minutes later, gave Eleanor the address.

Tom was still astonished that he'd actually brought her in. "I think the Lord made me do it," he said. Eleanor asked, "Could I hug you?" and they hugged and cried.

The next day, Sunday, the actress Susan Stafford called and said the Boones had been having a round-the-clock prayer vigil for Rock and wanted to come lay on hands. Susan had been a friend of Rock's since 1970, and was a born-again Christian and intern minister. Tom says, "I figured, they can't do any harm." Fifteen minutes later, the group was in Rock's bedroom, kneeling around the wooden bed with their hands on the sheet. Shirley Boone led the prayers while Rock slept. When they finished, Tom said, "Rock, there are a lot of good friends here. I want you to thank them." Rock opened his eyes, said, "Thank you," and went back to sleep.

Many of Rock's friends were angry when they learned that born-again Christians had been allowed to pray over him, and said, "Rock would never have stood for that if he'd been conscious." Tom said, "I never heard him say anything for or against religion. I'll do anything, I'm gonna fight and fight and not give up. I'll have a witch doctor here if you know one." The previous year, Mark Miller had asked

Rock what religion he was and Rock had said, "I guess, Congrega-tionalist." But Tom said Rock had been baptized a Catholic and had selected a Catholic service for his mother when she died. Tom de-cided Rock should see a Catholic priest. Susan Stafford brought a friend, Father Terry Sweeney, who sat with Rock and asked if he wanted to be forgiven for his sins. Rock nodded, received commu-nion and the anointing of the sick.

Tom began to hang religious medals and pictures sent by fans and friends on the posts of Rock's bed. "Tell me why not?" he said. Mar-tha Raye had given him a gold medallion, which, she said, "got me through two tours of Vietnam," and Tom put it on the bed.

On Friday, September 27, Clarence brought a fresh bunch of gin-ger up to Rock's room and placed it in a vase. "Good night, Rock, keep your faith," Clarence said in his gentle voice. "I'll see you Tues-day."

"Probably you won't see me Tuesday."

"I'm gonna see you."

On Tuesday, Clarence brought up an orchid from the greenhouse and set it, floating in water, on Rock's nightstand. "Here's your favor-ite orchid," Clarence said. Rock's eyes were open but they were fixed on the ceiling, and Rock did not respond. That night, Clarence could not sleep. Death is close at hand, he thought. No, it can't be, I must have been mistaken.

Over the weekend, Dean Dittman had come to visit after church. Tom had told him, "Rock's out of it," but when Dean walked into the bedroom, Rock said, "It's Dean!" Dean saw a smile that he felt was one of transcendence—a smile he had seen when Rock was lis-tening to great music or watching a film he treasured. Dean felt Rock was "letting me know he knew something—that from all the pain and anguish he'd had to suffer during that devastating year and a half, he'd learned something. In his mind, he was home." Rupert Allan came later and said Rock had "an aescetic quality I'd never seen. I thought he looked beautiful, like a Christ figure."

On Monday, September 30, I asked to see Rock, sensing that it might be the last time. His eyes were closed, his bare arms were above the covers and he was shivering. Tom leaned over and said, with tenderness, "Are you cold?" Tom pulled the blanket up to his chin. Rock's skin was transparent, he was a frail skeleton, yet as I stood there, he opened his eyes and gave a smile that was unearthly in its radiance. Where was it coming from, I wondered. His body had sunk to nothing, and it was as if all the brilliance of his being was in his eyes.

The next night, October 1, Toni Phillips, the night nurse, said to Tom, "I haven't told you this before, but I'm a member of the prayer vigil the Boones have been having, and they want to come again and pray with Rock."

"Get 'em over," Tom said.

Rock was unconscious, but Pat Boone placed a Bible on his chest and took his hand. Tom got in bed with Rock and held him, and Eleanor fell to the floor and began speaking in tongues. After the prayers, Pat Boone told Tom to lay out clothes for Rock, because a miracle would occur in the night and Rock would be feeling so well in the morning, he would want to get up and get dressed. Tom went to the closet and placed on the sofa a pair of gray slacks, a blue and white striped shirt, a sport coat, shoes and socks. "Those will be his happy clothes," Boone said, and instructed the nurse to put them on him in the morning.

On Wednesday morning, October 2, James was the first one up to Rock's room. There was Rock, lying on the bed with his arms straight out, completely dressed in his shoes and "happy clothes," which were now so big that Rock looked lost inside them. "He was lying there like a doll, not moving at all," James says. Two nurses were there because a shift was changing, and the nurses started carrying Rock to a chair where they propped him upright. James says Rock looked in agony as they moved him, and clear liquid was coming out of his mouth, dripping onto his sport coat. Tom Clark walked in at seven, and James said, "Mr. Clark, he doesn't look at all comfortable or well."

"Get him undressed," Tom said.

Rock seemed to revive once he was back in bed in his pajamas, and wanted to watch the *Today* show. James left to do some shopping—he needed more disinfectant for the sickroom and some Swiss Miss tapioca puddings that Rock liked. Tom had coffee with Rock, they talked about the news, and at 8:30, Tom said, "I'm out of coffee. Do you want some more?"

"No, not now," Rock said.

Tom went down to the kitchen and a few minutes later, the nurse buzzed him. "Could you come upstairs?" Tom walked into Rock's room and saw the nurse in tears. "We've lost him." They reached for each other and hugged, then Tom asked to be left alone with Rock.

Tom had been given instructions as to what to do when Rock died, "but I hadn't paid attention because I thought Rock was gonna live." Rock had stipulated that he wanted to be cremated and have his ashes scattered at sea, but Tom couldn't remember the procedure. Ironically, Mark Miller had flown to New York for that one day. Tom called Dr. Kennamer, then went and told Marc Christian Rock had died. "Do you want to see him?" Tom brought Christian up to the room—the only time since Rock had come home from the hospital that Christian had been allowed there. Tom tried to reach Mark Miller in New York and couldn't. He called Wally Sheft, he called Claire Trevor, and at 9:07, he called George in the desert. At 9:15, the news of Rock's death was on the radio.

To this day, Tom is baffled as to how the news got out so fast. There were only three people in the house when Rock died: Tom, the nurse and Marc Christian. Tom made three calls, and the people he called say they did not speak to the press. Tom concluded that the phones were tapped, but a month later, when the phone bill arrived, it showed that a call had been placed at 9:07 to a hotel in New York where Marvin Mitchelson had been staying. It's possible that Christian called Mitchelson, who alerted the press.

James came home with the groceries shortly after nine, and when Tom told him Rock had died, he put his hands to his face. "No, he can't be, he isn't!" He went upstairs to see Rock, and Dr. Kennamer arrived. Elizabeth Taylor called and said she was sending her security people over. "My God, the gates are wide open," Tom said, and quickly went and closed them. All four phone lines began to ring.

Stockton Briggle was getting dressed to go to the office when he heard the news. He called the house and reached James, and said, "Tell Tom I'm on my way over." He arrived at 9:50, rang the bell at the gate and when it opened, a yellow car drove in behind him. Shirley Boone and Eleanor got out of the car, brushed past Stockton and Tom and went upstairs to pray. Eleanor lay down on the floor and spoke in tongues, and, Stockton says, "I was stunned at the impropriety of it—they were blubbering and carrying on. It was as if a medieval king had died and the women were chanting over his body."

Stockton called his office and said, "There's no one here but James and Tom. Cancel my appointments for the day." Stockton told Tom, "I'll take care of this," and started to answer the phones: "Mr. Hudson's house." Stockton says he took over because "there was no one else to do it. I'm a director, and I ended up directing Rock's last appearance. You know what?" He patted the arms of his chair. "I feel a great deal of pride and happiness that I was able to do that in his service."

At 10:45, the van from Pierce-Hamrock-Reed Mortuary arrived and could barely get through the gates because there were so many photographers, reporters and TV crews in the street. They were hanging on the gates, jamming microphones and flash guns through the bars. Several started to climb over the gate and Stockton yelled, "Get back, you're on private property, we'll call the police!"

Stockton saw that the van had two windows in back. Photographers would be able to shoot through the windows, and Tom was determined that no one be allowed to take a picture of the body. Tom said he would stay with Rock all the way to the crematory. "I insist that Rock have the dignity he deserves."

"Get some towels," Stockton said. "We'll cover the windows." The two men from the mortuary asked, "Where's the body?" and began putting on masks and gloves to place Rock in a body bag.

"Do they have to do that?" Marc Christian said.

"No." Dr. Kennamer said, "but let them, it's easier not to cause a problem."

James brought out two of his own towels that were brightly colored with diamond patterns. Stockton said later, "The towels were hideous. That house is full of beautiful things, and Rock was going to his final reward with the tackiest towels in the world draped over the windows." James was miffed when he heard Stockton's description. "They served their purpose," he said.

As Stockton and James were taping the towels on the truck, Ross Hunter came through the gates. He had called earlier and said, "Jacque and I are coming, make sure we get through the gates," but their Rolls-Royce had been blocked by press vehicles. "Jacque is caught in the Rolls! You've got to get Jacque! He's caught in the

Rolls!" Ross cried. One of the security men left to see if he could help Jacque Mapes.

Stockton ran back upstairs to Rock's bedroom just as the men from the mortuary were starting to carry Rock out on a gurney. Tom, Marc Christian, James, Dr. Kennamer and the nurses were following down the stairs. Shirley Boone and Eleanor had disappeared. As the procession reached the landing, Ross Hunter came into the red room and started hyperventilating. "Oh, Rock, Rock! . . . Oh, no! . . . Oh, Tom . . . Oh my God . . ."

"It's okay, Ross, it's okay," Tom said.

They carried Rock out through the garage to where the van was parked, lifted the body into the van and put a chair beside it for Tom. Ross said, "I'm going with you," and tried to get in the van.

"No, no, you stay here, I can take care of it," Tom said.

They tried to close the doors of the van but couldn't because Rock's feet were sticking out.

"Get his feet!" The men pushed and pulled at the gurney, and just as they got the doors closed, Ross fainted. "He collapsed like a bloody sponge," James says. Marc Christian ran to get a pillow, which a nurse placed under Ross's head. Dr. Kennamer looked at him briefly and said he would be fine.

Jacque Mapes came through the gates, calling, "Where's Ross?"

"He fainted."

"Oh, no! Oh, no!"

"Let's get going," Tom yelled form inside the van. "It's a hundred degrees in here!" Tom was wearing a blue sport shirt, khaki pants and the I LOVE ROCK button. Stockton said, "Don't you want to put on a sport coat?"

"No, Rock doesn't care," Tom said.

Moshe Alon, who was Elizabeth Taylor's head of security, said there should be a backup car to follow the van to the crematory. He sent a guard to get his car, but it took him twenty minutes. Ross Hunter was on his feet again, going back and forth between the house and the gates where the press were, crying and saying, "He was the best friend I ever had!" Tom shouted from inside the van: "Let's get out of here, it's broiling, we're dying! I don't give a damn about security!"

Finally, the guard returned with his car and the van began moving out the gate. The press surrounded it and started climbing on the van, while Stockton yelled, "Don't you people have any decency? Don't you have families!"

Inside the van, the driver said, "I sure hope they don't open the back door."

"What!" Tom said.

"You son of a bitch, get off of there," Stockton yelled.

"We can't lock it," the driver said.

Tom bolted to the door, grabbed the handles and held them closed. He rode all the way to the crematory on his knees, clutching the doors, straddling Rock's body.

When they reached the crematory, the gates were locked to keep out the press. Tom and the driver put Rock on a gurney and carried him into the building where there was a cardboard box that said ROCK HUDSON. They put him in the box, put the box back on the gurney and rolled it into the oven. "I saw the box catch fire. I stood there watching it, then they closed the oven and I left," Tom says. "It was the hardest thing I ever had to do, but I did it and there weren't any photographs taken."

The next morning, I found Tom sitting on the red-tile patio, staring out over the swimming pool. "There's such a void," he said. "I had such energy going into making him well, and I really thought we were gonna lick it. Damn it! I'm cross we didn't." He opened a can of beer. "I have all this energy and suddenly I don't have any floor to wash."

Tom sipped his beer. "I feel pleased, at least, that Rock was here in his own bed. I brought the dogs in every day and he wasn't in pain. I'm gonna go back to my house today, think on this, then get on with it." Within a few weeks of Rock's death, Tom went to a twelve-step program for alcoholics and did what he had never been able to do while Rock was alive—stop drinking. He became, in his friends' words, "a different person. The negative qualities dropped away and all the positive things we loved about Tom were at the forefront—his humor, charm, warmth and caring."

On October 20, 1985, thirty-five people met in the fog in front of the Wherehouse Restaurant in Marina Del Rey. They wore windbreakers and hats and held bunches of flowers as they climbed up a ladder onto the motor yacht *Tasia II*. When all were aboard, the boat headed for the Catalina Channel where the ashes of Rock Hudson would be scattered.

The night before, there had been a memorial service and party at the Castle for three hundred people. Rock had not wanted a memorial service, he had wanted his friends to have a party on a yacht with champagne and mariachis. But there were too many guests to be accommodated on a yacht, and Rock's inner circle had decided to have the party at the Castle.

It was to be the last great party at Rock Hudson's house, and Tom was to plan it. Then Elizabeth Taylor stepped in and decided there should be a Quaker-style memorial service where everyone could share their memories of Rock. She wanted pink and white flowers, where Tom had ordered bright colors. She wanted coffee and a sweet table, where Tom had wanted Mexican finger food—passed. She wanted no writers or public-relations people present, even if they had been friends of Rock, and names on the guest list were crossed off and reinstated all the way up to the day of the ceremony.

A white tent and rows of chairs were set up on the croquet lawn behind the house. The ceremony had been called for five, and at 5:15 Elizabeth Taylor walked in wearing a navy and white dress with a long rope of pearls and the service began.

Constance Towers and John Schuck sang a medley from *I Do! I Do!* Father Sweeney called for a moment of silence, when everyone might pray for Rock. Then Elizabeth Taylor stood and talked about the night she and Rock had invented chocolate martinis. One by one, other friends stood up and talked. Carol Burnett told how she had persuaded Rock to do *I Do! I Do!*, and how it had been "the most fun I ever had on a stage." Faye Nuell, who had co-produced the show, described the way Rock had shouted, "I got my step!" Susan Saint James talked about how Rock celebrated Christmas, and Stockton Briggle described the "ten-snot scene" in *Camelot*. Roddy McDowall spoke about Rock's great instincts as an actor, and Tab Hunter described his generosity. Everyone mentioned his laughter—how he loved to break people up. Don Morgan, one of Rock's publicists from the early years, told the story of when Rock met President John F. Kennedy. "They were seated next to each other at a fund-raising dinner, and President Kennedy had obviously been briefed. When he sat down, he said to Rock: 'We have something in common—we're Irish, and they say all the Fitzgeralds are related.' Rock said 'Oh?' and paused. 'Ella will be happy to hear that.'"

Elizabeth Taylor closed the service, saying, "Rock would have wanted us to be happy—let's raise a glass to him." People streamed through the house and out to the patio, where mariachis were playing and waiters were passing margaritas and miniature tacos and there were flowers everywhere and paper lanterns in the trees. As darkness fell, the candles and fires came on, making the house warm and romantic, with its comfortable oversized sofas and log ceilings. It was a unique setting, transporting one to grand old Spanish days in California. Small groups gathered in the rooms, and in every circle, someone said it was a shame Rock's house would have to be sold.

Sunday morning, among the small group that gathered at the marina, there was not one person whose name was a household word or who could be recognized by the two photographers who, despite elaborate ploys to throw them off, had managed to show up at the harbor for the burial at sea. The code word for the event had been "George Nader's birthday party," and in fact, it was George's birthday. The guests included the entire staff of the Castle, Rock's attorney and business manager, four female cousins who had lived with Rock in the house of Grandma Wood, a dozen male friends and three of Rock's lovers: Tom Clark, Marc Christian and Jack Coates. (Inadvertently, Mark Miller had forgotten to invite Ron Channell.) Mark suggested that the three lovers all hold the container of ashes, but Tom wouldn't hear of it. He alone would scatter the ashes.

"By what right does he . . . ?" someone asked.

"He just does," Mark said.

There was a festive spirit on the way out—everyone laughed and talked as the boat sailed through the fog to the open sea. The motors were cut and the group gathered on the foredeck. In the hush, broken only by the lapping of waves, Susan Stafford read the Twenty-third Psalm. The air was gray and the water was an opaque green. Tom sat at the prow, holding a brown plastic container that said on the lid, ROCK HUDSON. He touched it to his chest, bowed his head, then dumped the contents all at once into the water. The ashes settled on the surface like a powdery cloud, and in seconds they were gone. We tossed roses, lilies, carnations, and Tom threw a maile lei that a group of Green Berets in Hawaii had sent. The captain started the boat and drove in a slow circle around the flowers. They had been tossed helter-skelter, but to our surprise, they fanned out and formed an almost perfect ring, bobbing on the water. Everyone leaned over the rail, staring at the flowers as we sailed around them in wider circles.

No one spoke on the ride back to shore. John Dobbs wept silently, and Dean Dittman held the hand of Jack Coates, who clutched, in his other hand, a bunch of small white narcissus. Much later, Mark Miller would tell how, at the moment the ashes were dropped, a seagull had crapped on his blue cashmere sweater. Mark felt it was Rock, "having the last laugh."

The house on Beverly Crest kept running as if Rock still were alive. There was a flurry of scheming and meeting to try to stave off a lawsuit by Marc Christian and the sordid publicity it would bring. Susan Stafford met with Christian, Rupert Allan took him to lunch, George Nader had a heart-to-heart talk with him. All of them promised to help Christian obtain the money and insurance he needed, and Christian assured them he had no intention of suing, he had only gone to Mitchelson because he needed a powerful ally. Yet even as he was making these assurances, papers were being drawn up for the court action. The drama was running on its own engine now, like a Greek tragedy that, once begun, has to play out to the end, until the stage is littered with bodies and everyone is bloodied.

Marvin Mitchelson told Rock's attorneys that Christian wanted a substantial settlement. Wally Sheft told James to have the locks changed at the Castle, to ask Christian for the keys to the Seville and to deny him kitchen privileges. Christian started moving out on October 25, and the next night, James found that the playroom had been stripped bare of electronic equipment, films and records. In a cross-complaint against Christian, the Hudson estate would charge that he took three video recorders, approximately seven thousand records, 150 videotapes of films, eight pieces of audio equipment, a computer, a video camera and the most elaborate needlepoint rug Hudson had made. He had tried to take a large-screen television, but

Moshe Alon, the security chief, pulled it out of Christian's station wagon. Christian said, "Most of the things I took, Rock had given me before I moved into the house. He told me the records were all mine and said, 'Anything you need, just consider it yours.'" Tom Clark asked Christian to return the records because they were a priceless collection that should be donated to a public institution. "Rock never gave you anything and you know it."

On November 2, Christian and Mitchelson held a press conference, announcing they were suing Hudson's estate, Mark Miller, Wallace Sheft and two unnamed doctors for $14 million for conspiring to endanger Christian's life. At the Castle, the staff watched it in the kitchen and James turned pink with rage. "How dare he drag Mr. Hudson's name through the mud!"

Christian said in an interview later, "I don't care if I win money in court. I made my point; I didn't let them treat me like an ant or a non-person."

Mark and George left the desert and moved into the Castle to guard it until it was sold. James continued his routines, going to Theodore's in the morning and shopping for supplies. John Dobbs came in to clean the house, and Clarence was there every day, pruning and trimming plants.

One afternoon in late November, I found Clarence in the kitchen, fixing himself a bowl of ice cream. On the counter, he had stacked sprigs of ginger, with their exotic yellow blossoms that possessed the most intoxicating scent. Rock and Clarence had planted the ginger and nurtured it together, and Rock had always looked forward to the summer when it would bloom. "He was some man, as far as I'm concerned," Clarence said. "He loved his fellow workers. He treated me like I was one more member of the family."

"He never paid you very well," one of the staff said.

"That doesn't matter. It's not the pay but who you work for."

Clarence finished his ice cream and gathered the ginger in his arms, wanting to take it up to the room where Rock had slept for twenty-four years. "It was one of his favorite flowers," he said.

"How long does it bloom?" I asked.

"From July to September fifteenth."

"But . . . it's November."

"This is a very unusual year. It never happened before." Clarence's sage eyes flickered with amusement. "I think maybe Rock's spirit is in the flower. That's Japanese philosophy." Clarence calculated how long it had been since Rock had died. "Fifty days? That means he's already crossed the first river." Clarence smiled, bowing his head as he did. "He's on his way to Nirvana."

CHAPTER NOTES

CHAPTER 1
p. 18: Rock Hudson to James Wright, July 1985.

CHAPTER 2
p. 37: Rock Hudson in an interview with Gordon Gow, *Films and Filming*, June 1976; Rock Hudson interviewed by Ronald L. Davis, Southern Methodist University Oral History Project Number 276, August 24, 1983.
p. 41: Letter from Rock Hudson to Jim Matteoni, February 22, 1944.
p. 44: Rock Hudson to Sara Davidson, September 9, 1985.
p. 47: Southern Methodist University Oral History Project.

CHAPTER 3
p. 51: Rock Hudson to Dean Dittman, 1984.
p. 60: Rock Hudson to Sara Davidson, September 1985.

CHAPTER 4
pp. 65 and 71: Southern Methodist University Oral History Project.

CHAPTER 5
p. 79: Rock Hudson to Dean Dittman and to Mark Miller.
p. 91: Southern Methodist University Oral History Project.
p. 103: *Coronet*, June 1976.
p. 104: Gordon Gow interview, *Films and Filming*.

CHAPTER 6
p. 111: Southern Methodist University Oral History Project.
p. 119: Rock Hudson to Louella Parsons, October 25, 1959.
p. 121: Gordon Gow interview, *Films and Filming*.

CHAPTER 7
p. 129: Rock Hudson to Jack Coates; Rock Hudson to Clarence Morimoto; "Rock Hudson from A to Z," by Robert Osborne, columnist-critic, *The Hollywood Reporter*.
p. 141: Roy Newquist column in *Chicago American Magazine*, February 19, 1967.

CHAPTER 8
p. 145: "Rock Hudson from A to Z," by Robert Osborne.
p. 155: Rock Hudson to Mark Miller.

CHAPTER 9
p. 170: Southern Methodist University Oral History Project.

CHAPTER 10
p. 178: Rock Hudson to Sara Davidson, September 1985.
p. 190: *Coronet*, June 1976.

CHAPTER NOTES

CHAPTER 11
p. 196: *McCall's,* February 1967.

CHAPTER 12
p. 212: *Chicago American Magazine,* February 19, 1967.

CHAPTER 13
p. 228: "Rock Hudson from A to Z," by Robert Osborne.

CHAPTER 14
p. 261: "Rock Hudson from A to Z," by Robert Osborne.

CHAPTER 15
p. 284: Rock Hudson to Sara Davidson; Southern Methodist University Oral History Project.

ROCK HUDSON CREDITS

FILMS

1948: Fighter Squadron
1949: Undertow
1950: I Was A Shoplifter
One Way Street
Winchester '73
Peggy
The Desert Hawk
Shakedown
1951: Tomahawk
Air Cadet
The Fat Man
The Iron Man
Bright Victory
1952: Here Come the Nelsons
(aka Meet the Nelsons)
Bend of the River
Scarlet Angel
Has Anybody Seen My Gal?
Horizons West
The Lawless Breed
1953: Seminole
Sea Devils
The Golden Blade
Back to God's Country
Gun Fury
1954: Taza, Son of Cochise
Magnificent Obsession
Bengal Brigade
1955: Captain Lightfoot
One Desire
All That Heaven Allows
1956: Never Say Goodbye
Giant
Written on the Wind
Battle Hymn

1957: Something of Value
The Tarnished Angels
A Farewell to Arms
1958: Twilight for the Gods
1959: This Earth Is Mine
Pillow Talk
1961: The Last Sunset
Come September
Lover Come Back
1962: The Spiral Road
1963: A Gathering of Eagles
Marilyn [Narration]
1964: Man's Favorite Sport
Send Me No Flowers
1965: Strange Bedfellows
A Very Special Favor
1966: Blindfold
Seconds
1967: Tobruk
1968: Ice Station Zebra
1969: A Fine Pair
The Undefeated
1970: Darling Lili
The Hornet's Nest
1971: Pretty Maids All in a Row
1973: Showdown
1976: Embryo
1978: Avalanche
1980: The Mirror Crack'd
1986: The Ambassador*

*All dates based upon premiere in Los Angeles except The Ambassador, which has been shown only on local cable TV.

THEATER

1973–75:	*I Do! I Do!*
1976:	*John Brown's Body*
1977:	*Camelot*
1979:	*On the Twentieth Century*

TELEVISION

1971–75:	*McMillan and Wife*
1976–77:	*McMillan*
1978:	*Wheels*
1979:	*Martian Chronicles*
1981:	*World War III*
	The Starmaker
1982:	*The Devlin Connection*
1984:	*Las Vegas Strip Wars*
1984–85:	*Dynasty*